Everyday
Revolutionaries

2/98

Everyday Revolutionaries

Working Women and
The Transformation of American Life

Sally Helgesen

DOUBLEDAY

New York   London   Toronto   Sydney   Auckland

PUBLISHED BY DOUBLEDAY
a division of Bantam Doubleday Dell Publishing Group, Inc.
1540 Broadway, New York, New York 10036

DOUBLEDAY and the portrayal of an anchor with a dolphin
are trademarks of Doubleday, a division of
Bantam Doubleday Dell Publishing Group, Inc.

Library of Congress Cataloging-in-Publication Data
Helgesen, Sally, 1948–
Everyday Revolutionaries: working women and the transformation of
American life/ Sally Helgesen.
p.   cm.
Includes index.
1. Women—Employment—United States.   2. Women—United
States—Social conditions.   3. Married women—Employment—
United States.   4. Married women—United States—Social
conditions.   5. Working mothers—United States—Social conditions.
6. Telecommuting—United States.   I. Title.
HD6058.H395   1998
305.42′0973—dc21   97-17941
CIP

ISBN 0-385-48025-3

Printed in the United States of America

January 1998

First Edition

1   3   5   7   9   10   8   6   4   2

In memory of my mother
Ann LaFollette Helgesen

ACKNOWLEDGMENTS

My deepest gratitude goes to Sandy and Charlie Alcorn of Glen Ellyn, Illinois, who helped me with every aspect of this book and opened their wonderful house to me. I could not have done what I did without them, and I feel that the work was worthwhile for bringing me their friendship.

I am also indebted to Bob Wilson, vice chairman of Johnson & Johnson, who persuaded his organization to give me a timely grant; to the Ragdale Foundation, in Lake Forest, Illinois, where I wrote my first draft; to Kelly Morgan of Evanston, who shared her insights and lent me her house; to my editor, Bill Thomas at Doubleday, who gave constant encouragement and steered me in the right direction; and to my enthusiastic and always-available agent, Anne Borchardt.

The women whom I interviewed for this book were generous and insightful. They speak in their own eloquent voices—there are no disguised names or composite characters. I want especially to thank Carol Dunn Brown, former dean of Continuing Education at North Central College, and Judy Wagner, reference librarian at the College of DuPage. I am also indebted to Adair Waldenberg, associate dean of the College of Arts and Sciences at Northwestern University, who arranged for me to have access to the university's library;

Acknowledgments

to Paul Numich at North Central College; and to Beth Kilmer and Lucy Ehrbar, who provided meticulous help with research.

This was a demanding project, and friends both got me through it and provided invaluable insights. In particular, I want to thank Julie Anixter, Elizabeth Bailey, Stanley Crouch, Sharon Evans, Bart Gulley, my sister, Cece Helgesen, my brother, Chuck Helgesen, who found me the perfect car, and my beloved father Charles Helgesen, who died the week I finished this book. I have been blessed in my relationships with all these people.

The real consequence of emerging science and technology is not gadgets, whether hydrogen bombs or silicon chips, but radical social change: ever-increasing diversity and complexity in the way people live and work.

—Dee Hock
Founder, VISA International

I am an American, Chicago-born, and I go at things as I have taught myself, free-style, and I will make the record in my own way.

—Saul Bellow
The Adventures of Augie March

CONTENTS

PROLOGUE:
Voices from an Improvising Chorus

"My life has almost nothing in common with my mother's. I'm having to make everything up as I go along."

"I created my job. It wouldn't exist if I hadn't. I just saw something that needed to be done, and I did it. Everything else flowed from that."

"I believe that women right now are changing the world, and I'm thrilled to be part of that. But some days, I just want to crawl into bed with a stack of Martha Stewart magazines, and stay there for about a month."

"I told my boss I want to work from home two days a week so I can get away from all the interruptions. Also, I can make the beds if I have a little downtime instead of wasting precious minutes trying to look busy to impress other people."

"What I see for myself in the future is employing more women who are like me. By that I mean talented women who do great work but want to have families and lives as well. Most companies ignore these women or treat them like slackers. But my own success is proof that if I hire them my business will thrive."

"I don't know how to describe myself anymore. I don't have a job just now, because my two girls are still toddlers. But I always worked, and I'll be working again in a few years, and I'll probably keep working until I'm in my seventies. So I can't quite view myself as a stay-at-home mother."

"When I took five years off from work to stay home with my kids, I became incredibly active in the community. And the experience I got, and the contacts I made, led to a whole new career that never would have evolved if I hadn't taken that time off."

"I'm twenty-eight and already on my third career. If I'd known how things were going to go, I would have gone to our community college instead of spending all that money to go to a prestigious school out of state. As it is, I've still got at least eight more years of paying off student loans to qualify for a career I transitioned out of three years ago!"

"My husband just got downsized after twenty-five years, and it's like the end of the world for him. We're lucky that I've been through a lot of job changes, because now I can really help him."

"The women in my neighborhood have all these incredible organizational skills that they developed at work, and now they're using them to run things at home. So everyone around here is scheduled up to their eyeballs, even the three-year-olds! Our refrigerator door calendars look like something you'd find on a corporate executive's desk."

"When I look around at the business world where I am now, all I see is priorities out of whack. I think that, as a woman, I have a clearer view of this, because I haven't been pro-grammed to accept it. And I won't accept it! I'm willing to make big financial sacrifices in order to have a life that makes sense to me."

"One of the great things about the way people live now is also one of the problems: there is just so much variety and choice. Life today is like Starbucks: you don't just order a coffee, you specify precisely what kind you want. A tall double decaf skinny latte—that seems like the perfect metaphor for our times."

The voices in this chorus belong to contemporary suburban women, all between the ages of twenty-eight and fifty-six. What they have to say echoes what I have heard from thousands of other women over the past few years, women who describe their lives in tones that mingle excitement with wonder, uncertainty with exasperation, deep satisfaction with occasional nostalgic regret. These women—ordinary Americans—are having to improvise their existence in a world very different from the one in which they grew up, a world that expects more from them than they could ever have anticipated, a world so complex and diverse that it renders the very word "ordinary" obsolete. This book is about these women, about how they are improvising solutions to the challenges that face them and changing our world in the process. For it is their improvisations, both individual and collective, that are altering the way people now live, pointing the way and giving direction to a common future.

Life on the Postindustrial Frontier

The large-scale entry of women into the workplace over the last thirty years, and their subsequent assumption of positions of influence and authority outside the home, is changing how businesses are run, how families are structured, how communities are organized, how children are raised and taught, how goods and services are conceived, marketed, and sold. The role women are playing in the public sphere, which not so long ago was assumed to be almost solely the preserve of men, is reshaping every organization and institution: business, political, legal, medical, educational, military, religious, and familial. This reshaping is in turn transforming values and ethics, altering cultural presumptions, introducing new notions of what is possible, and forging a new understanding of what really matters in human life.

The changes wrought by the movement of women into the public arena are drastic, structural, and profound. And their effect is compounded, strengthened, and deepened because they are taking place at the exact same time that the basis of our economy and the shape of the technology that supports it is undergoing a fundamental shift. The long-familiar industrial order is giving way to the confusing uncertainties of the post-industrial era, with its emphasis on knowledge and information, its inexorable speed, and its capacity to destroy established hierarchies. The advent of a truly global economy and the development of technologies that entirely reconfigure how we do our work are altering our world in ways no one fully understands.

That this major economic and technological upheaval should be occurring *at the precise historical moment that one half of the human race is also entering the public realm* dramatically hastens and intensifies the pace of change. The economic and technological transformations of the last thirty years have created new social conditions that have mandated women's participation in public life, but women's participation has also shaped these transformations. Women have altered the nature of the economy, new technologies have been developed to support this altered structure, and organizations are being transformed as a result. All these changes work together; nothing can be understood in isolation, since cause and effect are both cumulative and mutually reinforcing. And yet there has been no attempt to look at the advent of the postindustrial economy in terms of how it has shaped and been shaped by the changing role of women, and little effort to understand the social causes and consequences of the technological revolution.

It often seems as if a kind of fortunate confluence exists

between the entry of women into the public arena and the recognition that virtually every organization and institution is having to undergo radical change in order to succeed in the new environment. Certainly, if women had entered the workplace in the same numbers and achieved the same levels of authority even thirty years ago, they would never have had the chance to influence the broad direction of our society that they have today, for the simple reason that American organizations thirty years ago were fat and happy, institutions seemingly secure, and the industrial economy at its confident late high tide. This is simply no longer the case. Although this nation is by many measures more prosperous than ever, the end of the century is nevertheless also distinguished by a pervasive sense of unease, which is inevitable given the rapid pace of economic and technological change. Over the last few decades, seemingly invulnerable industries have collapsed, major companies have lost markets almost overnight, and both scandals and astonishing inefficiencies have corroded the common faith in public institutions. Much of this instability has resulted because, while the shape of the technology that determines how people work has radically shifted, most organizations continue to operate in a fashion suited to the industrial era.

The pervasive sense of dislocation that many feel is further heightened because the private and public spheres, so long kept rigidly separate and presided over each by a single gender, are losing their sharp definition, melding together in ways that alter the texture of people's lives. What many formerly regarded as strictly private concerns—divorce, child support, medical decisions, sexual behavior, the difficulties of reconciling workplace demands with those of family, even workplace jokes—have become matters for recurrent and intense public debates that often prove inflammatory and divisive. Indeed, on a scale unimaginable in the sixties, when the phrase first gained currency in this country, the personal has become the political in everyday life.

Men and children have been affected by all these changes, but it is women who have been most transformed by the confluence of economic and social upheaval, women whose sense of self and possibility has been most transfigured, women who have most benefited but have also been made most insecure. Women today find themselves having to forge identities and carve out lives with little precedent to guide them, lives that demand constant reshuffling and improvisation, lives that may be enormously satisfying but are also very demanding. And they must do so bereft of clear models that might provide direction and often without much in the way of support, because community is hard to come by in our transient and work-harried culture. Indeed, traditional notions of community in America have long depended upon women having the free time to build informal networks; now that fewer have this time, our communities are less cohesive.

The extraordinary increase in opportunity, and the insecurity that attends it, is affecting contemporary women in every situation, not just those who work outside the home. Indeed, as later chapters will show, the line between women who work and those who don't (often portrayed in the popular media as the basis for some kind of "war") is becoming ever more difficult to distinguish. This is in large part because people today move in and out of the workplace, often spending periods of time working from home, working part-time, or taking a few years off to prepare for a new career; as a result, the rigid boundaries that once separated work and home are breaking down. In addition, the instability that characterizes today's institutions forces people continually to reinvent themselves in response to changing circumstances, whether a layoff at their company or a divorce. These trends affect all adults, but are far more marked among women.

The fluidity of the culture is also accentuated by the fact that Americans are more fragmented, more self-consciously *different* from one another, than at any time in the recent past. This is true not only because of the great increase in immigration in recent decades, but also because ethnic differences are more apt to be emphasized and valued than in past decades, when rapid assimilation was widely accepted as the only proper goal. In addition, the big, established, comfortably homogeneous organizations that once bound large numbers of people together—major political parties, large unions, mainstream churches—are far less powerful and cohesive than in the past. Even big corporations, whose power remains strong, now employ fewer people, tend to undergo mergers or spin off established divisions, and are in general less firmly tied to the communities from which they draw their managers and staff.

The mass popular culture that only recently instilled the comfortable sense among the middle classes that "most people" agree on fundamental issues has also begun to erode. As one of the women in our chorus noted, we live in what might be called the Starbucks society, in which the accent is firmly upon individual choice. Today's marketplace requires people constantly to make decisions: what kind of coffee to drink, what magazines to subscribe to, how to exercise, what kind of sports their children should play. People do not wish to be, in the popular and metaphorically apt phrase, mere "white bread," like those complacent and generic Americans on television re-runs from the 1950s. People today want to shape every facet of their lives, and the commercial emphasis upon niche marketing enables them to do so.

These developments all have broad and long-term implications, as well as diverse causes. Yet none can really be understood without recognizing the extent to which the changing role of women has helped to shape these trends, while also being shaped by them. Women today occupy the uncertain and shifting ground where issues of economic and social change collide—issues that will not go away and must find resolution. Because of this, women are the ideal lens through which to view the evolution of postindustrial life and work, and, in doing so, get a glimpse of our common future. Women thus provide the century-end counterpart to the suburban junior executives who were the subject of William Whyte's 1956 *The Organization Man,* that classic of a more easy-going era.

In his book, Whyte examined the middle-class men who worked for the large, confident, highly bureaucratized and prosperous organizations that dominated the late years of the industrial era. He showed how the men's lives were influenced by the shape, form, and needs of their organizations and how the men's values, prooccupations, and concerns influenced their organizations in turn. Tracing the effects of this reciprocity, Whyte showed his men to be *the* paradigmatic figures of mid-century American civilization, the prism through which our culture as a whole might be viewed and understood.

Women today occupy this position. For just as Whyte's "great freemasonry of transients" transformed the social and economic landscape of America at mid-century, so the challenges faced by women today are transforming the nature of American life. Women, living at the point where public and private concerns collide, are both influencing and being influenced by the fluid and fragmented organizations to which the postindustrial era is giving birth. It is women's entry into the workplace that has blurred the lines between public and private spheres, and made the personal political in everyday life. Women—working women in particular—are thus *the* paradigmatic figures of the late-century American life and the key to understanding our diverse and confusing culture as a whole.

We all have our stories of how the social and economic landscape has shifted around us; some are wrenching, others trace a more gradual course. My own encounter with what would become the new reality for women probably began on the day in 1963 when my mother checked out *The Feminine Mystique* by Betty Friedan from our public library in Kalamazoo, Michigan. Reading that book, my mother, a well-educated and intellectually curious woman who had stayed home to raise five children and tried occasionally to fill leisure hours with unsatisfying neighborhood barbecues and bridge games, quickly recognized the scope and cause of her dissatisfactions. Within the year, despite a new baby and the firm disapproval of her own mother, she was back in school, and upon graduation she for the first time joined the workforce, teaching at our local university.

Thus, in a private way that did not at the time seem to presage any great social movement, my mother joined the first wave of middle-class women who decided that their education, intelligence, and skills should not be restricted to the home. This being the high point of American middle-class prosperity, most joined the workforce primarily in search of personal fulfillment, the desire for which took real courage to declare. In 1960, 21 percent of married women worked outside the home; by the decade's end, 33 percent did.

During the 1970s, the cost of living began to rise as a result of inflation, brought on most dramatically by a series of oil embargoes, but more far-reachingly by a drop in workplace productivity and the decline of the industrial Midwest. For the first time since the Depression, many Americans began to feel financially insecure and to doubt the premise that upward mobility was a kind of birthright that would continue on unchecked. As a result, middle-class women began to view work not simply as a means to achieve greater fulfillment or a greater measure of social equality, but as a necessary supplement to their family's income. Women might, and often did, stay at home when their children were small, but fewer viewed this as indicating a life-long commitment to solely domestic concerns. And so in that anxious decade, the entry of women into the workforce continued and picked up speed; by 1980, 42 percent of married women were employed outside the home.

Also during these years, the divorce rate steadily increased, in part in response to the sexual revolution that sparked a more experimental attitude in many aspects of life, and made both husbands and wives more willing to question the value of remaining in a troubled marriage. Women's growing participation in the workplace was both a cause and a result of the escalating divorce rate, because it convinced many women that they could survive financially even if they left an unhappy marriage—and persuaded at least some men that they could leave their wives with less guilt. Whereas in 1960, 22 percent of American marriages ended in divorce, by 1985, the figure was 44 percent. Unable to ignore this reality, many younger women began to regard the acquisition of professional skills and experience as their primary form of protection in the event of domestic dissolution.

As the 1980s gave way to the 1990s, the competitive pressures wrought by the global economy and the increasingly fickle nature of capital investments led many companies to make huge cuts in their staff and to continue cutting freely whenever management perceived the need to do so; the new practice of tying executive compensation to stock performance exacerbated this trend. Knowledge workers began to learn what manufacturing employees had discovered in the previous decade: that open markets and rapidly evolving technology are not necessarily consistent with expectations of lifetime employment, particularly in an era when greater wealth is increasingly concentrated in fewer hands, and CEOs often reap both widespread praise and immediate financial rewards for even the most ham-fisted cutting. In such an environment, men could no longer assume that joining a good company would keep their families financially secure; thus the permanently unemployed wife came to seem an unaffordable luxury to most in the middle class. Given the uncertain nature of contemporary employment, the two-wage household became the primary strategy for families seeking to spread the risk.

By 1996, more than 74 percent of all women over the age of eighteen were in the workforce. That figure is continuing to grow. Over the last two years there have been a number of articles in the popular press purporting to show that women's entry into the workplace has begun to slow during recent years, but, as Bureau of Labor Statistics economist Howard Hayghe has decisively shown, women's participation in the labor force has in fact increased steadily throughout the 1990s, even as men's has begun to decline. Hayghe notes that figures that *seem* to reflect the stabilizing of women's workforce participation actually result from higher school enrollment among women under nineteen, which of course bodes well for women in the labor force in the years ahead. Hayghe also notes that the nation's share of 1950s style married couples has continued to decline even as women's workplace participation has appeared to level off. In 1994, only 18 percent of all American households followed the traditional 1950s pattern of dad at work and mom at home with the children. It is a proportion that has declined every year since the early 1960s.

No one knows precisely how the social, economic, and technological changes that are presently taking place will transform people's lives. The future of everything, from the configuration of the workplace to the role of public education, is unsettled, open to question. Yet precisely because women are taking their place in the public sphere in so uncertain and transitional an epoch, they are in a position to determine the nature of what lies ahead, to stamp upon it the mark of their attitudes, values, hopes, and beliefs to an extent inconceivable in even the very recent past.

These circumstances have created a new social and economic frontier, one of a succession that have periodically redefined the nature and scope of American life. Americans have a long tradition of being skilled and resourceful when adapting to frontier conditions. Our notion of life as progress, the ceaseless urge to transcend limits and conquer obstacles, the constant expansion of notions of what is possible: these all result from the American sense of being a frontier people. Indeed, the steady movement of women into public life over the last thirty years has been a consequence of our frontier penchant for ceaselessly redefining what an individual might aspire to be.

Americans flourish during frontier epochs because such times free them to improvise responses to circumstances that have not been met with before. Unsettled periods give everyone a chance to leave footprints on the land, to be the shapers of the times they live in. As the historian Sharon O'Brien observes in her study of Willa Cather, "The essential quality of America resides in its unsettled wilderness . . . and in the opportunities that such a wilderness offers to the individual as the medium *upon which he may inscribe, unhindered, his own destiny and his own nature.*" But with rare exceptions—the Willa Cathers, the Eleanor Roosevelts, the Jane Addamses— the privilege of blazing a frontier path and leaving one's mark on the public world has been the prerogative of men.

In the classic myth of the American Western, frontier settle-ments were founded by men intent on escaping predictability and the triviality of safe and circumscribed lives in order to seek their fortunes under extreme conditions. The places that men carved out in the wilderness were violent, unstable, and wild, the frontier being a place of danger as well as a potential paradise. Only when women arrived did these settlements be-gin to acquire the trappings of civilization: schoolhouses and churches were built, a library society formed, and the minister became a force in town along with the sheriff. Lace curtains appeared in windows, prostitutes were chased to the town's periphery, and children became the settlement's future, its rea-son for being.

Implicit in this mythology is the notion that, once women arrived, *the actual conditions of the frontier disappeared.* As carriers of the arts of civilization, women were the implied destroyers of those frontier Edens where ruggedly individualis-tic men might roam free from the fetters of established cul-ture. This equation of women with civilizing values and men with the rough world of ready action forms the root of a partic-ularly American brand of romantic antifeminism, which both idealizes personal freedom and implicitly equates it with an escape from female society. It lies at the heart of this nation's unending conflict between the exaltation of untrammeled indi-vidual rights—usually envisaged as the rights of *men* (to carry a gun, to protect their home, to exploit the resources in their possession)—and the need to build strong communities that serve the common good, an activity usually identified as a woman's province. The tension that results from this conflict has long been a defining aspect of the nation's unique history.

Those who have studied the dynamics of frontier settlement know that the image of the lone conquering white male was often contradicted by truth; pioneers came in couples, or even as single women, and there were black as well as Mexican pioneers, for the conditions of the wilderness were complex, not at all simple. Nevertheless, the individualistic frontiersman remains a stock figure in our national mythology. And when one visits regions where the footprints of the early settlers are still visible on the land—say, West Texas—it is the men, the Dan Waggoners and the Burt Burnetts, who haunt the landscape, for it was they who wrested the land from the Comanche, they who signed the treaties, they who named the ranches and then the towns and counties of white settlement after themselves. The women who stood with them have vanished without a public trace, vivid only in the memories of their immediate descendants.

It has been this way because the divide between public and private, between work and home, has fundamentally derived from the divide between men and women, who have long presided over rigidly separate domains: men the world of enterprise and civic responsibility, women the province of kitchen, nursery, and garden. But as women have begun to enter the public world, and as the basis of our economy has begun to change, this divide has become permeable for the first time. Women are most immediately affected by the dissolution of the divide (which kept them powerless but also protected them), and so it is they who are improvising the solutions that will shape our lives in the years ahead. It is they who, in the words of Saul Bellow quoted on page ix, are teaching themselves, freestyle, the things they need to know and so creating the record of our era. That record is one of revolution, and women are the revolutionaries of everyday.

CHAPTER ONE

The Landscape of Change

The women whose voices make up this book's prologue all live in or around Naperville, Illinois, a prosperous suburban metropolis of 110,400 people that lies thirty miles west of Chicago. Naperville is one of the ten fastest-growing cities in the nation and is the only city growing at this speed in the northern part of the country. Naperville and the towns around it—Oak Brook, Lisle, Aurora, Downers Grove, Wheaton, Bolingbrook, Glen Ellyn—together constitute a true edge city, one of those sprawling centers of commerce and ideas that the writer Joel Garreau has described as "the workplaces of our new information age."

Naperville and its surrounds, the borders of which are always expanding and shifting, do not form a suburb in the traditional sense of being a residential satellite dependent upon a much larger city. As an edge city, it is a place where people not only live but also work, shop, and spend their leisure hours. As such, it is one of the new hearths of our civilization, a frontier zone where Americans are creating the future and improvising new ways of life amid the rampant opportunity and bewildering chaos that we have historically been so expert at negotiating. More of us every year live in places like Naperville, and so it was to Naperville that I went to study the role of women in shaping today's social and economic transformations, and to see how women are in turn being transformed.

Naperville is in many ways the perfect contemporary counterpart to Park Forest, Illinois, the 1950s bedroom community about thirty miles to the southeast where William Whyte studied his Organization Men. Whyte chose Park Forest because it was typical of the new postwar suburbs in which junior executives, who defined so much of mid-century culture, were beginning to settle with their families. While the complexity of our culture at the end of the century makes it difficult to confidently label any place as typical, Naperville is nevertheless characteristic of the fastest growing kind of American settlement today. I have focused my study of contemporary women in this locale both in order to accentuate the connection with Whyte's classic work and because the Chicago area's diverse and heavily suburbanized economy is representative of that of the rest of the nation. I am indebted to an insightful essay by Nicholas Lemann in *The Atlantic Monthly* for first pointing out the Park Forest–Naperville parallel.

From Park Forest to Naperville

While it is upper middle class and on the west side of Chicago, Naperville is different from Park Forest in ways that vividly illustrate the changes that have taken place over the last half century in how people live and work. Park Forest was a true bedroom community, a residential haven for commuters and their families, with few services, no major businesses, and little public life. The Park Foresters as chronicled by Whyte adhered to fairly rigid patterns, determined entirely by gender. The men worked for large organizations, headquartered in downtown Chicago, that rewarded loyalty and team spirit and offered security in return; they advanced through their careers in predictable stages and expected to stay with their companies until they retired. The women stayed home looking after the 3.7 children that were the household average; in their ample leisure, they visited with their neighbors. In terms of how they spent their days, the men and women had almost nothing in common.

Virtually all the adults in Park Forest were married (Whyte notes as the only exception a few "girl teachers"), as were 87 percent of American adults over 21 at the time. Couples tended to be about the same age as their neighbors and to have children of similar ages, all of whom went to the new Park Forest public school. Residents shared conventional values and subscribed to similar political beliefs, with most describing themselves as moderate Republicans. They belonged to the mainstream churches, overwhelmingly Protestant, into which they had been born, and they shared similar beliefs about how to raise their children. They watched the same television shows, subscribed to the same general interest magazines, and bought the same cars and household appliances as their neighbors. Almost all the Park Foresters came from somewhere else and would move elsewhere as the men's careers advanced. In this, they followed a tame version of the timeless settler narrative that has built this country: the men made the settlement in the course of seeking their fortunes, while the women, at home, made the place *a place,* defining a common culture and enforcing community values. Then when the time came, the family moved on.

Three things strike the contemporary reader of *The Organization Man.* First is the absolute, almost unquestioning faith and trust in large organizations that so obviously prevailed. Whether it was the companies for which the men worked, the developers who built the community, the established churches in which the residents had grown up, or the governmental bureaucracies that oversaw everything from the building of highways and the implementation of the tax code to the curricula for the children's schooling, the Park Foresters assumed that these entities knew best and could be trusted to guard the interests of those they served. In today's more skeptical and combative environment, when every new road or change in school policy is likely to be fervently championed by one part of the citizenry and fiercely opposed by another, this willingness to trust those in authority seems almost childlike, emblematic of a far simpler time.

Also striking is the homogeneity of the Park Foresters, defined not only by race, age, and profession, but even more by the similarity of their interests and way of life. People seemed content to have generic interests and ambitions, shunning the display of any individual taste or aspiration that might distinguish them from their neighbors. A comment made in the community newspaper in the 1950s by a resident of Levittown, New York, a comparable bedroom community, describes this homogeneity succinctly: "Our lives are held closely together because most of us are within the same age bracket, in similar income groups, live in almost identical houses, and have common problems." By contrast, few of us today can automatically assume that we will share the values, tastes, interests and ambitions of our neighbors.

Finally, one notices the sense of leisure and unhurried ease that pervades the lives of Whyte's suburbanites. The men, like commuters in a John Cheever novel, arrive home regularly by 5:30, so that evening ballgames and family barbecues are a regular event. They rarely travel for business, so there are none of the 5 A.M. departures for the airport or midnight returns that are so familiar a feature of corporate life in our era. The women seem to have unlimited hours for informal visiting, for the kaffee klatches and Tupperware parties that have become a proverbial feature of early suburban lore. The children, when not in school, seem always to be off amusing themselves, playing on front lawns or riding bicycles around the neighborhood, their activities rarely giving their parents cause for second thoughts. The sheer sense of the *spaciousness* in people's lives is like the remembrance of summer in childhood. Life today seems anxious, frantic, and overscheduled by contrast.

Whyte was concerned that the complacency, easy acceptance of communal values, and lack of enterprising spirit that characterized mid-century suburban culture as exemplified in Park Forest would make it difficult for America to produce the kind of dynamic individualists who had shaped this country and made it great. This fear seems largely irrelevant in an economy as fragmented, diverse, and driven by entrepreneurialism as ours has become; in a society where people tend to define themselves in terms of individual differences rather than broad similarities; and in a culture where insecurity is a major aspect of organizational life. In retrospect, it seems clear that the homogeneity that Whyte observed among his Organization Men in large part resulted from their living at the high noon of the era of mass production and mass consumption, a time when commentators frequently agonized over the spread of conformism and the emergence of "mass man."

Given today's complex and shifting circumstances, the large-scale entrance of women into the public world has not resulted in some ubiquitous present-day Organization Woman, a single representative type who easily epitomizes the spirit of the era. Rather, women's growing participation and leadership in fields from business to religion has only added to the variety of experience we find in an already decentralized and fragmented environment. The extent to which diversity and complexity now shape daily life becomes clear when one contrasts mid-1950s Park Forest with a place like Naperville today.

Naperville lies near the end of a commuter railroad line that runs alongside the old Burlington-Northern route, which bisects midwestern farmland from Chicago all the way to Denver. Commuters still use the line to travel to Chicago, but most people in Naperville these days work in the surrounding suburbs and so drive to work. The majority of the workforce is employed within DuPage County, of which Naperville is a part, or in Kane County to the west or Will to the south. These are the fastest-growing areas in Illinois and indeed among the fastest growing counties in the nation.

The region's sprawl of housing developments, office parks, corporate campuses, small towns, open land, commercial strips, and massive malls is webbed with highways. The most frequent approach to Naperville is from the East-West Tollway, also known as I-88. Developers grandly call the land on either side the Research and Development Corridor because of the many technology enterprises that have sprung up in the region since 1964 when the federal government established the Fermi Laboratory to study applications for atomic energy on a nearby patch of farmland. The corridor presently exceeds all other single-area suburban markets in the nation in both total office building space and offices under construction. Not coincidentally, farmland in DuPage County has decreased 93 percent since 1950.

To the east of Naperville, the silvery blue towers of Oak Brook and Downers Grove loom above I-88. Just off the Naperville Road exit is a large campus belonging to Lucent Technologies, formerly part of AT&T. Naperville has been deeply affected by AT&T's reorganization, although the companies that formerly comprised it together remain the largest employer in the region. It was in fact the Bell Labs division, which settled in Naperville in 1968, that set the city on the path to suburban boom.

Ogden Avenue is the main commercial street through town, an undistinguished series of strip malls leading to the old main route, Washington Street, which crosses the railroad tracks. To the east lie leafy old neighborhoods where the houses have front porches, and North Central College, a small but thriving private school whose campus is distinguished by tall elms and a wonderful old stone gothic main building. To the west is a small and lively downtown clustered around Jefferson Avenue, with its restored Victorian storefronts. Adjacent to downtown, the Riverwalk jogging and bike path winds along the DuPage River, which widens at one point into a large community swimming pool that was built by the WPA on the site of an old stone quarry. The humble older houses east of downtown are a reminder of the days when the Kroehler furniture plant was the big employer in town, and workers lived within walking distance. The old brick factory has recently been transformed into an indoor mall of restaurants and cafes, and other small industrial enterprises have also been gentrified.

Mary Jo Lenert, a long time resident who with her husband ran a local plumbing business, has watched Naperville change rapidly over the last thirty years, both in size (it had a population of 12,933 in 1960) and, perhaps more fundamentally, in nature. She says, "Up until the sixties, this was a real little midwestern city, a place with a bit of everything: agriculture, education, manufacturing, small entrepreneurs. You had factories, farmers all around, people who worked for the railroad, local business owners, tradesmen, rich people—a lively mix. There were corner stores in the neighborhoods, and you heard factory whistles during the day.

"That began to change when the corporations started moving in, bringing in a lot of people, but shifting them around all the time. Land prices went up, the farmers sold off, and the countryside was turned into housing. Things got very transient; at one point in the late seventies, I heard that the average family stayed in the area for 18 months! Since people were always selling their houses, they got very concerned about property values and didn't want factories or even stores nearby. Now it seems like everyone wants to turn Naperville into this pristine fantasy, like it used to be a quaint Victorian village, when it was really a gutsy little town."

South of Riverwalk is one of those attempts at the quaintness to which Mary Jo refers, a well-done restoration of the neat clapboard buildings that formed the original 1820 settlement; here teenagers in pioneer costumes lead weekend tours. To the immediate south, the 1960s subdivisions begin, ranch houses and occasional clusters of apartments set on winding streets beneath trees that now have 30 years of growth. The developments become newer to the south and west, the houses seeming to grow larger with every mile. South of Chicago Avenue lies the real boomtown, known by town planners as Sector G, the most recently annexed part of Naperville; seven new schools opened in this 14.7-square-mile area in 1996, with four more planned for 1997. Sector G nearly doubles the land area covered by Naperville.

The newer housing developments, none of which connect with one another and all of which can be reached only from narrow and traffic-choked country roads, have names like Ashbury and Amhearst, and feature houses that start at about 4,000 square feet. Many are under construction and stand alongside stretches of bulldozed earth or in the midst of fast-disappearing cornfields. These neighborhoods are still mostly bleak and treeless, with unsold muddy lots bordering fully oc-cupied streets. The beauty and drama here belongs to the wide, magnificent prairie sky that arches broadly over the unre-lentingly flat earth. But nature did not intend the prairie to support dense development, for the violent storms that these flats attract can only be absorbed by deep and spongy land. And so large stretches of open space border the new neighbor-hoods, and big retainer ditches have been disguised as ponds, all efforts at reducing the fierce and raging floods that spring, nevertheless, often brings.

Plainfield Road, which runs south to Joliet and is known locally as "tornado alley," forms Naperville's western edge. The old county road is now in the process of transformation. On Sunday, traffic is fierce, thanks to the new Calvary Temple, a 2,500 seat amphitheater that rises incongruously amid barns and silos, its design a cross between an airport concourse and a college fieldhouse. Beyond it, Sector G fades into Aurora, an old industrial city that has been troubled by crime, gangs and an eroding tax base, but which is nevertheless rapidly growing more suburban. New subdivisions are rising fast here, for houses are less costly than in Naperville, where the public schools are considered among the best in the nation. The city of Aurora actually cut off the water supply for a large subdivision that advertised itself as belonging to Naperville, although it lay very much within Aurora's boundaries.

READING THE LANDSCAPE

Naperville differs dramatically from Whyte's Park Forest in many ways, most obviously because it is a place where people work as well as live. Indeed, it has been employment, rather than the mere availability of housing, that has drawn settlers to the region. AT&T, McDonald's, Motorola, Amoco, Kraft Foods, Nalco Chemical, Allied Van Lines, Hewlett Packard, General Electric, Travelers Insurance, and Boston Market have either headquarters or major corporate offices in the area, and thriving new technology enterprises such as Tellabs, NexTel, and Spyglass all started here. The region has thus followed the development model pioneered by California's Orange County, where residential, commercial, and business development are mixed yet rigidly separated by zoning in a suburban mileu.

Comparing Naperville with Park Forest, one notes immediately the extent to which the barriers between men and women have broken down. One sees men and women in business attire drinking coffee at Starbucks at mid-morning, and men and women in leisure clothes scanning the shelves in the Barnes & Noble superstore on a weekday afternoon. The Mexican restaurants on Jefferson Avenue are filled with groups of men and women as well as students during the lively lunch hour, and men and women join the 6 A.M. traffic jams along arterial roads. Barbara Knuckles, vice president for advancement at North Central College, notes that several fathers are always in attendance at the 3 P.M. weekday soccer practice at her son's school. With 68 percent of the region's women in the workforce, and both men and women working flexible hours or working for themselves from home, old patterns of gender separation are fast eroding.

Demographic variety is another key characteristic, in contrast to the homogeneity that William Whyte both noted and lamented. Life in Park Forest was entirely dominated by couples about the same age, but in Naperville there are young people just starting out, retired couples, divorced men and women, as well as people who have never married. Pam Lenert, Mary Jo's daughter, an international group manager at Lucent Technologies and a single mother, says that her primary support system on the job has been a loose network of single parents, who take over for one another in emergencies. "We give our names as the contact person at our kids' schools," she explains. "Last month, one woman was tied up in a conference, so I got the call that her son had fallen at school. I told my boss, then left my job to pick the kid up and take him to the hospital. I don't know how we'd manage without one another." Sue Ross, a self-described "social worker for business," who is also on staff at Aurora University, started the mockingly named Spinsters Club for local unmarried women and found the gatherings larger than anticipated. Karen Keough, a senior manager at Lucent, notes that there are four single women in her four-unit apartment building and "not all that many kids in the neighborhood."

Linda Mellen, a transplant from Los Angeles who runs stress workshops for corporate clients and teaches yoga privately, has found it unexpectedly easy as an unattached woman to make friends in Naperville. "There are lots of cafes right in town—Starbucks and the Green Mountain—and that really makes a difference. There didn't used to be anywhere you could just hang out in the suburbs, but now you can go to the same cafe every morning and read the newspaper or chat, and people can get used to seeing you in a casual way." Linda has also joined the DuPage Unitarian Universalist Church in Naperville, as has Jean Ellzey, a divorced woman of seventy. Jean notes that the church "seems more geared toward individuals instead of couples." The diversity in age and condition one finds in Naperville reflects the broader demographic shift of recent decades, particularly the 22 percent decline in the number of married people over the age of 21 that has occurred since the Organization Man era.

Ethnic diversity is also evident. American-born blacks may be underrepresented, comprising only 5 percent of Naperville's residents (though a much larger percentage of its workforce), but they rank sixth in per capita income among all blacks in the metropolitan area. There are many recent immigrants from around the world, particularly Asians. This reflects a national trend, as newcomers during the last decade have begun settling directly in prosperous suburban centers instead of first moving to large cities. Professionals from Iran, Argentina, Pakistan, Singapore, and Hong Kong live in the $350,000-and-up dwellings in the new sections of town, while a whole colony of Russians recently bought into a condominium complex in Danada, a cluster of subdivisions just north of town. There is a Korean Baptist church, several Pentecostal Iglesias, a number of mosques, and even an elaborate Hindu temple looming incongruously over a strip mall.

Variety also characterizes the local business culture. Large corporations inspired Naperville's growth in the sixties and seventies, but the real boom now is in smaller enterprise. Although DuPage County is home to 26 companies with over 1,000 employees, there are more than 4,000 companies of less than 250 employees in Naperville alone, and an increasing number of people who work for themselves. The decentralizing of the economy and the boom in entrepreneurship are the major workplace trends in the region, as in the nation as a whole. Thus, to a degree unimaginable forty years ago, the balance has shifted toward *precisely* the kind of small enterprises that William Whyte feared were on the verge of disappearing and away from the large bureaucracies that he, along with other commentators at the time, saw as inevitably growing ever larger and stronger. What those observers could not have foreseen is the extent to which increasingly powerful technologies have grown ever cheaper, enabling entrepreneurs to challenge big companies without investing large amounts of capital to do so. The fact that an individual in 1996 could purchase for $2,500 the same amount of computing, word processing, information and communication power that would have cost *one million dollars* in 1986 has unleashed a surge in entrepreneurial activity such as has not been seen since the early years of this century. That surge is having a profound impact on places like Naperville.

Many local entrepreneurs have come from the ranks of downsized managers, professional service providers, and executives. These people were initially drawn to the region by large organizations but elected to stay on after they lost their jobs. Naperville's sprawling, vital, and complex character makes it hospitable to independent ventures, because the region provides many resources for those who go out on their own. The Business and Professional Institute at the College of DuPage, the largest single campus community college in the world, pairs aspiring entrepreneurs with successful local business owners who serve as mentors, while the local chamber of commerce works with North Central College to develop programs that serve local entrepreneurial needs. Naperville has one of the nation's most active chapters of the National Association of Women Business Owners, and the region has the fastest growing number of women entrepreneurs in the state.

Naperville has also become increasingly accommodating for home-based businesses, of which there are now 20 million in the United States. Patricia Kummer, a freelance history editor and writer, began working from home in the mid-1970s, following the birth of the first of her three children; she is enthusiastic about the entrepreneurial infrastructure that has grown up in recent years. "It used to be so hard, working from home. The only Xerox machine was in the library, and you had to hand feed it one sheet at a time! Plus you had to rely on expensive messenger services or else the mail in order to get your work to clients, so you were always running to the post office and waiting in line. Now Office Depot and Kinko's are five minutes away, and Federal Express makes everything convenient. Also, when I started out, there were no professional groups in the suburbs; if I wanted to meet people in my field, I had to drive into Chicago. Now there are lots of networks here, so it's easy to expand my contacts." Patricia adds that "it used to feel downright weird, working from home in a quiet suburb. You were so isolated, so invisible. But now lots of my neighbors are doing it. The man across the street runs a sales office from his basement, and a few doors down is a commercial artist. Also a woman with a day care center and someone with Mary Kay. We're all around during the day, and for some reason just knowing that makes things easier."

The accent on variety and choice that characterizes the business community is also evident in the variety of neighborhoods and housing choices in Naperville. In 1950s suburbs like Park Forest, houses tended to be similar or even identical in size and design, their cookie-cutter sameness betraying their buyers' wish to conform to prevailing standards. In Naperville, particularly in the newer neighborhoods, houses are so various that many seem to be straining to distinguish themselves. The postmodern pastiche reflects the pervasive desire among residents to stand out from the crowd, to make individual statements that both reveal their personal taste and suit their particular needs.

The variety results both from the large number of housing models that builders offer and the extent to which these can be customized. When Judy Wagner, chief reference librarian at the College of DuPage, moved to the area from nearby Shaumberg, she was confused to hear several women discussing their "Elizabeths." She assumed that they all must have daughters of that name, but soon discovered that the "Elizabeth" was a popular model of house. The options offered with these models are so extensive, however, that each woman's Elizabeth was as distinct as each one's daughters.

The consumer markets in Naperville also offer residents an opportunity to customize their surroundings to an extent undreamed of by Whyte's suburbanites, who had to content themselves with the standardized offerings at mass market emporiums such as Sears. In addition to the many local enterprises geared to satisfying particular niches, the trend toward mass customization reflected in our 500-channel culture permits upscale chains and franchises to tailor their offerings to every kind of consumer. The Fox Valley Mall off Plainfield Road, with its 150 stores, and the commercial "town center" in Danada, offer locals a range of choice for which they would formerly have had to travel to Chicago. Indeed, in Chicago one increasingly finds the same upscale niche chains—Williams Sonoma, Banana Republic, Barnes & Noble superstores—that were first established in suburbs like Naperville. Local choice has thus both exponentially expanded and at the same time become globalized. Yet because distribution takes place through national chains, local variety, although great, still occurs within a larger context of sameness.

The sheer multiplicity of choice available in an edge city like Naperville provides people with the means to have different experiences throughout the course of their days to an extent unimaginable in Park Forest, where the homogeneity of people's daily patterns both mirrored and reinforced the homogeneity of their tastes and values. For example, the increase in entrepreneurship, combined with the continuing upheaval in large companies, means that people in Naperville now work for many different kinds of organizations, in terms of size, culture, security, and benefits. This creates a diversity in terms of work life that is compounded by the frequency with which people change jobs and even careers. Also, people commute in every direction, often at very different times from one another, as a result of unpredictable hours and flexible schedules. Taken together, these changes mean that the particular situation of any individual is likely to differ distinctly from that of his or her neighbors.

People's domestic lives are also characterized by complexity and variety, in part because men and women now begin a family at different ages. It is not uncommon these days to find a couple in their mid-forties with two young children living next door to a couple of the same age whose children are in college. And because divorce is no longer uncommon in the suburbs, families no longer necessarily conform to a single pattern, but may be compounded out of previous families. Step-siblings may be far apart in age, children may travel back and forth between parents, and mothers or fathers may be raising children on their own.

This variety in work and home life is compounded by the accent on individual taste and preference that characterizes postindustrial life. Flexible and easily programmable manufacturing techniques and a sophisticated marketing approach that targets individual "lifestyle" demographics have combined to spawn products and services tailored to very specific tastes. People do not simply buy sneakers today, they buy Adidas for tennis and Nikes for running; they do not just have a phone installed, but buy a package of communications services that fits their specific needs. The emphasis today is on choice, options, and alternatives, those bywords of the 1970s counterculture that have now become fully absorbed into the texture of middle-class life. This customization brings richness and variety, but also increases the pervasive sense of fragmentation, the awareness of the differences among individuals.

The working mother of two school-aged boys who recently moved into a development in Sector G describes how this accent on individual interests affects life even in her new neighborhood, despite its classic "kids and cul de sac" demographics. "Everyone here is really pressed for time. That means most people only want to get involved with activities that *really* interest them, so everything breaks down into different groups. If you're a jogger, you meet other joggers. If you're into Bible studies, you meet people who do that. If you're part of an AA group or into gourmet cooking, that's where you focus. It's the complete opposite from the suburban neighborhood where I grew up, where the neighbors would get together for cake or just to watch TV."

FOR RICHER AND FOR POORER

The accent on variety and choice results in part from Naperville's relative affluence, which has increased dramatically over the last two decades. Until the late 1970s, Naperville was a solidly middle-class bastion, but during the last twenty years its neighborhoods have experienced rapid growth in both size *and* wealth, with the most affluent zip codes growing the fastest. In

1976, mean income for all households here was $32,548 compared with a national mean of $38,362; by 1996, it was $66,943 compared with a national mean of $44,938. What has occurred in Naperville has happened across DuPage County, and indeed in most of Chicago's western suburbs: communities like Oak Brook, Barrington, and Burr Ridge are growing ever more prosperous, while towns like Lombard, Elgin, and Aurora are falling farther behind.

This polarization reflects what has occurred in the society as a whole. Reports by the U.S. Department of Labor have warned for a decade that America is increasingly a two-tiered nation, in which many are growing richer and many are growing poorer; meanwhile, the center that defined the country at mid-century is disappearing. As Robert Reich has argued, a fundamental fault line now divides workers by virtue of education and skills. In 1979 a college educated man earned 49 percent more than one with high school education; today, that gap has grown to 83 percent, too wide to sustain the illusion of common membership in a middle class. The growing wealth we see in Naperville is in large part the result of its transformation from Mary Jo Lenert's "gutsy little midwestern city" into a sprawling center of the new information economy. Indeed, the upheaval attendant upon the transition to this economy (which has been strongly influenced by the entry of women into the workplace) is primarily responsible for the decline of the American middle class. If there is no precise counterpart to Whyte's solidly middle-class Park Forest, where modest income and aspirations coexisted with a sense of security and achievement, it is because such settlements, like the economy that supported them, no longer exist in proximity to major metropolitan areas.

Economic polarization is evident in Naperville's housing, especially in the newest and fastest growing neighborhoods.

Whyte's Park Foresters settled proudly into those standard-issue two- and three-bedroom "little boxes" that have now become emblematic of postwar suburban innocence. But while there are still some relatively modest 1960s- and 1970s-vintage ranch houses and split levels in the older neighborhoods near Naperville's core, the new houses rapidly filling great swaths of land are increasingly huge.

Gary Jamnicki, chief of construction for Joe Keim, one of DuPage County's largest developers, says that when he started with Keim in 1987, the average new house was 2,100 square feet; in 1996, the average was 4,500 square feet, and even 10,000 square feet is not unheard of today. "People seem to believe that bigger is better," he shrugs. "We went from selling $230,000 to selling $450,000 like a *shot*. Now four hundred is considered almost moderate around here and sells very quickly. A spec [a house built without a buyer lined up in advance] won't stay on the market more than six months if it's in that range. And the bigger they are, the faster they go." Jamnicki notes that in a Keim development in nearby Geneva, "we've got houses from two hundred to two-forty just sitting on their lots. But we put a seven-fifty up for sale, it's gone." As a result, developers are beginning to tear down smaller houses of fairly recent vintage in order to erect mini-mansions in their place on half-acre lots, which of course only further diminishes the availability of affordable housing.

Barbara Knuckles, who is on the board of a local bank, notes that real estate agents and developers often work together to create an illusion that only expensive housing is available in Naperville. "They keep insisting that you *must* pay $300,000 if you want to even consider living in this area, but that isn't true. There are less expensive houses around, but nobody wants to show them." Setting the entry level high creates a kind of self-fulfilling prophecy, boosting the average market price and discouraging those who work in local service jobs from even thinking of living in the area. The municipality, of course, has little interest in encouraging less expensive housing, because high property costs mean more money to support the local schools. And so while Naperville's booming economy and mix of high tech jobs enable it to attract increasing numbers of the new economy's winners, its escalating housing costs also help to winnow out those perceived as losers, further eroding the base of the middle class.

The increasing emphasis on affluence, and the perceived need that winners feel to differentiate themselves from those being left behind in an insecure and fast-changing environment, have resulted in a growing demand for both privacy and private services. Stockade fences have become popular in many neighborhoods, and anticruising ordinances keep Naperville's downtown streets quiet at night. And despite the city's outstanding public schools, the number of students who attend private academies is growing, as are private transport services in this region without public transit. In Whyte's era, children rode their bikes in the street or frolicked in front yards in the summer and after school; today, they attend private camps and enroll in an extraordinary range of after-school classes.

What one sees today might be characterized as the democratization of what was formerly an upper-class way of life. Nannies, au pair girls, landscaping services, caterers, winter ski vacations, weekend cottages, teenagers heading south for spring break—these were indications of genuine wealth in Whyte's unassuming era. The increasing prevalence of such luxuries in an edge city suburb like Naperville is both a measure of the growing affluence of those whose skills are shaping the information economy, and proof of the economic fault line that divides them from those whose skills are of less value in this time of transition to the postindustrial era.

Whyte felt confident that the hopes, aspirations, and limitations of his suburban junior executives reflected those of mid-century Americans as a whole. In so assuming, he was taking his place in a long tradition of social chroniclers who have drawn conclusions about the nation's direction by observing those considered to be representative of the larger populace. But attempting such a portrait today is tricky, since the belief that any one group can serve as a vehicle for understanding the nation as a whole began to erode at sometime during the late 1960s.

Indeed, one reason it has become difficult to depict with accuracy the nature of social and economic change in this country is the lack of any common consensus on just who "the typical American" might be. The belief that such a person exists seems to require a greater confidence in the commonality of people's lives and situations than is possible in an era when the social emphasis is on diversity and difference, when commercial interests promote the importance of the niche, and when economic polarization is on the rise. Of course, the notion of the typical American always reflected a certain innocence and presumption, assuming a homogeneity of experience and purpose that never did exist. Blacks, immigrants, Native Americans, even white factory workers never appear in studies such as Whyte's, except as supporting characters. Indeed, he presents women only as the *wives* of typical Americans, never as typical Americans themselves. People are too sophisticated for this kind of blindness today.

But it is not only a heightened awareness of race, class, and gender that makes it difficult to draw a generalized picture of contemporary American life. In places like Naperville, even people with similar demographic profiles who live in the same neighborhood and have similar professions are apt to have less in common with one another today than in the past, thanks to a great diversity in work and family life. People at mid-century tended to experience the major events of life at roughly similar times: If one was forty in 1964, one probably had a teenager living at home. By contrast, people today no longer move together through life in similar stages, but instead do different things at different times. It is above all the demise of this *predictable progression* through life, this discernible general pattern, that has led to a pervasive sense that no such thing as a typical American exists today.

Sandy Alcorn, dean of the School of Social Work at Aurora University and a resident of Glen Ellyn, which borders Naperville to the north, was quoted in our prologue describing the kind of fragmentation she finds in her region as a manifestation of "the Starbucks Syndrome" in American life. And indeed, just as the old generic order for "a coffee to go" has been replaced by the highly individualized request for "a tall double skinny decaf latte," so also has the proliferation of choice made people in general less generic and cut the ground out from under notions of typicality. As Alcorn notes, one does not walk into a Starbucks and simply order coffee; rather, one specifies exactly what kind, since variety not only offers but *demands* that one make a series of decisions and then articulate a customized choice.

The Starbucks analogy serves as a convenient handle for describing the kind of diversity and complexity we find in Naperville, where people are free to pick and choose from a smorgasbord of easily available options and package them together in particular and individual ways. And so it is that the new mother in Sector G finds not the undifferentiated neighbors she nostalgically recalls from her suburban childhood, when a barbeque pit seemed sufficient basis for making friends, but rather individuals segmented into highly specific lifestyle groups: joggers, Bible readers, recovering alcoholics, hockey mothers.

Life in this era of many choices offers broad opportunities for individual satisfaction, but it also makes everything more confusing, for it demands that people figure out just where they belong. The need to do so is exacerbated by the instability of today's business, professional, educational, political, and religious institutions. In the world depicted by William Whyte, these institutions were stable and predictable, and the society they dominated was capable of imposing firm limits on personal choice, while also offering people a clear place in the world and a sense of belonging. By contrast, the flexible and fluid organizations in Naperville today force people to develop a more flexible and fluid sense of self, one that is always subject to redefinition. This requires individuals to construct their identities out of more individual and fragmented material, and in circumstances where they have less in common with one another. Just as William Whyte was concerned with the long-term effects of the conformity he found among his suburbanites, so today's concerns must instead center upon whether people leading diverse and often stressful lives can find the sustenance they need in communities that are even more fragmented than frontiers in the past. The complexity and variety of life in the contemporary edge cities offers individuals more opportunities than ever, but also places upon them the burden of having to customize every aspect of their lives.

CHAPTER TWO

Why Women Are Leading the Way

Driving around Naperville, one sees evidence of the complexity, fluidity, taste for entrepreneurial ventures, vast array of choices, and emphasis on the niche that are hallmarks of today's decentralized, flexible, and knowledge-based economy. These characteristics are there to behold on the surface, etched onto the face of the constantly changing landscape of this booming end-of-the-century edge city; they reveal in chaotic outline both the nature of the economy and the configuration of the technology that supports it. What is not so immediately obvious, however, what one is not able to discern just driving through town, is the role that women are playing in shaping this landscape. And yet every trait examined in the previous chapter that distinguishes life in Naperville from life in Park Forest exists in substantial measure because of women's increasing participation in the public sphere.

In 1978, *The Economist* carried an article outlining the events that have had the greatest impact on the history of the world over the past 135 years. The list included the conquest of space, World War II, the rise of Communism, the elimination of slavery, and the invention of television. But the item that topped the list was "the vast change in the status of women." This change, perhaps the greatest and certainly the most rapidly evolving social movement in human history, is being played out in places like Naperville, where individual women are creating unprecedented lives.

As I interviewed them, I was struck by the verve and commitment of these everyday revolutionaries and the dramatic contrast between their attitudes and the familiar picture of today's citizenry as angry and apathetic, cynical about the future and doubtful about the ability of individuals to control their lives. Clearly, there is a chasm between the popular images of a populace that feels overwhelmed and frightened and these pioneers who are consciously fashioning new ways of life. Sue Ross, the management consultant who started the Naperville Spinsters Club, expressed a common sentiment: "I feel pretty optimistic most of the time. I feel that I can have a real impact, both in terms of shaping my life and making the world a better place. I see other women in this area who are doing extraordinary things, and I feel very much part of that, part of a really monumental change. But it's still kind of restricted; it hasn't reached the big political arena yet. Let's face it, Henry Hyde is still our congressman. In a way, if you looked at it on the surface, you might say nothing much was going on. But I know it is. Women are changing the world for the better."

The End of Uniformity

Whyte's Organization Men were above all homogeneous. Their family lives, the kinds of jobs they held, their beliefs and aspirations, their tastes as consumers—all these bound them together and identified them as belonging to a specific group. By contrast, life in Naperville is heterogeneous and diverse. Although demographers and real estate brokers continue to try, it is increasingly difficult to categorize people living here as belonging to clearly identifiable groups. This is in part because the postindustrial economy thrives on variety and change, but it is also because of the breakdown in the divide between men and women. Without the rigid boundaries that prevailed in the past, people are becoming less alike in regard to their outer circumstances.

The variety in domestic life is an example. I first became aware of the extent to which women's advent into the workplace is reconfiguring family life when I participated in a retreat for women in upper management at Baxter Healthcare several years ago. Baxter is a $6.4 billion company headquartered in Deerfield, a northern Chicago suburb that shares many of Naperville's edge city demographics. The women at the conference were all successful working suburbanites between the ages of 38 and 50, yet their family situations were dramatically different. One woman was 46 and had just given birth to her first baby; a colleague of the same age, divorced with two teenagers, had recently married a widower with six young children. A woman of 48 was about to be married for the first time, while yet another of 42 had two sons in college. The women belonged to the same generation, but there was no predictable pattern in their lives. Each had made an individual choice.

Comparing this diversity with the uniformity documented by William Whyte, I began to recognize a profound truth: that the breakdown in family uniformity *is almost entirely the consequence of women's entry into the workplace.* Rigid patterns thrived upon and resulted from the equally rigid separation of the genders. With few alternatives, women at mid-century married early and began quickly to have children; by contrast, women today, who have many alternatives, increasingly delay doing both. Statistics tell only part of the story: in 1956, American women married on average at 20 years of age and bore a first child fourteen months after marriage; in 1996, women married on average at the age of 24 and bore a first child three years after marriage. But the real change lies in the dramatic increase in very long delays: Almost 30 percent of college educated women today reach the age of 35 without having borne any children.

This causes great variety in life patterns and is a primary reason that the generations no longer move together through predictable stages. The variety in family life has been further augmented by the rising rate of divorce, which has increased both the number of single parents and the number of families composed of children of very different ages. Although the frequency of divorce today has many causes, the change in women's status has played a major role by making women far less dependent on marriage; indeed, the more money a college educated woman earns today, the more likely she is to have been divorced. Thus have the social consequences of women's entry into the workplace led directly to the kind of diversity in home life that I first recognized at the Baxter conference.

This diversity is evident in Naperville. A counselor at Illinois Benedictine College, which lies on the border between Naperville and Lisle, notes, "I find it impossible these days to guess what kind of family situation someone has. It no longer has anything to do with age or background or income. Everyone's situation is different, and it's always changing." Judy Wagner, the reference librarian at the College of DuPage, observes that it no longer makes sense to assume that women of the same age have the same experience. During women's history month, she says, the school sponsored a series of roundtables, organized by decade—women in their forties at one table, in their thirties at another. The idea was to discuss what they liked best about their respective decades and also what they liked least. "We found it impossible to generalize about the women or fit them into categories based upon age, because the span of their experience was enormous and often very different."

Sandy Alcorn, dean of the School of Social Work at Aurora University, a few miles to the west of Naperville, laments that sociology textbooks still divide adult life into a series of sequential "stages." The model, based originally upon the work of Yale sociologist Daniel Levinson, posited a kind of developmental ladder, whose steps constitute an orderly progression through life's stages and transitions. The model was popularized by Gail Sheehy in her best-selling *Passages: The Predictable Crises of Adult Life*, which dressed Levinson's stages and transitions in catchy phrases—the Breakaway Years, the Deadline Decade— and made the sequential view of life a feature of daytime television as well as of psychology courses. Sandy Alcorn says, "We still use Levinson's books in class because there isn't much else, but our students, especially the women, can't relate to what he reports. They all say, 'My life hasn't been like this! I didn't have my kids then! I don't view myself as being in that slot!' " Alcorn believes that the linear approach to adult development is going to have to be rethought. "People's lives unfold more like spirals than ladders these days. And this is especially true for women." Alcorn's colleague, Fred McKenzie, adds that, "We've gotten used to thinking of these stages as if they're rooted in the human psyche. But all along they've really reflected the larger culture, especially our system of economics."

Just as domestic life today is more diverse, so is life at work, and here again the changing status of women is a primary reason. Global competition and the pace of technological change have made organizational instability a continuing fact of life today, but this instability has been augmented and accelerated by the entry of women into the public sphere. By breaking down barriers between work and home, drastically increasing the competition for jobs, and creating demand for a broad array of new services and products, women have simultaneously exacerbated, reaped benefits from, and been casualties of today's organizational upheavals. Thus, it is hardly surprising that women are leading every trend that characterizes postindustrial work life: They are more likely than men to shift jobs and careers, to start their own businesses, to telecommute, to assume work on a project basis, to work from home, to integrate periods of education with periods of employment, and to plan for longer work lives punctuated by periods away from work.

The greater variety, fluidity, changeability, and discontinuity experienced by women in the workplace is occurring for a number of reasons, all of which we see reflected in Naperville. Women have a long tradition of moving in and out of the workplace in order to care for children or for aging parents; they generally feel less stigma than men when they take these periods off; with less seniority, women have less job security and so are often the first to be cut in a downsizing; they are driven from large organizations at a faster rate than men by the persistence of the glass ceiling; and they are more likely than men to seek retraining on their own time and using their own money. Thus, some of the very disadvantages that held women back in the industrial workplace are now often proving advantageous, enabling women to adapt more quickly to the realities of the information economy, and pushing them to improvise individual solutions to the pervasive instability that confronts us all. And women's experience in negotiating the uncertain shoals of economic change often proves a resource that is valuable for their families.

Joan Gunzberg, an arts administrator who runs a foundation in Chicago, lives in Evanston, a suburb to the city's immediate north. She made the point about women serving as a resource for others as she sought to put her own experience in a broader context. "My career has gone through major changes," she says. "I started out as a teacher, then left to raise my kids. I was part of a group of women all about the same age—we lived in Buffalo, New York, at the time—who all stayed home when our kids were small, and who in the years since have ended up doing very different things, from being a college president to selling real estate." After she and her husband moved to Illinois, Joan decided to return to work, but had no interest in being a teacher. She knew she wanted something different but had to discover what it was. "There was a lot of struggle around making the shift. I had to learn a lot of different skills and think about how to market myself. Really, I had to figure out how to create a job that would suit me. Now my husband, who's in his fifties, is without work for the first time—the company he'd been with for many years was recently sold. I'm a real resource for him, because I've been where he is, I know how to handle being without work, how you create yourself all over again when the situation demands it. And I see the same thing happening with my friends. The women have already been through their big career shifts, after being out of work when the kids were young, and now their husbands are losing their jobs. So the husbands are having to learn from their wives, because we've been there first."

Just as Sandy Alcorn's students are finding that schematic and linear "stages" do not describe their family lives, neither does the linear approach reflect their work lives. I spent some time in one of Alcorn's classes and found that the students, the majority of them women and all candidates for a master's degree in social work, represented an extraordinary variety of situations, while also ranging in age from mid-twenties to mid-sixties. Among the students were a former marine colonel with a full pension, a full-time mother with three young children still at home, a nurse with 32 years experience who wanted to switch to less physically demanding work, and the female superintendant of a juvenile prison who also moonlighted as an aerobics instructor. Most were either starting new careers or seeking credentials that would enable them to make a major transition. When asked, few saw the changes and transitions they were in the midst of as being tied either to predictable events or to their specific ages. Glenda Blakemore, the corrections officer/aerobics instructor, seemed to echo Bellow's Augie March, quoted in the prologue, when she said, "Things just come at you, and you keep responding, try to keep on top. And you learn from that, and that creates what happens next. But I can't see it as some neat pattern."

Alcorn finds that the women in her classes "view their work and family as integrated, inseparable aspects of who they are and how they have developed. They have a holistic approach toward life that is very different than what I saw in years past." She notes that the women's focus is both broad and diffuse, at times centering on family, at times more on work, depending upon what the immediate situation requires. Because they are always having to respond to evolving circumstances, the women's careers don't unfold predictably, hence the enormous variety in background and experience.

The economic polarization one sees in Naperville has also been profoundly influenced by women's entry into the workplace, because the income provided by women contributes substantially to the growing disparity in household wealth. This is true both because families with two incomes usually have more money than those that do not, and because women who work tend to have fewer children. But it also reflects the growing tendency of men and women with high income potential to seek one another out, a phenomenon that sociologists call "assortive mating." Male doctors today are more likely to marry professors or executives than nurses, while male lawyers marry other lawyers instead of their secretaries as they did in the past. Indeed, the large increase in the prosperity of the professional and managerial classes in this country over the last decade derives in substantial part from the double incomes earned by such couples. Thus, the practice of "assortive mating" has played an important role in hollowing out the middle class, widening the gap between those at the top and those at the bottom, because low-income women also tend to partner with low-income men. This has contributed to the greater spread in the range of household incomes, even as it has also given families in different brackets less in common.

Women's participation in the paid economy has also led to another characteristic of life in Naperville today: the democratizing of upper-class ways of life. A significant portion of the income earned by professional married women goes toward helping their families afford weekend houses and expensive children's camps, luxuries unknown to the middle class in the Organization Man era. Dual-career professional couples in Naperville drive the market for high-end services such as gardening crews, cleaning women, and private vans to chauffeur children to after-school classes. The demand exists in part because these couples have higher discretionary incomes, and in part because they are hard pressed for time. As Barbara Casey, owner of a successful advertising agency in Naperville, puts it, "Our family doesn't have a lot of time together as it is. So when we *are* together, we really want to enjoy it." The demand for personal services has created a boom in a broad range of low-wage jobs, which further contributes to economic polarization.

One of the great, though rarely acknowledged, supports of the middle class in William Whyte's era was the national consensus on the desirability of the "family wage." Conventional wisdom today holds that only women's salaries have enabled millions of families to remain in the middle class. This is true, but it is also true that women were kept out of the workforce for most of this century because of a widespread commitment to the belief that every man was entitled to a job that earned him enough to support an entire household.

The concept of the family wage has a telling history. It was adopted in the years just after World War I, both in order to force women from the workplace so that their jobs could be given to returning veterans, and because it satisfied a peculiar convergence of interest between capital and labor. Union leaders recognized that women's participation in the workforce tended to keep wages lower by expanding the pool of mostly unskilled workers that the industrial economy demanded. Thus, if women could be persuaded to stay at home, unions would be able to win higher wages in collective bargaining. Business owners, for their part, feared socialist revolution and were eager to discourage workers from revolt. The more pragmatic among them recognized, in the words of one prominent factory owner, that "the working man who is the sole support of his entire family will be more malleable and less prone to strike." Thus, an informal policy of paying a family wage was adopted during the early 1920s and renewed after World War II in order once again to provide jobs for returning veterans. American dominance in the world economy and the stability of mid-century organizations in an uncompetitive environment permitted the economy to thrive despite this extraordinary restriction on the labor force.

The writer Barbara Ehrenreich argues that the consensus for the family wage began to break down in the early 1960s, not in response to the women's movement, but as a result of a male revolt against being typecast as the exclusive breadwinner— forced into the straightjacket of the Organization Man. Ehrenreich notes that many men in that decade began to reject the notion that supporting an unemployed adult female for the entire course of her life was compensated for by the fact that she "made him a home." It hardly seems coincidental that the task of running a household had become far less demanding than in the years following World War I, when the notion of a family wage was first introduced, or that the size of the average family had substantially diminished in the intervening years. Ehrenreich believes that this male rejection of bearing the entire financial burden for a family was an early cause of the rise in divorce that began in the 1960s, which in turn spurred the entry of women into the workforce. In any event, the family wage has been a casualty of the last three decades, its abandonment giving women a strong incentive to remain in the workforce while also contributing to the growing polarization of wealth.

THE DISAPPEARANCE OF TIME

Another aspect of life in Naperville that cannot be discerned by a simple drive through town might be characterized as the disappearance of time. That "nobody has any time anymore" has become a commonplace, a cliché of our era, something people accept and discuss without really considering all the reasons that it might be so. And yet upon examination, it becomes clear that the disappearance of time is also very much the result of women's participation in the world of work.

In retrospect, it is apparent that the sense of spaciousness and leisure that pervaded life in the Organization Man era existed in large part because the division of adult labor allocated exclusively to women the care of household and children. By contrast, the work of raising a family, keeping a house, and building the community today must be squeezed into people's (particularly women's) off hours. Women's dual roles are almost entirely responsible for this phenomenon, the impact of which has, of course, fallen primarily upon them. Arlie Hochshield's well-documented *The Second Shift* details the extent to which women are overscheduled and overworked as a result of often having to bear the burden of two demanding jobs.

The woman quoted in the prologue who prefers working at home because she can make beds whenever she has a few minutes of downtime is typical of those I interviewed for this book. Many women mentioned that they were always concerned with making every minute *count*, constantly battling to get more done during the course of each day. But making minutes count demands tight scheduling, both at work and at home, and this constant scheduling creates a condition of stress. Indeed, Nicholas Lemann, in his *Atlantic Monthly* article on Naperville, noted that stress was the problem most frequently mentioned by residents.

The disappearance of time that characterizes life in Naperville is also the result of the longer hours that Americans in general are working, a phenomenon that will be examined in Chapter 3. But it should be noted here that women's entry into the workplace is itself an important, if not immediately obvious, cause of the lengthened work hours that are making contemporary life ever more harried. The greatly expanded pool of skilled labor that results from women's workforce participation has given employers greater leverage in making demands upon workers' time. In addition, the trend toward self-employment, which is especially strong among women, contributes to longer working hours, because business owners have always toiled more than the 40 hours each week.

Finally, the diversity of work and family life wrought by women's changing roles has contributed to the pervasive harrowing of time. The need for individualized goods and services that arises from more particularized circumstances, and the ability of the niche-driven marketplace to meet them, give people the means to tailor their purchases to suit their desires to an extent that Whyte's more generic suburbanites would have found unimaginable. Yet this very proliferation of products and services, evidenced in everything from the variety of soaps available to the extraordinary selection among home computers and the range of decorating choices for the house, also makes life infinitely more complex and time-consuming. Again, just as women's entry into the workplace is a major reason for this vast increase in options and choices, so are women also most profoundly affected by it, because they make most major purchasing decisions as well as 75 percent of all shopping trips. In our Starbucks culture, even the most mundane purchases demand a series of decisions. And so while choice may be welcome, it puts still further constraints upon people's time.

A TIME OF OPPORTUNITY

The nature of the new economy, while influenced by women's increasing participation, also favors their continuing involvement. The emphasis on the value of knowledge in particular enhances opportunities for women, as organizations recognize the need to draw talent from a broader base. A generation ago, membership in the right club or graduation from the right school was enough to virtually guarantee a man lifetime employment in a prestigious company, even if he displayed little aptitude for the job; top positions were closed to outsiders of any kind. But the new economy is becoming too competitive and too reliant on knowledge and expertise to routinely tolerate such exclusionary policies. This is not to say that old boys' networks have disappeared, but the favoring of established elites has been eroding since the 1960s, when talent became more important than having the right connections in high-stakes fields such as investment banking and the then-infant business of computers. That erosion of privilege has created more opportunities for women, as doing outstanding work becomes more important than fitting in.

Pam Lenert, describing her successful though occasionally stormy fifteen year tenure at Bell Labs (now Lucent Technologies), notes that she has thrived both because of her company's emphasis on knowledge and expertise and because of her own skill in transcending cultural limitations, which she attributes to her outsider status. She says, "When I came to work here, it was the kind of place where, if you weren't at your desk, people would feel your chair to see how long it had been cold. It was all about making the right impression on your higher-ups, proving to them that you could fit in. If you were skilled at playing that game, you got ahead. Now, that sort of thing is over. Nobody cares if you're away from your desk or if you don't fit some mold. What matters is how well you do your work." Pam is currently managing a major software development project for Lucent. "I've got all of Asia, our most volatile and fastest growing market, so the results of what I do really count. My value to this company can be measured. I'm very good at organizing complex projects, and that's what's making me successful."

Pam also believes that the global nature of the new economy provides many opportunities for women because, as outsiders, they are often more sensitive to cultural nuance. "I see it all the time, working with Asians, how our white male executives act in ways that aren't appropriate at all. For example, at the beginning of a meeting, you often see these guys preening, talking in loud voices, establishing how important they are—peeing on the territory, I call it. Well, that kind of in-your-face behavior is extremely offensive when there are Asians present. They value being polite, honoring other people's space. One time it was just incredible. We had a group of Japanese executives over for a very high-level meeting, and our guys insisted on throwing around a lot of football lingo, talking about fumbled passes and Monday morning quarterbacking, that kind of stuff. They were trying to show off and be macho, but they just looked *ridiculous*. The Japanese had no idea what they were talking about. I had to take time with them afterward, so I could translate what had happened. I think men exhibit this kind of behavior because they've been dominant for so long—it gives them the idea that they're at the center of things. But it's just not effective anymore, not in the global economy, not when you've got so many different kinds of people."

The increasing integration of work and life that characterizes the postindustrial economy also presents particular opportunities for women. As the technology people use to do their work becomes less costly, more plentiful, and more widely scattered, work has become less compartmentalized, and the barriers that separate work from home have begun to erode. This can be especially useful for women, who have traditionally played a more active role at home, for it permits them to organize tasks in a more coherent and sensible way. Pam Lenert has begun working from home two days a week, managing her global project from the powerful workstation that Lucent has installed in her living room. "I can be here when my son comes home from school. I can be working and helping him with his homework at the same time. My phone calls from Asia come in at 4 A.M. anyway, so it doesn't matter if I'm not giving my job my full attention at 4 P.M."

This integration of work and home also supports the desire of women to see themselves as whole persons, whose rounded identities do not depend entirely upon their status in the workplace or the fact of their motherhood. While researching an earlier book, *The Female Advantage: Women's Ways of Leadership,* I found that even the most successful women executives viewed themselves as having complex identities that encompassed the various roles that they assumed in both public and private life. "I am the leader of this company, but I am also a mother, a sister, a daughter, and a friend," one divorced woman told me. "I think the role I play at my church is as important as what I do at work." By contrast, Henry Mintzberg, in his study of successful male executives, found that the men's sense of who they were derived almost entirely from the high positions they held. Mintzberg saw this as a major weakness among these men, which made them vulnerable during times of uncertainty and transition. It would seem that the more flowing and holistic approach to work and life exhibited by the women I studied is better adapted to a world in which change is constant, in which people must be prepared to move between companies, jobs, and even careers with great frequency. The instability of such an environment means that many people will spend at least some of their prime years either out of work or acquiring new skills. For those who derive their primary sense of identity from the position they hold at work, this can be demoralizing in the extreme, and indeed a recent *Wall Street Journal* report documented the growing problem of serious depression among male executives who have lost their jobs.

If a more rounded view of life's possibilities is particularly suited to life on the postindustrial frontier, it was also a feature of the *pre*industrial order, in which virtually no divide existed between public and private, work and home. Since the compartmentalization of the human life span resulted from the industrial revolution, it seems fitting that new forms of technology should have the effect of returning people to an earlier, more integrated conception of life's meaning and purpose. It also makes sense that women, who have been historic outsiders to the industrial order, should both be leading and benefiting from this reintegration.

The great social thinker Max Weber, in his classic work *The Protestant Ethic and the Spirit of Capitalism,* noted that women never became fully acculturated to the industrial system. They never entirely accepted the belief that the accumulation of capital was a proper goal for life; its reliance upon abstract figures for quantifying and measuring individual success; or its ethic of unceasing competition that, at its most extreme, conceives of economic endeavor as a kind of game. Sequestered in the domestic sphere, women, in Weber's view, kept alive the preindustrial approach to life as an integrated whole, an awareness of the embeddedness of an individual within family and community that is at odds with the larger culture's exaltation of individual achievement. This more rounded view of human life and its purposes has long been viewed as a handicap for women. Yet as the nature of the economy shifts, breaking down the divide between public and private, it begins to look more like an advantage.

Because the uncertainty of work today forces people to improvise and adapt, it also provides an opportunity for them to customize their work lives to align with their individual talents, skills, and interests. As Barbara Knuckles, the vice president for advancement at North Central College, says, "I've always tried to figure out what interested *me,* and then find a position that would let me explore that." Sunny Fisher, the advisor to Chicago philanthropists who is quoted in our prologue ("I created my job. It wouldn't exist if I hadn't. I just saw something that needed to be done, and I did it.") takes this one step further, viewing the public world as an arena for manifesting who she is and what she wants to achieve in the world. Her approach is not uncommon, for many women, as latecomers to the public sphere, seem to regard their work not simply as a job, a means of earning money, but rather more as a vocation, a *calling,* a means of expressing and satisfying individual gifts (a theme that will be explored more fully in Chapter 3). This shaping of work to suit personal tastes, which is benefiting both men and women, was almost impossible in the rigid world chronicled by William Whyte, where organizations had far more power to determine and regiment the shape of work.

In today's more fluid environment, women often benefit from having strong personal networks. Peg Price, the former mayor of Naperville and a present member of the city council, describes the workings of her own support group, which is typical of many in the area. Peg moved to Naperville in the late 1960s, when her husband was hired by the then-new Bell Labs division. "Those were the early boom years, when things were just getting started, and there was lots of excitement," Peg recalls. She remembers how she relished the feeling that the slate was clean, that she could have the freedom here to carve out a place for herself. Naperville struck Peg as a particularly promising place for a woman looking to improvise a life. "Because the R&D community plays such a role here, the emphasis is not on who you are, but on what you can do. And there aren't the social expectations you find in more settled regions—especially for the wives of executives."

Having moved frequently within the Bell system, Peg and her husband had learned "to be real proactive. We got involved in whatever community we were in right away." Instead of getting a job immediately, Peg began volunteering for the League of Women Voters; she was invited onto the board, then joined the Naperville Planning Commission, which later led to her being elected mayor. She attributes her success to two things: not holding any preconceived ideas about what she should be doing (not much of an option, since her original desire to be an engineer had been stymied in college by a professor who advised her that a woman engineer could never even hope to find a job), and relying on a closeknit clan of other women for support and guidance. "We have this regular group," Peg says. "We're a banker, an attorney, a consultant, and a college administrator. And, of course, me. Two of us are married, two are single, and one is divorced. We get together regularly once a month, that's a commitment we never miss. But we meet more often if one of us needs to. We really hash things out and make an effort to come up with solutions that will help each other. The process is very fluid: we serve as one another's mentors to some degree, but we each take on the opposite role as well. It works because we can talk about *anything*. We discuss our jobs, but also our most personal problems, and we don't hold anything back. So it's a personal and professional support system at the same time. But that makes sense, because, when you come down to it, it's all part of the same thing anyway."

It's all part of the same thing anyway: that holistic sense of public and private life being one exemplifies the approach of the women I spoke with in Naperville. The importance of groups such as that to which Peg belongs was another constant theme in the interviews I conducted. Carving out unexpected lives in a world with few precedents, women here have had to create from scratch an environment that gives support to their aspirations. Some of the groups, like Peg's, are informal, essentially gatherings of friends that through the years have gained a defined sense of purpose. Others are more structured, part of established organizations, such as the Women's Business Network of Naperville. A surprising number of the longer-running gatherings originated in the 1970s as "consciousness-raising" sessions, in which the women first groped to articulate their dissatisfactions. Over the years, as their members have gained more experience in the public world, these groups have come to assume a more constructive and dynamic slant.

What makes these gatherings helpful, according to the women who belong to them, is the quality of relationships that they nurture, for relationships are what enable these women to negotiate the unpredictable changes and opportunities that confront them. One member of a long-running group described the process perfectly when she said, "It's like the women in my group have found our paths together, although our paths are really very different. It's because of each other that we've developed to the point that we have." Given the institutional disorder that confronts people today, this view of personal development as evolving within a web of relationships seems particularly appropriate. In a fascinating way, the process mirrors what is known from quantum physics about how change occurs in the natural world. Quantum theory teaches that massive changes occur rapidly and unpredictably, rather than unfolding smoothly over time, and that they always do so within the context of relationships. In her seminal study, *Leadership and the New Science*, Margaret Wheatley writes of an "unseen fabric of connectedness" in which everything functions as a "bundle of potentiality," the power of which can be unleashed only through a series of interactions, which occur differently in different settings. The workings of the new science thus describe the nature of people's lives today far more accurately than the mechanical models that have long shaped our notions about how change happens.

A TIME OF RISK

Along with opportunities, there are also risks on today's constantly shifting frontier, some of which particularly affect women. Chief among them is the prevalence of divorce. Whyte hardly mentioned divorce in his study of Park Forest, but it would be impossible to write about life in Naperville today without doing so. Although precise figures are impossible to find, the divorce rate in DuPage County has stabilized at a slightly lower rate than the national average of 40 percent. And owing primarily to divorce, a growing number of DuPage households are headed by women. Edge city suburbs like Naperville can be particularly difficult places for divorced women, because of the lack of affordable apartment housing, which can provide living space during times of transition, and because driving requirements in such spread-out regions are particularly onerous for single parents.

Although college-educated women who are divorced earn on average more than their married counterparts, divorced women are nevertheless likely to experience downward mobility as the result of the loss of their husband's income, a real difficulty in an era when two incomes are often needed to maintain a middle-class way of life. Divorced men tend to be less affected by the loss of their wives' incomes, not only because they typically earn more money themselves, but also because they are more likely to remarry and to remarry sooner, which enables them to replace the lost second income. Thus, just as the phenomenon of assortive mating contributes to the disappearance of the broad middle class by raising the net worth of dual-earner families, it does so also by impoverishing those who are no longer part of such families.

Jean Ellzey, who lives alone in one of Naperville's older neighborhoods in a modest ranch house on a block shaded by tall oaks and maples, is an example of what divorced women in the area can face, especially in their later years. Jean, now 70, grew up in Texas, earned a degree in music education, married directly out of college, and moved with her husband, a theological student, to Chicago's north shore. She worked as a secretary to support his studies. When he found work, first as a Methodist minister and then as a college instructor in religion, Jean stayed home to raise the couple's three children.

"When my oldest daughter moved away from home," says Jean, "I began to get a sense of what it would be like when the others left. I saw women ten years older than I was, and their lives were *over*. I knew I needed to do something new, but didn't know what. I'm from a generation of women who didn't really develop as adults until we reached our forties, so I had no clear picture of who I was at the time." She had just taken a part-time job in administration at a local college, when her husband received the chance to do parish development work at a thriving Methodist institute in Naperville.

Transplanted to the western suburbs, Jean returned to school full time, studying for a master's degree in clinical psychology. She says, "I was beginning to feel more like a part of the wider world, more sure of myself as a person. But as that happened, I could also sense my husband withdrawing from me. It was as if he couldn't stand the shift in the balance between us." For a required course on contemporary marriage, class members were asked to bring their spouses. Jean brought her husband, who became involved with a younger woman in the class. On the day Jean graduated, he asked for a divorce. "My whole world just collapsed," she says.

Because Jean could not imagine anyone wanting to hire someone with so little workplace history, she devised a program based on her own experience and readings for women who were returning to school after many years at home. Based upon the proposal, she created a job for herself at a community college on the south side of Chicago. She taught steadily, then retired in her early sixties, only to discover that she had no pension. Community colleges had been exempt from pension requirements for the precise years during the 1980s when she had taught. Yet because she had been employed at the time of her divorce, she was denied any share in the pension claimed by her husband, whose younger wife (he soon remarried) also has a salary.

Again using her experience to create a role for herself, Jean became active in the Older Women's League of America and put together a workshop that she now teaches on the subject of women and retirement income. It is drawn from her own experiences and those of women she has taught through the years. She is now a paid speaker on the subject and is working to build her entrepreneurial skills in order to better market herself. To that end, she has attended classes at the College of DuPage's Business and Professional Institute and is a member of nearly every woman's network in the area. Money is very tight, though, and Jean has no security at all. "It seems I'll have to work until the end of my days," she says. Yet she also believes that her ongoing trial by fire has given her a self-confidence and resilience she never would have developed if circumstances had not constantly challenged her to grow. "I've been forced out of the nest. It has not been easy or comfortable. But I've learned to reach out to people as a result. So I've established this incredible network of friends—they're not just contacts, they're people I really love. I also feel that I'm part of something important that is happening for women. So in a strange way, I'm really grateful for my experience."

Cheryl Lockhart, a full-time teacher in the public school system in Aurora, has also had to stretch herself, but is less sanguine about the value of doing so. A single parent whose son now lives at home while he attends the College of DuPage, Cheryl is a classic example of the downward mobility occasioned by divorce. In order to make ends meet, she supplements her teacher's salary slicing meat at night at the delicatessen counter at Jewel's, a local grocery chain. Cheryl, who lives in the Naperville house that she and her ex-husband, a successful lawyer, bought in the early 1970s, has seen her finances drained in court battles over alimony and child support that have dragged on through many years. In order to keep possession of the house ("I don't know where we'd live if we didn't have it"), she negotiated an agreement to assume the cost of her own legal fees, which is the primary reason she has had to work at Jewel's. Cheryl says, "It's been incredibly difficult and exhausting, but I also think it's set a good example for my son. He sees that you can either moan and groan, or you can do something about your problems."

Cheryl is also studying for a master's degree, which will entitle her to an increase in her teaching salary of $200 a month, and enable her to cut back on her hours at the deli counter. She says, "I can already see that I'm getting ready to do something else with my life." She originally wanted to go to law school but thought it was not appropriate for a woman who wanted to marry and have children back in the early 1970s. "I like teaching, but it doesn't pay enough for a single parent in a place like Naperville. It's hard enough to live on one salary, much less what a teacher earns."

Cheryl says that while divorced parents are no longer a rarity in the area, they were when she moved back to town after her marriage failed in the late 1970s. "When my son was in school, I was always at Little League sign-up or basketball games. It was always just me and all the dads. I only knew one other single mom in those days, although now there seem to be a lot of us. Most women with kids who got divorced then ended up going back to wherever they came from, because it's too hard to make it without a support system. You really need your family when you're a single parent. Just the demands of driving are so great. When my son turned sixteen and I was able to buy him a car, it changed my life. Also, it's hard to keep up the expense and maintenance of a house by yourself. But it did give me something to talk about with the dads at Little League, since I was the one who took care of the lawn and dealt with burst pipes!"

Despite the difficulties, Cheryl says, "At least I have a profession. If you don't, divorce can be a disaster." She mentions a recent feature in the DuPage newspapers about local ex-wives reduced to living in their cars, despite their husbands' substantial incomes. The women kept up appearances by using mall dressing rooms and health club showers, but they were both indigent and utterly impoverished. Most had not worked steadily before their divorces, relying on their husbands for support while they stayed home with the children. They were unprepared for life alone on the suburban frontier. Cheryl believes that the local court system has done a particularly poor job of protecting divorced women, a situation she attributes in part to backlash.

———

A good number of the women I interviewed felt that their careers had in some way been shaped by backlash, thwarted by the jealousy or resentment of male coworkers, which became particularly fierce when the women made demands because of family. Barbara Casey, who runs an advertising agency from her house on Naperville's south side, spoke for many of the women when she described her former job. "They just weren't comfortable with a woman being successful. They resented my popularity with my clients. It's like they were always waiting for me to screw up." Susan De Young, a local lawyer who now has her own one-person practice, echoes Barbara. "The firm I used to be with just wasn't a good place for a woman," she says. "Three female attorneys in a row had left. The only one who stayed was a woman who never once talked to me, or to anyone else that I know of. She had no social skills, but she worked day and night, so the partners liked her. I realized that the firm just didn't value who I was. I got reprimanded for having lunch with my secretary, that sort of stuff."

In her 1992 best-seller *Backlash: The Undeclared War Against Women,* Susan Faludi chronicled the undercurrent of resentment against women's accomplishments that has attended the success of the women's movement, creating a workplace atmosphere sometimes characterized by antagonism and scapegoating. And indeed, in the years since the book's publication, the political phenomenon of the "angry white male," and the growing divergence in political views held by men and women, has been fueled by the widespread perception among certain men that women's growing presence in the work world has deprived them of the secure and well-paying jobs to which they, as men, are somehow entitled. The reality is of course far more complicated, since the primary reason for the disappearance of Organization Man era jobs is the advent of the global economy and the galloping pace of technological change.

Nevertheless, there *is* demographic evidence that as women have become more successful in the workplace, men have become less so—not surprising when one considers that men formerly had a monopoly on well-paying jobs. In 1965, 81 percent of all men over 18 were employed full-time, while 26 percent of women were; by 1995, full-time employment for all men had fallen to 67 percent, while rising to 58 percent for all women. Both men's declines and women's advances have remained steady for two and a half decades, so that when the figures are plotted on a graph, the lines almost mirror one another in reverse. The growing trend toward the permanent dismissal of workers from large organizations has had a particularly adverse impact upon men, because they always held the largest share of these very good jobs. Fully three-fifths of the long-term unemployed today are men, and these rates are increasing. Early in the decade, this was widely attributed to recession, but in fact the relative decline in male employment reflects a fundamental change in how companies are managing their labor resources and the extent to which they now favor temporary positions, outsourcing, and limited-contract work.

As women's workforce participation has grown, the gender gap in earnings has also fallen. Over the last decade, earnings for all men, except those with postgraduate degrees, have declined, while earnings for all women, except those lacking high school diplomas, have risen. Even the incomes of men who hold advanced degrees are not rising as fast as those of women with comparable schooling, although these are still not equal. Further, studies show that women, along with Hispanics, are the most satisfied American workers, whereas baby boom men and native-born blacks are the least content. As one demographer observed, "On nearly all counts, women appear more 'at home' at work, and happier to be there, than do men." Women also exhibit a greater sense of commitment to their workplace and a greater support for company values.

No one knows what the ramifications might be if men continue to lose jobs while women gain them. Such a circumstance has not occurred since the start of the industrial era, when the very notion of "jobs" first came into being. It *is* known, however, that periods of high male unemployment have traditionally been times of social unrest, and that in specific areas where male unemployment has remained high for many years (Glasgow, South Central Los Angeles), disproportionate numbers of men succumb to alcohol and drugs, resulting in family disintegration and domestic violence. Considering this, one may well ponder if societies have in the past implicitly understood that life is safe only when men are employed in substantial numbers, and have thus favored male workforce participation out of some self-protective instinct. This leads to some uncomfortable questions. For example, to what extent has men's monopoly on secure employment throughout the industrial era served to protect the larger society from the anger of idle men? And what might be the long-term consequences of this anger in an environment that no longer automatically favors male labor?

Such speculations seem remote from the thriving situation one encounters in an edge city such as Naperville, despite private miseries that may have been inflicted by downsizings at major employers. Yet in light of the potential for social distress that could result from continuing backlash, it is particularly fortunate that the new economy has been able constantly to spawn new jobs. The independent and entrepreneurial ventures that have enabled knowledge workers in places like Naperville to continue to earn a living in the face of major corporate shrinkage may have also ameliorated an unacceptable degree of social stress. Women's greater willingness to leave the world of large organizations to seek self-employment may also have contributed to women's greater social safety, by fore-stalling some of the male exodus from well-paying and secure jobs. It is conceivable that the economy had to wait until tech-nology could provide proliferating opportunities for self-em-ployment before fully integrating women into the world of work. The self-correcting nature of the new economy, its ex-traordinary capacity for both creativity and destruction, may have brought society to the point where we can live safely with less secure male employment.

Customizing
Work Life

L ife in the industrial era was circumscribed by rigid barriers: between men and women, work and home, public
and private. But by entering the workplace in substantial numbers during the last three decades, women have breached the
fundamental basis for the divide. As a result, the very nature of
work—what constitutes it, how it gets done, by whom, with
what means, when, and where—must be reconceived, because
a system of labor built upon the separation of the sexes cannot
survive the reversal of that condition.

Technology has always determined the nature of work, for it
provides the tools. Before the start of the industrial era, in the
last half of the eighteenth century, these tools were simple,

inexpensive, owned by their users, and widely dispersed. As a result, almost everyone—farmers, weavers, bankers, administrators, merchants, tanners, scholars, and scribes—worked in the same place where they lived. The domestic sphere, whether cottage or estate, was thus also the site of commerce and production, and men and women worked side-by-side, although at different tasks. Barriers were more permeable than they would later become, and life less compartmentalized. To recognize this is not to idealize the past, when class divisions were almost unbreachable, most labor physical, and life circumscribed and short. Yet the miseries of preindustrial work have been overstated. As Juliet Schor has shown in *The Overworked American*, people in preindustrial agricultural societies labored relatively short hours and at their own pace, spending nearly a third of the year in holidays.

The industrial revolution reversed this ancient rhythm. The invention of large, complex, and expensive machinery—from the steam engine to the giant loom—made the basic tools of production unaffordable for their users and too cumbersome to be located in the home. And so work had to be centralized, moved from the home to a separate place: thus were the factory and, later, the office born. This separation of work from domestic life then became the basis for the rigid division of public and private, which evolved into entirely separate domains for men and women. The notion of a woman's "place" being exclusively in the home was a sentimental attempt to explain this compartmentalizing but was not its cause; the divide existed because the expense of industrial machinery demanded that many people work together in a single place.

In the Victorian era, the ideology of separateness was expressed in the cult of the wife as "the angel of the house," who was imagined to be too delicate to face the rigors of the outside world. During the first half of the twentieth century, this notion was reinforced by a host of male and female "experts" who predicted disastrous social consequences if women were to work outside the home, although of course poor women had always done so. The insistence on separate spheres for the middle class reached its extreme in the 1950s, when it was intensified by families moving to the suburbs: work and home now took place in separate *towns*. This was the situation William Whyte depicted, and it was against this circumscribed and rigid world that early readers of *The Feminine Mystique* (my mother among them) began to rebel.

The maintenance of separate spheres for men and women, work and home, persisted into the early years of the computer era, when centralized and hierarchical mainframes continued to reflect the basic technological shape of the industrial age. But the development of inexpensive, powerful, and highly portable personal computers, and their establishment as *the* primary means by which people do their work, has begun to reverse the logic that led to the separation of paid labor from domestic life. By enabling people to do their work at any time and in any place, the networked PC has begun to make the need for distinct and centralized workplaces obsolete. Thus, the new technology permits a reintegration of work and home and the breakdown of barriers between men and women that industrial era economics enforced. In addition, by distributing access to information and computing power far more broadly and at a far lower cost, PCs have played *the* pivotal role in the creation of a knowledge-based economy in which individual human skills have greater value than capital equipment *or even capital itself;* this is why Peter Drucker speaks of a "post-capitalist society." As was seen in Chapter 2, the fact that this technological transformation is occurring at precisely the same time that women have begun taking their place in the workforce has created an unprecedented confluence between social and economic change: both forces work upon and modify one another.

It is worth noting that traditional barriers between men and women are also being eroded because both now use the same primary technology in their work. Until about fifteen years ago, most women who worked in offices used typewriters; even those rare women who achieved high positions usually began their careers working on these machines. By contrast, few men except those who wrote for newspapers had any notion of how to type; it was considered a feminine skill, taught to girls in high school while boys took "shop." Typewriters thus served as a fundamental symbol of men and women's very different status and were evidence of the restricted and specific roles that women who did enter the workforce were expected to play.

This of course has changed. Now virtually everyone, from executives to architects to administrative staffers, makes use of software programs run on networked PCs to do their work. Those who manage volunteer efforts from home also use computers; indeed, over 35 million Americans now have space set aside at home where they do some or all of their work on a PC. That both men and women now share the same basic technology of production gives them more in common than they have ever had: they share a language of work, and must develop similar sets of skills. This is a situation that has *virtually never existed in human history,* for since time immemorial men and women have used different primary tools, which has made the texture of their days distinct from, and even mysterious to, one another.

By returning people to a world of cheap and physically dispersed tools whose effectiveness depends upon individual expertise, the rapidly evolving knowledge economy is beginning to create a high tech version of an essentially preindustrial way of life, in which work and life, family and employment, are not rigidly divided; in which people determine the shape and scope of their labor; in which the texture of life feels more integrated, more whole. This may sound idealistic, especially given the stress that many working people experience today, the complex balancing required to meet the demands of work and home, and the extent to which the physical structure of many communities makes cohesion more rather than less difficult. Yet despite such difficulties, it is also clear that a transformation is occurring in the nature of work, which is indeed in the early stages of becoming deindustrialized.

This transformation is particularly evident in communities like Naperville, given their status as workplaces of the information age. For in such edge cities one finds all the major trends that are beginning to reshape workplace life—trends that to a large extent are being led by women. It is women whose lives are most dramatically affected by the disintegration of the old barriers between work and home, and women who have the most to gain from the change.

DECOMPARTMENTALIZING WORK LIFE

The most immediate means of integrating work and home is erasing the physical barriers between them. Pam Lenert, the single mother and Lucent Technologies project manager we met in Chapter 2, began to do this when she persuaded her company to let her work from home two days a week. The global nature of her job, which requires 4 A.M. phone calls from places like Taiwan, makes the notion of a specific work *time* obsolete; when this occurs, the notion of a specific work*place* becomes correspondingly less important. The portability, power, and relative cheapness of Pam's primary household tool, a workstation networked to a powerful server, make it possible for her work to come to her rather than mandating that she travel in order to do her work. And so, in the small apartment built onto the back of her mother's ranch house on a quiet street near downtown Naperville, Pam manages a global technology project while her ten-year-old son lies on the floor doing his homework. It's a far-from-startling picture in America in the late 1990s, one that people have come to take for granted, yet it exemplifies a historic shift away from the centralization of work that began with, shaped, and typified the industrial era.

The most dramatic example of decompartmentalizing work is of course the growth of home-based business. The flexible, decentralized, niche-oriented, and primarily knowledge-based nature of the new economy has made this era unusually hospitable to entrepreneurial efforts, while the speed of cheap and powerful technologies has made individual ventures more feasible than at any time in this century. In 1996, 20 million Americans earned income from a home-based enterprise. Naperville, with its highly developed infrastructure, plethora of professional networks, rich opportunities for advanced education and training, and wide array of organizations in need of a variety of specialized services, offers particular opportunities for self-employment. This has contributed substantially to the decrease in mobility throughout the region during the last decade, as people who are asked by their companies to relocate choose instead to remain where they are and sell their expertise on the open market. Thus is the present economy's emphasis on individual opportunity beginning to rewrite the typical settler narrative, in which those who have settled a frontier zone almost inevitably move on.

Barbara Casey, 32, operates an advertising agency out of the front den in her house in the Ashbury development in Sector

G on Naperville's south side. She did not initially envision herself as an entrepreneur and says the notion of being on her own "scared her to death," but she felt driven to it by her experiences in the work world. Barbara grew up in the suburb of La Grange, not far from Naperville. After graduating from Indiana University, she married her college sweetheart and took a job at a small agency in Downers Grove, adjacent to Naperville. "I'd always wanted to be in advertising, and it was a good job for learning," she says. "I did everything, from washing the president's car to writing ad copy." She began quickly to pick up her own accounts, but by the time she was 24, she realized she would have to leave the company. "My boss was an alcoholic and totally irresponsible—we'd have lawsuits from creditors, and he'd be out buying a Porsche. But I had some good clients, and a good team, and I knew that together we had some value. So I just took a big breath and called the president of a national agency that I had read was opening a local branch. I said, this is what our team is billing, give us a home!"

Barbara's boldness paid off. She describes the CEO who hired her as "a boss from the old school—gruff and profane, but with a heart of gold. I learned *so* much from him! We had a great relationship, and I was consistently first or second in sales." Then her boss retired, and a new successor was chosen, just when Barbara discovered that she was pregnant. "I was the first person in the company to get pregnant who planned on coming back, but I don't think anyone there really believed I would work again. Certainly not my new boss." Barbara took six weeks of unpaid leave, then returned to her job, with an agreement to work three days a week. "Our son James had some serious health problems just after birth," she says. "It turned out to be just a blister from the caesarean, but the doctors didn't know what it was, and my husband and I were constantly going in with him for tests. It was a very stressful period, but I managed to keep up with all my work, although people in the company were very skeptical about what I was trying to do. Whenever I'd have to go to the hospital for some test, someone would always say, why can't your husband go? And I'd say, we're both going! We both need to be there for this!"

After several months, Barbara asked to be allowed to work four days a week. "I was bringing in very good money for the company, really taking care of my clients, and there was no reason I had to show my face five days a week. But my boss hated the idea: he didn't want me setting an example, just in case some other woman—or some man!—started wanting to spend more time with the family. The idea in the company was that you had to constantly prove your loyalty. You did that by sacrificing everything to work. So I was put on straight commission, no salary, as a punishment for wanting to work four days a week. Even with that, I continued to bill top dollar in sales, which just seemed to make my boss angrier. He began complaining because I didn't hang around in the evening like the other managers, who were all men. So as a next step, the company took away my office, then my car. Finally, they put in new accounting rules that particularly killed me because I was only on commission. Basically, they were trying to squeeze me out."

When her son was nine months old, Barbara quit her job. "My boss and the other guys expected me to go away with my tail between my legs and be a full-time mom, which of course meant being a complete failure in their eyes. But my clients kept telling me I should go out on my own. I had learned *so* much: electronic advertising, billboards, radio, TV. So I decided to start my own company, even though I had a noncompete clause. I consulted an attorney, and he said the way I had been treated constituted harassment, so I let the company know that. They were *furious*, but they must have known I had a case, because they didn't give me any trouble when I went on my own."

Barbara describes a painful transition. "I was a total wreck. I had friends at the agency, and now I was cut off from them. Plus I was financially scared. I did have my husband to fall back on, and that helped a lot, but I was still afraid of failure. I also had a lot of learning to do, and fast! I didn't know anything about accounting, I had to find an artist I could work with, and I had to make a name for myself." The easiest part was setting up an office. "My only real business costs were $2,500 for a Mac and a fax," Barbara says. She set up at a desk in the bedroom of the ranch house on the north side of Naperville where she was living at the time. "Basically, I left my job on Friday and was in business for myself on Monday morning." She got plenty of referrals, and her business grew quickly. By the end of her first year, Barbara had done $400,000 in billings; she finished her second year billing $600,000.

Confident about future earnings, Barbara and her husband bought a four-bedroom, 3,300-square-foot house on a corner lot in the Ashbury development. They chose it in part because the front den made an ideal home office, but more important was the fact that "there are tons of kids in the neighborhood, and we can see the grade school from one of our front windows." Barbara especially likes knowing that she will be close to her son's activities once he starts school. "I plan to do scouts. I want to be the mother who bakes cupcakes. And I'll be able to do it if I'm this close to my son's school." The remoteness of Sector G from downtown Naperville has not been a problem because Barbara's clients are increasingly located in the far southern reaches of the western suburbs; her client base has now expanded as far south as Joliet.

Barbara is more comfortable setting her own hours than she was "always trying to show up just so I could please my boss."

She now works between 30 and 50 hours a week, depending on the week, dropping three-year-old James off at his playgroup at 9 A.M., and fetching him home at 4:30. "That's the end of my day, though I may still take some calls. And maybe twice a week I do a few hours of paperwork after he's in bed." She finds the rhythm of self-employment particularly constructive, because she is able to take time during the day to attend to needed chores. "I can stop at the grocery on the way back from a client. I can pick up the cleaning if I have ten minutes extra. Now that I work from home, I can't figure out how *anyone* gets things like laundry done when they have to go to an office every day."

Last year, Barbara hired her sister-in-law to work part-time as an assistant, bringing her infant daughter along to the office. "My sister-in-law was a customer service rep at a shipping company, but after her baby was born she decided she'd rather work for me. She saw all I went through with my job after I had my son and didn't want to try that route herself. Having her baby here has been fine, though once she starts walking, we'll need another arrangement. We don't know what it will be yet, but we'll work it out. There are lots of playgroups in the neighborhood."

Barbara believes that as her business expands she will be able to profit by hiring "a lot of women like myself, women who don't want to work sixty hours a week, who need flexibility, who are convinced they can be good mothers and good at business. Women who don't believe that they have to live and breathe their work in order to be successful. That's one of my goals. I know that I was of great value to my company even if I didn't work tremendous hours—it's just mind-boggling that they let me get away, let all that money walk right out the door! I know there are lots of women out there who are talented but who think like I do. There are men like that too—the artist I use likes to work at night so he can take his son to the park during the day. If I can continue to hire people like us, I should do very well."

Barbara Casey is one of many women in Naperville who found the rhythm of traditional employment incompatible with her notion of active motherhood. Many have told me that they couldn't imagine *not* working, and would do so even if they did not need the money, but that being employed by someone else was too rigid and confining to suit their needs. Jenny Potanos, the mother of three and a speech therapist who specializes in children with autism, works from a suite of offices in the basement of her home in a new development in Wheaton, which borders Naperville to the north. She spends several days a week seeing private clients and also acts as a consultant for local schools trying to mainstream children with communications disorders. She teaches a course on autism each semester at a local college and organizes training seminars for social workers, teachers, and parents who are dealing with autistic children.

Jenny's schedule is very busy, but she feels she has more control over her days than before she was self-employed. "Being a volunteer at my kids' school is important to me, but a lot of working mothers just don't have the time. I *make* time by taking every Monday off and doing something at school on that day. I couldn't do that if I worked for someone else." Jenny's husband owns a trucking company, and the flexibility he enjoys enables him to be with the children after school on the two evenings a week when Jenny works. "We're partners in this," she says. "It works because we both control our own schedules. I don't know how we'd manage if we didn't."

Susan De Young, a lawyer specializing in divorce and mediation, has found working from home a satisfying alternative to more traditional employment, in part because it allows her to "be there when my girls get home from school," but also because it lets her shape her practice to reflect her skills and interests. Susan, who is married to the pastor at a local First Presbyterian church, lives in Danada, the development bordering Naperville and Wheaton, in what she calls "your standard ugly suburban subdivision." Before she and her husband moved to the area from the East Coast five years ago, Susan had served as a public defender and then been a partner in a small firm.

"When we came back to the Midwest, I decided to take a year off and just be at home. I was burned out from my previous job, and I'd had a terrible time as a lawyer trying to keep my hours manageable. The idea was that I would relax, fix up the house, and spend more time with the kids. But pretty soon I was waking up wondering what I was going to do with the day. I felt useless and depressed. I was very crabby, and I didn't think it was good for the kids to see me like that. Also, my husband is a minister, and ministers don't make a lot of money. I realized that I needed to get a job."

Susan found the market for lawyers glutted, but finally accepted work as an associate in a local firm, a part-time position. "I wasn't making much more than a legal secretary, but I figured at least I'd be able to keep my hours down and have a life. I was wrong. I was given a *lot* of work, but I was still considered part-time because I wasn't willing to work eighty hours a week like the men in the firm. When I tried to get a raise, they said I didn't bill enough hours. After a year, I saw that it just wasn't going to work. The firm was simply not a comfortable place for women."

Susan decided to open her own practice in order to exert more control over her life. "I wasn't at all sure that it would work, because there are so many lawyers in the area. But I figured I had been unhappy in my last two jobs, so it was worth a try." At first, she assumed that she would need to rent office space. "That seemed like a big expense, and I didn't really want to do it, but I thought people wouldn't see me as professional if they had to come to my house." But a friend who worked at home urged her to try it, so Susan set up an office in her living room. She hired an assistant, who serves as office manager as well as secretary, set her up in the dining room, and bought computers, desks, and software.

Because she works for herself, Susan has been able to restrict her practice to family law, and to concentrate on mediation. "It suits my style, my way of operating. I don't like going to court, I don't enjoy the litigation process. I think most issues within families can be worked out without taking things to court, and I work with clients who agree with this premise. If I were part of a larger firm, I wouldn't have the luxury of doing this." Being clear about her professional preferences has enabled Susan to choose clients with whom she is comfortable. "If people are eager to litigate, I suggest they find somebody else. They're not going to be satisfied with me." Not having to pay overhead for a separate office has made Susan comfortable limiting her practice in this way, and within the parameters of a one person shop she has thrived. "I am very people oriented, which a lot of lawyers aren't, and it turns out there are a lot of clients who really appreciate having a lawyer like me."

Being home during the day has also worked out well for Susan's family. "I am here when my daughters (aged 9 and 12) get home from school. I can have a snack with them and then go back to work. I don't schedule client meetings for after 3 P.M., because the kids are going to be here. It's not always ideal, and the girls often want more of my attention than I can give them, but we do touch base and that makes a difference." The convenience of the Danada development, with its central location, has been an advantage. "This is not the kind of neighborhood I would ideally choose to live in, because I like more diversity. But there are lots of kids here, so you can do carpooling, and the girls can take a bus to and from school. If they have lessons, I try to find someone in the neighborhood who will come here, so we don't have the problem of who will drive them. And I don't let the kids get involved with certain activities, like traveling soccer teams, that would require we do a lot of driving. Because of our work, we have to prioritize."

The women I interviewed who worked from home all stressed the necessity of having their children out of the house in order to do so. After-school programs, regular playgroups, and day care for the youngest children were crucial to the women's success. Kim Weeks, now 30, who lives in the Naperville development of Hunters Grove, is the one woman I spoke with who had been unsuccessful working from home, and she had attempted to do so with small children in the house.

Kim grew up in nearby Glen Ellyn, got a journalism degree from Iowa State, then worked for a newspaper in Texas. In 1989, her husband, an engineer, was transferred to Amoco's corporate headquarters in Downers Grove, a few miles from Naperville. Kim was glad to return to her home region. She found a job with the Naperville Chamber of Commerce, writing a newsletter and brochures, working on advertising, marketing, and member relations. "I had a broad range of skills, so it was a good job for me. I like writing, but I can't say I *just* want to write. Being with the Chamber, I got to know a lot of people here fast. I began to feel like I was in the thick of things." In 1991, Kim had her first child, followed by a second two years later. She put the first in day care when she was small, but care for two children cost more money than Kim was earning after taxes. That is when she decided to try to work from home.

"I then proceeded to go slowly beserk," she says. "My husband does a lot of traveling, and I was home alone all the time. There I was trying to make calls and write, so I stuck the kids in front of the TV, which I knew was wrong and made me feel very guilty. I felt *so* isolated! We had just moved to a new neighborhood, and I didn't know anyone. But I didn't try to make friends, because I always felt I *should* be working. Even though I was home, I was never free. There was constant pressure, always something I felt I needed to do. I was absolutely miserable."

Although Kim continued to write for the Chamber, being at home meant that she had to forgo membership on various committees. "I could hardly bring the kids along with me. But the committes are where things happen, where decisions are made, and so I fell completely out of the orbit. I found I started forgetting peoples' names, things like that. When you're always around small kids, you forget how to meet people. You really lose the skill of being around adults. I got used to showing my emotions right up front, and that made it hard to be diplomatic. Being home made me lose confidence in myself."

After six months, Kim decided she could not continue. "My state of mind was so bad! It got so my son would start crying when I came in the room." By this time, her son was a toddler and her daughter no longer in diapers, so the cost of day care would be somewhat lower; Kim decided to return to her job three days a week. Still, she says, "I'm paying for having been out, and I'm definitely paying for working part time. I can't do things with real continuity, so I miss a lot of opportunities. I see other people moving ahead of me. I'd like to go full time now, but the Chamber can't afford it." Being back "in the world," Kim feels her self-confidence returning and has now "reached the point where I really enjoy being with my kids. But being at home taught me a lot about myself. I find I am even more interested in a career than I thought I was, and I can't ignore that side of myself. Also, of course, your kids *do* get older, so things get easier as you go along."

FLUID AND CUSTOMIZED CAREERS

Life in the Organization Man era was segmented into discrete and separate periods: youth was for education, adulthood for work, and maturity meant it was time to retire. Thus the stages of life for those who worked were predictable, even generic, unfolding in broadly similar ways. One might have paraphrased Tolstoy by observing that successful careers at mid-century were all basically alike; only unsuccessful careers showed conspicuous and individual features.

This is no longer so. Notions of what constitutes a career path are being profoundly altered by the end of expectations of lifetime employment, the need for people to reinvent themselves in response to fast-changing conditions, the creation of new disciplines and markets, and the demand for the continual upgrading of skills. As choices multiply, not only jobs but entire careers assume a more customized and fluid shape, with individual designs replacing generic patterns. More and more, people find themselves doing different things at different times in their lives, shifting careers mid-course, and taking time away from work to seek more education. And so, just as mass production and consumption are giving way to a consumer market that is ever more dominated by the niche, so individuals are beginning to craft work lives to suit themselves.

Women are leading this process, in part because their lesser seniority often means that they are less secure in the workplace, and in part because they have a long tradition of taking several years off from paid employment when their children are young. This movement in and out of work has long been considered an impediment to women's success, and companies have penalized women with irregular histories of employment. Yet today's pattern of continual downsizing, along with the trend to periods of self-employment, are rendering old notions of what constitutes irregular work patterns obsolete. And so the female tradition of taking some years away from the workplace, far from always being a hindrance, can in fact be highly adaptive in the new scheme of things, providing women with a time in which to reconfigure their careers.

The fact is that women who leave the workplace today overwhelmingly return to it—*and go on to have proportionately longer careers than most men.* While labor force participation at age 59 drops substantially for men, it rises for women, and professional women are apt to keep working well into their seventies. The time that many women often take off is thus made up for later; their leaving is a hiatus from, not an abandonment of, paid employment. To portray it simply as "dropping out," as the mainstream media often do, is to take an either/or view of life best suited to the industrial era, with its strict dichotomies and insistence upon compartmentalization.

In Chapter 2, the arts administrator Joan Gunzberg noted that she, like many women, had invented a whole new career for herself after taking some years off to stay home and care for her children. I found similar patterns among many women in their forties and fifties, whose temporary retreat from the workplace (often a time of active volunteer service) gave them a chance to rethink youthful goals in light of real-world experience. Many women had used this time to shift direction, to create careers better tailored both to their changing tastes and to the changing market. A number said that they felt more freedom to reinvent their lives than their husbands did. They noted that the men in their lives, bound by the belief that they must not abandon the role of breadwinner for even a few years, were reluctant to take the time away from work that making a major change might require. Because the women didn't feel ashamed of having their husbands temporarily support them, they were more willing to shift course as adults—a flexible stance well suited to life in today's ever-shifting economy.

Even long periods away from work are not necessarily a hindrance for women eager to fashion entirely new ways of working when they reach their early forties, that classic mid-career point in the Organization Man scheme of things. Bonnie McLaren, director of the Business and Professional Institute (BPI) at the College of DuPage, devises programs and services for people in the Naperville area who are seeking a better match between their skills and the marketplace. She believes that women have a particular talent for making successful mid-career shifts because of their "ability to metamorphize them-selves." Because women are accustomed to playing multiple roles, Bonnie says, "they are more comfortable constantly drawing on a variety of skills and recombining them in different ways."

Bonnie herself is an example. A former grade school teacher, she stayed home for many years while her children were growing up. During that time, she volunteered in local school libraries, served as treasurer for her church, and took a wide variety of courses. In 1991, she returned full-time to school. "I went back with a vengeance. It was a choice, I really *wanted* to be there. I was hungry to make a big change." She earned a master's in adult education, then applied for a job devising programs for the BPI, which was just starting up. Echoing Kim Weeks, she notes that at first her years at home made her feel awkward and shy. "I was full of fear that I couldn't keep up because I'd been away from work so long." Yet she also found that her volunteer work had helped her to develop important skills. "For example, because I had worked in libraries, I was very comfortable with computers and had a real feeling for the internet. As it turned out, I had a lot more to build on than I thought." As Bonnie "metamorphized," she began to understand that she was hardly alone in finding it difficult to accommodate herself to change, and this knowledge freed her to be inventive. "No one can keep up with the changes that are going on today. *That's the big secret!* It's because the technology is changing so fast. We're all just struggling to keep up, no matter what our career experiences have been." Bonnie has come to believe that taking time away from work is not disadvantageous in today's shifting environment, in which skills are constantly being made obsolete. "Its just a matter of always working to develop new skills and then constantly building on what you have. You don't really lose points for taking time away."

Not all women making major career shifts do so after spending years at home, of course; many cannot afford it, and others have no wish to do so. But even those who have worked continuously plan new, and more meaningful, kinds of work at midlife. Many are laying the groundwork for whole new careers while still holding down full-time jobs. Such women are exemplars of the trend toward what Wendy Reade Crisp, president of the National Association of Female Executives, has termed "casserole careers," carefully layered work lives in which the various ingredients overlap and blend. Most of the adult students I met in Sandy Alcorn's graduate course in social work were adding another layer to what were already complex casseroles, creating a whole new stratum of skills that would help them fulfill the ambitions they had developed as they had become more mature.

Glenda Blakemore, the corrections officer and part-time aerobics instructor in Alcorn's class, is an example. Glenda, 48, grew up on Chicago's south side, studied psychology and sociology at Northern Illinois in De Kalb, and earned her master's in community mental health from that university. Her goal afterward was to "get out of hickland and back to Chicago," but instead she married the athletic coach at De Kalb, and settled with him in Aurora, which was halfway between. Glenda's primary interest at the time was in dance: she had been part of an Alvin Ailey performing group, but she could not envision earning her living as a dancer. "A girlfriend told me about a job with the corrections department, and I thought why not apply?"

As a black woman interviewed only by white males, Glenda was skeptical at first, but she landed a position doing evaluations at a state prison. "That was twenty years ago," she says. "And it's hard to believe, but I've been with the system all this time. I've never been a company person, I just always did a good job and so I got promoted." In the late 1980s, Glenda became highly visible as both the first African American and the first woman to serve as superintendent of the largest adult male facility in the state, in nearby Saint Charles. She left the prison in 1991, to assume leadership of a smaller facility for juveniles just outside Aurora. "I left Saint Charles when my daughter started junior high school. The superintendent at Saint Charles had to live on grounds, and I didn't want Tamara in that environment." She also prefers working in the juvenile system. "Here we have actual success stories, by which I mean kids who manage to stay off drugs and out of jail. I get calls from all over from kids who used to be here and want to tell me what they're doing now."

During the last twenty years, Glenda divorced and remarried, and moved countless times with her job; she says she has lived at one point "in just about every small town between here and Springfield." Now, in two years she will be eligible for a pension, and she has decided that it's time for a change. "The only way for me to move up in this system now is to get a central administration job, and I don't want that, I'm a hands-on person." So Glenda is currently working toward a master's in social work, while also working part-time as a therapist. She needs all the money she can earn, because she wants to pursue a Ph.D. after she retires. "I want to do research and policy involving kids in the justice system and probably teach at a university. I don't care that I'll be starting a new career in my fifties. Age doesn't mean anything to me. It's demeaning even to consider it. I've always been independent about my work. I always figured I had the ability to create something that would be right just for me."

Women like Glenda, who view mid-adulthood as the time to make a major career shift to an especially fulfilling kind of work, seem more the rule than the exception in Naperville. But one also finds much younger women taking the casserole approach. Debbi Sawyer, 28, recently left a well-paying job as a CPA with Arthur Andersen in Chicago, after deciding that she really wanted to be a grade school teacher. She says, "I was in the best possible situation at Andersen. I got a promotion every year. But I saw quickly that the high pressure route was not for me. I like to be physically active, but I couldn't work 60 to 70 hours a week. I hated all the traveling. Plus I found a lot of the work I had to do very boring. Looking around, I saw people whose priorities seemed out of whack—lots of stress, divorce, real unhappiness. I knew I didn't want to be like them when I reached my thirties. I think a basic problem was that making a lot of money just didn't motivate me strongly enough. I *thought* money was important to me—that's why I rejected the idea of teaching in the first place. But after a few years, it was clear that I needed to find work I could really love."

Debbi is now attending North Central College full-time in order to get certification, and working 30 hours a week at a clerical job at Andersen's Saint Charles headquarters. She has given up her own apartment and moved back in with her mother in Naperville. A surprising number of her high school friends are going through similar transitions. "One friend got a marketing degree, but now she's working with the handicapped. Another was a biology major. She had a good job but just went back to school to become a nurse. One of my best friends was a business major like me, but now she's studying to be a speech therapist. Also, a lot of the people I knew at Andersen have left—some voluntarily, some not. With all the downsizing, people are beginning to question the rewards: you come in and you're expected to work like crazy, but there's a good chance these days that you'll never make partner. That makes it hard to accept all the misery. Now that I've made this big switch, it seems I run into people all the time who have made a similar decision. I recently met two male teachers at Naperville High, where I went to school—one had been an attorney, the other had worked for Fidelity. And in my classes at North Central, most of the students are making some kind of career change. I think this is the wave of the future."

Almost two decades ago, Peter Drucker predicted that the advent of the knowledge economy would shift the balance of power away from organizations and toward individuals. He understood that, since people are the only repositories of knowledge, workers in a knowledge economy *would actually own the primary means and tools of production,* which are lodged in their own hands and brains. Drucker thus foresaw that organizations in the future would derive their real value from the expertise of those who worked for or with them. He did not envision a withering away of organizations, but rather a change in their function. People would use organizations in order to achieve their personal goals, rather than being used by organizations. This reversal essentially turns the presumptions of capitalism on its head—another reason that Drucker uses the phrase "post-capitalist society."

This reversal in the balance of power is under way in Naperville, where women like Pam Lenert, Barbara Casey, Jenny Potanos, and Glenda Blakemore are using organizations in essentially instrumental ways: to integrate work and home, to develop needed skills, to acquire clients and qualifications, to survive during times of transition. Organizations provide these women with the resources that enable them to fashion lives in which their imaginations, talents, and spirits can flourish, but they do not dictate parameters or mete out tasks. This "powershift," as Alvin Toffler calls this realignment in the balance between organizations and individuals, is still in its early stages, but its momentum is already transforming lives on the edge city frontier.

Shaping Companies

In the Organization Man era, people sought to fit themselves into specific slots, to adjust their needs to those of the companies that employed them. In return, their organizations offered them stable and clear career paths as well as a means of defining themselves in the world. What they rarely provided was any opportunity for an individual to shape the organization, because the confident and secure companies that dominated the mid-century landscape were usually run according to set policies and practices. But in today's wide-open environment, where change is a constant, individual efforts can have a real impact upon the shape and scope of organizations, even altering the way work gets done. People in fluid companies on the forefront of change have the chance to leave their footprints, while also building careers that reflect personal passions and strengths. This creates extraordinarily satisfying ways to work and is another manifestation of the shift in power taking place between organizations and individuals.

These trends are obvious in the career of Grace Pastiak, the director of operations at Tellabs, a sophisticated manufacturer of telecommunications equipment that was founded in 1974, now employs 3,000 people, and has sales of $870 million. The company is headquartered in Lisle, which borders Naperville to the east, and has a big new facility in Bolingbrook, which lies just to the south of Sector G. Grace is one of the most prominent women managers in her industry, having piloted Tellabs's shift to the just-in-time system of inventory and production before assuming the job of director of manufacturing.

Grace had moved around a lot within her company, but her big break came in the mid 1980s, when Tellabs installed a new software system for inventory. "It was supposed to be used by sales and accounting," she says, "but no one could figure out how to use the thing. So they put me in charge, and I got it up and running in two months." This gave Grace a lot of visibility within the organization, while also whetting her interest in the management of inventory, a facet of business that was starting to get a lot of attention. "At just about the same time," Grace recalls, "John Young, the CEO of Hewlett Packard, gave a talk in Chicago about just-in-time [JIT] inventory and manufacturing and the reasons it had worked so well for HP. Two of the guys who started our company heard him and decided that we should give it a try. Because of my success with the software system, they put me in charge of the pilot. The idea was to try out the JIT approach with one factory shift, so we could see if it would work."

Just-in-time is a revolutionary system that reverses the premises of industrial manufacturing. In an industrial factory, parts are stockpiled in inventory and then sent down the assembly line in a predetermined manner. Each worker on the line performs a single task in the assembly process; at the end of the line, finished products are stored. The system is efficient in that it breaks down tasks into the smallest components, so that the human effort involved is repetitive and requires little skill or training. But assembly line production also presents difficulties in times of rapid change and uncertain demand, for large inventories accumulate at either end. The just-in-time system puts an end to these pile-ups. Parts come into the factory, are assembled all at once by teams of workers, and then shipped out to fulfill a specific order.

"It completely changes how the factory operates," says Grace. "With just-in-time, you don't use an assembly line at all. The production people on the floor work together on every product, assembling it as the materials come into the factory and shipping it out right away. When you use teams, people have to be involved in every aspect of the operation; they can't just do the same things over and over. This means they have to understand the product. Before, we had the typical leave-your-brain-at-the-door mentality at the factory; people's main concern was trying to look busy in case the supervisor came by. It was the old batch mentality—the workers weren't very deeply involved, so they didn't take much responsibility for what they were doing. When you shift to JIT, you have to deal with all that. You have to change attitudes. It's very deep stuff, but when you start to make changes, it's incredibly exciting, because you are actually altering the way people think about their work. In cutting over to the pilot, we went from a factory where people were afraid to a factory where people are really involved."

Grace recognized that redesigning how inventory was handled had the potential to greatly improve work life, yet the changes faced strong opposition. "The technical operations guy *hated* what we were doing. He thought that we should be trying to robotize the factory and getting rid of workers instead of trying to get them involved. He kept pointing out that IBM had just spent $350 million to robotize production, installing big new belts and everything. He thought, if it was good for them, it should be good for us. I said, let's just do it this way for *two weeks*. Let's give it that chance, since it won't require a big investment."

To minimize the opposition, Grace chose to pilot the new process on the night shift. "I figured there would be less chance of other managers trying to undermine the effort if it meant they had to sit in on meetings at 4 A.M. So I was basically working from 10 P.M. at night to 3 P.M. the next day, being there all during the night shift, then also staying during the day to do my job. There was a lot of resistence, but it all turned out because the people on the floor wanted it to. They understood the possibilities and made it work." Within a month, Grace's team had cut production time on the company's major product from thirty days to six and a half hours. "At that point, the operations manager walked into my office and ripped up the plans he had drawn up to robotize the factory."

"It was *thrilling* work," Grace exults. "A real phenomenon, moving manufacturing from the bottom to the top of the pyramid. The workers are in U-shaped work cells now. There are no supervisors, only two layers: electronic associates and electronic technicians. The system is flexible and the workers control it. It's changed the whole notion of a factory. We have no clocks on the floor, people come and go, we don't have to check up on them. If we trust them with the product, we have to trust them with their time. They work in a clean environment that is spirited and efficient. Getting rid of the old emphasis on routine, on people sticking to their slots was incredibly rewarding. And once you start working this way, the whole hierarchy just starts to turn upside down, because you realize the most basic assembly jobs are really the most important—if you have errors there, the whole process gets derailed. But the people at the bottom of the pecking order are the ones who have those jobs! It makes no sense, when you think about it. So once you internalize the new process, everything begins to change. You are *actually altering the way work gets done.*"

The brilliant cultural critic John Kouwenhoven has pointed out that America's most important improvisations have always been in the area of process and method. The mass production *system,* rather than any specific piece of machinery, was this country's greatest contribution to the development of industrial work, whereas mechanical innovations from the jet engine to the computer originated in England. This emphasis on process contrasts with the aristocratic ideal, which has always relegated an interest in the means and methods of production to anonymous peasants and slaves. Kouwenhoven finds the American interest in process reflected in our music's focus on rhythm, on the beat: finding it, altering it, syncopating it, making it *swing.*

Because new technologies require new methods, individuals like Grace Pastiak will increasingly have the opportunity to improvise new processes in the workplace, thus "actually altering the way work gets done." Those who do this have the chance to leave their own stamp on even very large organizations, rather than simply adapting to work as they find it. Those who participate with them in these efforts, like the night-shift workers on the Tellabs floor, will also have a chance for creative expression, for leaving the imprint of their footsteps. In periods of rapid change, individual efforts can have a greater impact than in settled periods, when established methods prove equal to most challenges. This is why even work in large organizations is becoming more satisfying for many people, offering scope for innovation and new ideas.

FROM JOB TO VOCATION

Talking with hundreds of women around Naperville, I was struck by the frequency with which many of them spoke of their work as something they felt "called" to do. Nancy Chicernia, a psychologist who uses art as part of her therapy, describes her decision to restore a natural prairie on a piece of land west of Naperville and then build a house where she can hold workshops as "a change in my life that I was drawn to make." Linda Mellen, who teaches yoga and stress management at large companies in the area, speaks of starting her own business after moving from Los Angeles to Naperville as "something I was *meant* to do." Susan Calomino, an independent financial planner who works from home, declares that, when she looks back at the evolution of her work, she gets the sense that "everything I did was leading me to where I am now."

Sue Ross, the organizational consultant who started the Spinsters Club, has also been struck by the propensity of "women who feel good about their work to regard it in an almost mystical way. I hear them describe the paths their careers have taken as inevitable, part of a larger pattern. They really conceive of their work as a manifestation of their fate." When asked to speculate upon why this might be so, Sue says,

"Maybe our intuition makes us comfortable with the idea of searching for a path or regarding that search with a sense of destiny. Maybe the unexpectedness of many women's lives seems fortuitous when you match it against the experience of their mothers. Or maybe our general culture has just been influenced by the notion of life as a journey."

Regarding work as something one is *meant* to do seems especially characteristic of women who begin new careers at mid-life. Kendyl Gibbon, pastor of the DuPage Unitarian Universalist Church, a fast-growing congregation in Naperville, believes that women are leading the way in seeking out more meaningful kinds of work after the age of forty and thinks that this inclines them to conceive of work within the context of a calling. A humorous woman with a warm voice and a masterful preaching style, Kendyl has long felt a sense of what she was meant to do. She grew up in a Unitarian household, decided as a teenager that she wanted to be a minister (the denomination has a long history of women pastors), and entered seminary right out of college. In 1980 she became assistant pastor at a large congregation in Chicago, then came to Naperville as pastor in 1988. Kendyl and her husband Mark, who helps full-time with parish work, share a house with another couple who have two children.

Kendyl is an adjunct on the faculty of Meadeville-Lombard Theological School, which serves a number of Protestant denominations, and from this vantage point she has witnessed a remarkable evolution. "When I entered seminary in the mid-seventies," she recalls, "there were very few other women. Most of the men in my classes were like me: in their twenties, just out of college, and very sure of what they wanted to do." By the early eighties, however, Kendyl noted, "things had begun to change very fast. All of a sudden, the seminary had about 35 percent women students. But the really interesting thing was the difference between the men and the women. The men still tended to be in their twenties, but most of the women were in their forties or fifties; they'd had other careers, and they'd raised their children. A good number of them had been divorced—dumped, usually—and that had sent them into a major crisis. Or a parent had died, or they'd had breast cancer. Whatever the impetus, they had gone through what could only be called an awakening. They had realized that life was short and that they had to do something meaningful. That impelled them to enter the ministry."

The mid-life women Kendyl began seeing in seminary had different concerns than their youthful male counterparts, and she believes that their presence is changing the ministry profoundly. "The women brought this extraordinary depth of experience, often the experience of real pain, to their work and studies. They were truly in the ministry because they wanted to heal. The result was an increased emphasis on caregiving, something that I think was neglected when mostly young male seminarians focused on the ministry primarily as a career." The number of women in the seminary has continued to grow, but by the early 1990s Kendyl had noted another change. Substantial numbers of men had begun to follow in the women's footsteps, and were entering the ministry as a second career.

"Now, when you look around in the seminaries," says Kendyl, "you see almost equal numbers of men and women in their forties and fifties, along with a smaller group of men and women in their twenties. The older people have had their time in the world. Particularly among the men, you find those who have unexpectedly lost jobs or careers that consumed the best years of their lives. Often, they've been disillusioned by the way in which they have been fired. They've begun to realize that they made these sacrifices which weren't appreciated. So now they're following their hearts and doing what they *really* want to do. They have found, in every sense, a vocation." Kendyl cites the theologian Matthew Fox's definition of a vocation as "the place where your heart's gladness meets the world's deepest need."

Kendyl also finds that women are particularly likely to view their work as a calling. "I think this is because our culture gives women permission to be unsure for a while about what they want to do. Permission to look around, to respond to their own intuition. Also, a sense of vocation develops most often when there's a combination of vulnerability and affluence. For many women, some basic financial security has been provided by their husbands, so they're more comfortable undertaking a search. But they also experience extreme vulnerability in the searching stage. Getting beyond that adds to the feeling of being on a journey."

The notion of a vocation or calling has long had religious overtones, yet women today speak of even the most secular work in this context. But perhaps this is not surprising when one considers the extent to which today's increasingly fluid and customized careers give people scope to express their "heart's gladness." This freedom, invigorating though it is, also throws individuals back upon their inner resources, and so requires them to attend to their intuition. In the Organization Man era, there was less need to do this. People could rely upon stable and often paternalistic institutions to make many of their decisions, and there was a basic blueprint they could follow for middle-class life. Today's environment, with its relentless accent on choice, provides no such blueprint: people must look to themselves and listen to their inner promptings. The clarity of these promptings depends upon the strength of their connection to their own spirit, which is perhaps why the language of spirit is increasingly finding its way into conversations about work.

What Is Work? What Is Passion?

Volunteer work provided women like Bonnie McLaren and Joan Gunzberg with experience and contacts that later helped them create satisfying paid careers. This is not unusual, for with people moving in and out of the workforce more frequently than in the past, volunteer work and paid employment are becoming more integrated, constituting different phases in a long continuum of work. Both help an individual to build a portfolio of skills and interests upon which to draw; both expand an individual's reach; both determine the shape and substance of one's journey through the public world.

In addition, volunteer work, now commonly referred to as forming a "third sector," is growing both in scope and in importance as other parts of the economy employ fewer people and perform fewer services. In his influential book *The End of Work,* Jeremy Rifkin warns that, as government slims down and scales back on its commitments, and as business organizations continue to downsize, nonprofits will either take up the slack or a kind of anarchy will prevail. Third-sector enterprises, Rifkin believes, will play *the* vital role in determining how our communities address the challenges of the century ahead.

This has particular significance for women, for women have long been energetic volunteers, especially those who take time off from work to care for young children. During the first years of the women's movement, this tradition of volunteering was often disparaged, and women's willingness to work hard without pay portrayed as a form of exploitation. However, in an era when a single job rarely suffices for a lifetime, the value of skills and networks formed while volunteering becomes more clear. Increasingly, the volunteer sector is where people express—and often discover—their real passion, which may then have a profound effect on how they earn their living.

We see this especially in the new kind of parental activism that has begun to reshape our institutions. The story of Susie Alberts, a Chicago-area mother whose daughter, now sixteen, has the genetic disorder known as Charcot-Marie-Tooth disease, vividly illustrates this point. When Susie's daughter Jamie was born, she had almost no muscles in her legs, arms, hands, or feet; what little she had was expected to degenerate quickly. "Every doctor we went to said the same thing," Susie recalls, "that there was absolutely nothing we could do. Our daughter would never be able to walk or do anything physical—we just had to accept it. But I couldn't do that; I was desperate."

Susie, a psychotherapist and counselor at a mental health clinic, had planned to work part-time after her daughter's birth but decided instead to devote all her efforts to helping her daughter. She joined a national organization devoted to exploring her daughter's disease and began reading everything she could find about the subject. "I also went to every conference that was held. Most of these were a mixture of health professionals and parents. Experts would give their talks, but what really helped was the informal networking. You heard about things that had helped, like a macrobiotic diet. When I put my daughter on the diet, I could see a little bit of improvement." That gave us hope that something could be done.

A colleague at the clinic where she had worked had a daughter with severe muscular disabilities who had been greatly helped by a kind of therapy known as the Feldenkreis Method, but there were no practitioners in Chicago at the time. The center for Feldenkreis development was in Israel, so Susie took her daughter to that country for three months; her husband, a

Chicago lawyer, remained at home. "Jamie had six sessions a week. You could see it working; the progress was not dramatic, it was bit by bit, but it added up." Returning from Israel, Susie sought out other practitioners, who were all on the East or West Coast. "My daughter and I spent seven years on the road." Confounding doctors, her daughter was able to attend a regular school. Today she can walk long distances and travels with her class. "The only limitation she has is with the finest motor skills," Susie says.

Once her daughter started school, constant travel was impossible, so Susie decided to train for Feldenkreis certification so that she could work on her daughter herself. This involved spending two months in California each year for four years. "I remember talking to a friend when I was doing all the traveling. I said I was losing my identity—everything was for her, nothing was for me. But once I got into the training, I saw it *was* for me, because I loved it. It was really what I wanted to do with my life." Drawing on the broad network of people with disabilities she had developed in her years attending conferences, Susie set up a private practice and also began the first Feldenkreis training program in the Chicago area. "It's been an incredible thing, really," she says. "I had chosen my original profession without any deep conviction, but I'd always wanted to do something that I was passionate about. Well, this is it, this is what I totally want to do. So what started as this horrible experience has turned out to be a fabulous blessing—both for my daughter and for me. She has grown up as the most extraordinary person, and I have found my real passion in life."

Susie Alberts's determination to help her daughter inspired her both to get involved in a grassroots effort and to acquire new skills that eventually led to a new kind of paid work. In effect, she found a way to professionalize her passion, to integrate her private concerns with the needs of the public world, to create a new kind of value that could then be sold in the marketplace. She created her work from the crucible of her experience and interest, as did Sunny Fisher, the woman quoted in the prologue, who invented her job as a philanthropy consultant after her experience volunteering in a battered women's shelter.

This professionalizing of grassroots passion has been a major trend in the last twenty years and has shifted unprecedented power to individuals seeking to change both policies and institutions. The availability of affordable computers, fax machines, and e-mail is enabling people all over the country to transform private crusades into influential public causes. One thinks of the change in attitudes toward drunk driving and the subsequent rewriting of laws brought about by Mothers Against Drunk Driving, or of the role of parents in drafting the Americans with Disabilities Act of 1990, which is changing the very infrastructure of this country. Jenny Potanos, the autism therapist in Wheaton, notes that substantial breakthroughs in the understanding of autism have been made by parents who refused to listen to conventional advice, worked closely with their children, learned from their efforts, and lobbied effectively for resources and support. As Jenny says, "Parents today are highly educated and very demanding, much more than in the past, particularly in a place like DuPage County. They want to be involved in anything that affects their children. So they regard themselves as partners when they work with someone like me, instead of seeing me as having all the answers." Such attitudes, of course, were uncommon in the Organization Man era, when trust in large institutions and experts of all kinds was widespread, and individuals responded to organizations rather than trying to shape them. As Virginia Thornburgh, a national activist for children with disabilities, has noted, parents in the 1950s tended to accept diagnoses that "nothing can be done," whereas today they are likely to search out solutions for themselves.

Stories like Susie Alberts's exemplify Peter Drucker's observation that in knowledge economies, people shape their environment through individual effort. Thus they make use of organizations rather than being used by them; they work *through* organizations as they seek ways to "meet the world's deepest need." This proactive approach blurs traditional definitions of work, for when private efforts that derive from an individual's passion to address a problem create measurable value in the public world, *why should those efforts not be defined as work?* One could well ask if Susie Alberts was "working" when she was traveling the globe to find help for her daughter, or when she was acquiring the skills that would help her child, and which would then serve as a resource for others. Did her "work" begin only when she began charging money for her expertise, or was she in fact working all along? And just how do we define what work really is?

Again, the Problem of Time

Today's niche-dominated knowledge economy gives people the chance to create work that satisfies their individual interests and talents to an unprecedented extent. But the fast-changing technology and lean organizations that result from this dominance of knowledge are also creating real problems. Chief among these is the sheer amount of work that many find themselves having to perform these days. Chapter 2 described the extent to which women's entry into the workplace has contributed to the pervasive harrowing of time. Beyond that, people are also working longer hours.

When speaking with people around the country, I am constantly struck by how onerous work hours have become. At a conference for senior women at Johnson & Johnson a few years ago, I found their major concern was the amount of work the people they managed had to do. Employees, they said, were becoming resentful and discouraged; as a result, the managers worried that the most talented among them would leave their jobs. "We're operating *so* leanly," one executive lamented, "and things are changing so rapidly that it's almost impossible to avoid burning people out. And if this is happening with *us*, one of the best and most humane companies in the world, I can imagine what the situation is like in other places."

Certainly the problem of overwork is endemic in Naperville, where the morning rush hour is under way by 6 A.M. with country roads clogged and approaches to the East-West Tollway bumper-to-bumper. Indeed, the whole Research and Development Corridor is paradigmatic of the disquieting increase in work load that is making many Americans feel desperate, despite the general prosperity. This is partly because the technology businesses that dominate the region are subject to the most punishing levels of competition, and partly because suburban edge cities like Naperville, spread widely over great tracts of land, are among the most difficult places to live in terms of commuting. Because much of DuPage County was until recently farmland, many areas are still served by local two-lane roads, and public transport except into Chicago is nonexistent. Describing her battle with morning traffic as she drives from her development in south Naperville to her new and "basically exciting" job in Elgin, one working mother said, "It's like being on a roller coaster. You just get on every morning and ride. I don't remember things being like this when I was young."

In fact, they were not. Since the late 1960s, the time Americans devote to paid employment has grown from an average of 39 to an average of 47 hours each week, an increase of 28 percent. At the same time, paid vacation days have been stead-ily shrinking, in part because vacation time in this country is usually tied to the duration of employment, and people are changing jobs more often. Added to this are ever-increasing commuting times (people now spend an average of 46 more hours each year in commutes than in 1976) and the far greater number of hours spent in training and upgrading skills. The result is that free time among adult Americans has fallen a full 44 percent since 1973. Simply to reach the 1973 standard of living, an American in 1996 must work 265 extra hours each year, which amounts to more than seven full weeks.

It was not supposed to be this way. As recently as the mid-1960s, economists were confidently predicting that the end of this century would herald the advent of "the leisure society," a notion that now seems as outdated as the belief that computers would bring into being the paperless office. At a 1967 hearing in the U.S. Senate, workplace experts testified that the average American would work only 22 hours in 1985 and would retire by the age of 38. Academics and think tank consultants ago-nized in those days about how people would fill all these luxuri-antly empty hours, one commission suggesting that the White House establish a Cabinet-level Office on Hobbies.

Several things conspired to undermine this pleasing sce-nario. First, productivity began to fall in the early 1970s, as overconfident American companies began to lose their techno-logical and manufacturing edge, and as huge, and highly lever-aged, sums were spent on consolidations, mergers, and acquisi-tions rather than on process improvements. By the 1980s, these miscalculations, combined with the imperative to com-pete in an increasingly tough global market and the computer-izing of many workplace functions, led to the start of wide-spread downsizing, which continued without regard to business cycles. Organizations began routinely distributing a greater work load among fewer people. Those who held onto their jobs in this fierce market had little choice but to meet their employers' increasing demands. Nor did the entrepreneurial ventures that have spared this country from high unemployment alleviate the situation. Small business owners and private consultants have historically worked much longer hours than other people, and those employed in small ventures must often assume multiple roles. Also, the escalating cost of providing benefits to full-time employees has made organizations of every kind eager to limit the size of their workforce, strengthening the imperative to get more work out of fewer people.

In her influential study, *The Overworked American,* Juliet Schor notes that the pressure to work long hours has always been strongest among those who earn salaries rather than wages, and these now make up a greater proportion of the American workforce than in the past. She also observes that the professional groups whose ranks have grown fastest over the last decades—medical residents, investment bankers, corporate lawyers, software engineers—have traditionally worked 60 to 80 hours a week. Finally, Schor reminds us that, as organizations trim hierarchical layers, managers must handle more people and as a consequence must themselves work much longer hours. Indeed, at Fortune 500 companies, senior managers now average 70-hour work weeks, *excluding* the substantial time they spend for travel.

Karen Keough is such a senior manager. She oversees a major document support unit at Lucent Technology's Naperville headquarters. Karen, divorced and in her late forties, has been employed by some part of the former Bell system since 1968. Flexible and in possession of a wide variety of skills—she has worked in everything from installation to training—Karen has managed to escape the repeated downsizings that have occurred as a result of AT&T's reorganization. Yet her pleasure in her survival, like her pleasure in her daily work, is undergoing a severe test these days. She says, "I like the work and I like the people here, but my job has gotten so stressful over the last few years. The budget cutting is endless: you realize it's here to stay. We are constantly losing people, either through transfer or attrition, but there's no backfill, we just close ranks behind them. That puts a greater load on all of us, as we pick up the pieces. My job now is just a mishmash, a lot of odds and ends, responsibilities I picked up when we lost this or that person. So it's hard to get hold of. The work feels very scattered, in addition to having too much on my plate."

One of the most irritating aspects of the situation, according to Karen, is that "you can never really do a great job. My people come to me and say, 'help me prioritize.' They realize they can't possibly do all their work; they have to choose what's most important. And I have to work with them. I see the strain they're under. The thing is, I prioritize myself. I used to try to get it all done, but I don't anymore. If I did, I'd be in the nuthouse. For instance, I don't open my mail anymore. That's not how I like to do things! It's just a matter of putting out the hottest fire on any given day. After a while, it saps your energy."

Despite enjoying the security and the fact that she is "paid very, very well," Karen says, "I know there'll be a point when the effort is not worth it anymore." The constant reorganizations have made it difficult for her to keep up her enthusiasm, despite the interest, even the passion, she often feels for her actual work. "I'm part of a team now that's reviewing how we do our business. It should be exciting, but everyone has a jaundiced eye. There've been so *many* new initiatives, and they all end up meaning more work. The VP is all fired up about this new one, and I'm supposed to help get my people excited, but a lot of them just view this as another way of the company trying to squeeze more work out of fewer people. As for myself, I'm in a sitback mode on this one. I'll wait and see what's going to happen."

The civilized pace enjoyed by William Whyte's Organization Men is clearly a thing of the past. In retrospect, one can see that it resulted from the high productivity of the postwar era and because the forty-hour week was then the unquestioned standard for both blue- and white-collar work. Juliet Schor notes that this occurred only because two generations of trade unionists and social reformers had campaigned with fierce effectiveness for the forty-hour week. Their struggle began to collapse in the 1940s; by the early 1970s, when productivity fell, the work week began its long and steady rise. As unions continued to lose strength, the nation no longer possessed a culture of resistance and so lacked any force that could counter the demand for longer work weeks. As Rosabeth Kanter has observed, "Enough is no longer defined by some preexisting standard like an accepted length of workday, but rather *by the limits of human endurance.*"

The scarcity of time people are experiencing today also results from the velocity of digital technology, which operates *at a speed beyond human consciousness.* Everything we do on computers, from processing information to calculating figures to making copies to communicating across space, happens at an exponentially faster rate than was possible in the past. On the face of it, this might be expected to give people *more* time, but of course it does not. The problem arises not only because the technology is fast, but also because it operates at a speed that is *infinitely expandable,* whereas humans operate in the natural world, in which time constitutes a finite resource. The disjunction between natural and technological time has begun to un-hinge the human sense of what is possible to accomplish, creating expectations of productivity that no one can ever meet.

Technology also complicates the human relationship to time because it enables individuals to do their work anytime, anywhere. One receives e-mail at home, picks up faxes while on vacation, works out the details of a business transaction by phone while driving a child to school. This dissolving of boundaries between public and private often makes life easier, saving time by detaching work from its office setting, as Pam Lenert and Barbara Casey have found. Nevertheless, by providing the resources to integrate work into private hours, today's technology also helps to erode the notion that certain things are best done at certain times. And so people are losing sight of the ancient wisdom of Ecclesiastes, which instructs that "for every thing there is a season, and a time for every purpose under heaven."

Anytime/anywhere technology sends the opposite message: that one is free to do anything at any moment. This dissolution of limits, this abandonment of time-honored notions of appropriateness, adds to the pervasive feelings of overload. Today's technology also encourages the tendency to do two or even three things at once: one eats lunch while printing out copies of a report *and* scanning voice mail; one listens to music on walkman *and* reads the paper while using the stairclimbing machine. Certainly, these strategies enable individuals to accomplish more, but they also remove them from the moment they are in, dissipating attention, diffusing concentration, and thus exacerbating the sensation of being scattered and harried.

Taken together, these changes create a multiplicity of urgent demands upon time, demands that require precise scheduling if one is to meet them. It is this constant need to *schedule,* as much as the actual dearth of hours in which to complete tasks, that is causing the stress and exhaustion that concerned the women executives at Johnson & Johnson, and that Karen Keough describes as destroying the joy and pride she has always taken in her job. Just knowing that one must move quickly on to the next task as soon as the present task is finished robs one of the satisfaction of completion. Further, when life is seen as a series of tasks to be checked off as soon as they are done, even pleasurable events come to seem like duties that must be gotten through.

It is unfortunate and supremely ironic that this painful squeeze on people's time should be occurring just now, when work has the potential to be far more satisfying than in the past because of the shifting of power from organizations to individuals. Much of the potential for satisfaction at work is being squandered, however, because so many feel overwhelmed by the sheer amount that they feel they must do. To further the paradox, this squeeze is occurring just as people are becoming more concerned about the quality of their private lives—a response to the integration of public and private that is a consequence of women's entry into the workplace.

Karen Keough, after spending most of her life in the Bell system, has experienced this paradox firsthand. "I know there'll come a point when I am just too tired to fight it anymore," she says. "When despite the challenges and the fun I have around this place, the stress just becomes overwhelming." Although she has found Naperville a rewarding place to work, Karen doesn't see herself staying in the area once she leaves her job. "As I've grown older, I've become closer to my family, most of which is still in California. I feel a pull to go back west. Lucent doesn't have much out there. So I see myself doing some other kind of work." To explore the possibilities, Karen has been taking courses at the College of DuPage in fields ranging from social services to running a travel bureau. "I get the feeling there could be a whole lot out there for me," she says.

There could be a whole lot out there for many people who are skilled and educated, and herein lies the positive side of today's dilemma. For until organizations and people can find a new way of defining just how much work is enough, and just how leanly staff should operate, the best people will simply continue to leave, taking their skills and their expensive training with them. Like Barbara Casey and Susan De Young, they will decide that they would be better off on their own or joining forces with like-minded colleagues. With the costs of setting up a business far lower than in the past and with the market focused on ever-more-specific niches, the knowledge economy offers opportunities that never before existed.

The pressure to find alternatives to overwork is particularly urgent for women, who seem to have less patience with the practice than men, perhaps because they have not been socialized to expect that they would have to devote all their best energies to work, but also because they have always regarded the private sphere as a place to seek deep satisfaction. Here Max Weber's observation that women never fully assimilated industrial era values can be helpful, for it highlights the scope and profundity of the changes that are taking place and are reshaping ideas of what work is and why it is important.

Home as Workplace and Haven

I n the large and far-flung developments rising fast around
Naperville today, the dominant kind of house is neo-
traditional. On the curving streets and in cul-de-sacs, the new
dwellings, most ranging from large to enormous, display gabled
roofs, many-paned windows, curlicued trim, and shutters,
while inside one finds carved newel posts, bead moldings, and
wainscotting. Curtains are tied back and bordered with ruffles
or fringe; baskets or wreaths of dried flowers hang on the
doors. Somewhat self-consciously, the dwellings evoke the values of an earlier era, when big solid families lived in big solid
houses for one or two generations, and people knew who their
neighbors were.

Many of the new houses have front porches, which suggest an easy-going way of life, people passing the hours as they watch the world go by. And yet, although I drove through these new neighborhoods hundreds of times, I never actually saw anyone sitting on the porch. I assumed that the families inside were too busy, which no doubt was true, but I soon learned that this was not the only reason. Most of the porches are in fact too narrow to accommodate even one person seated in a chair; they are decorative, not functional. Their true purpose is to evoke the ambiance of a more leisurely and communal era, rather than to help make it a reality.

The fake porches on the new houses in Naperville seem an apt symbol of the profound disjunction that lies at the heart of life in today's edge cities. A constant tension exists between the notion of home as a private retreat from the outside world and the desire for a warm and close community life; between the complex and highly scheduled routines that govern people's daily lives and the suburban ideal of finding freedom from the "rat race"; between a transient society and the longing for stable and established families; between the need for convenience and the pull of tradition. These are familiar tensions, reflecting a discord long at the heart of American life: the conflict between the excitement and demands of the frontier and the more settled rhythms and satisfactions of civilized life.

What has changed, of course, is that men formerly presided over the demands of the frontier, while women were cast as the guardians of civilized tradition. By contrast today, many women are trying to straddle the divide in their own lives. This often requires going to extraordinary lengths, employing professional skills and techniques to manage the sticky complexities of family life, while bringing a domestic concern for relationships into the workplace. Despite the burden, few women I interviewed, even those with exceptionally demanding jobs, seemed willing to abandon the attempt to re-create the kind of home life that they either grew up knowing or always wished that they had known.

And so women are building domestic lives that, like their houses, might be called neo-traditional. They hang curtains and make wreaths and organize block parties for the Fourth of July; they bake heart-shaped cookies for the school Valentine's party and create tableaus of corncobs and witches on the front lawn for Halloween. They do all these things, even though they also work long days at the office or labor regularly at their home computers. Thus, their homes are both retreats from the world and the places where they meet it—an extraordinary, demanding, and often ambiguous enterprise.

HOME AS HAVEN

Domestic life among Whyte's Park Foresters could hardly have been more different than that in Naperville today, which becomes apparent when one compares their houses. Not only were the Park Foresters' dwellings modest, utilitarian, and relentlessly modern, but people lived in them in a specific way. The Organization Men and their families spent their time in the fronts of their houses, gathering in living rooms that opened onto the world through big picture windows. Cars were also parked in front, and people saw their neighbors throughout the day as they went about their business. One gets the sense of front doors being continually opened, of neighbors always dropping in. Children played on front lawns or common sidewalks, in sight of everyone. While houses were entirely separate, neighborhood life as Whyte described it had a distinctly communal flavor.

By contrast, in Naperville's new neighborhoods, the accent is on privacy. Front rooms have atrophied or been turned into offices, and people live and entertain in the rear of their houses. Kitchens are huge, and often connected to "great rooms," a sort of upgraded den with fireplace and cathedral ceiling. Front yards are small, almost perfunctory, and back-yards often fenced. The main entrance to the house is through the garage, so casual encounters with neighbors are few. As the architectural critic Philip Langdon has noted, "Driving straight into the kitchen has become more than the standard in suburbia today. It is like an inalienable right, the absence of which is unimaginable."

Children in Naperville play mostly inside the house; their informal running around the neighborhood is a thing of the past. Indeed, the sense of lawns as common space that prevailed in the Organization Man era has been replaced by an emphasis on respecting the privacy of one's neighbors. "One thing that is absolutely frowned on in the new neighborhoods is kids crossing other people's yards," noted Lou Cabeen, the mother of two teenagers who, when I interviewed her, was living in Saint Charles, about twelve miles northwest of Naperville. "Letting your kids do that makes you unpopular very fast."

Gary Jamnicki, the contractor for DuPage developer Joe Keim, showed me around Marywood, a new neighborhood between Naperville and Wheaton. We started our tour with a model known as the "Savoy" being built for a working couple with two children; the house was being extensively customized. As we entered the almost finished house from the garage, Jamnicki pointed out the absence of a living room. "Living rooms are just disappearing," he said. "People don't have any interest in the front of the house. They want to spend their money on incredible bathrooms, huge closets, or in the kitchen. It's a way people have of removing themselves from the world, of not having to be social when they're at home. I think it's also because there's a lot of paranoia." He nodded to a house across the way. "See that big place over there? The guy's a doctor and she's an accountant. They didn't even want anyone to know their names while we were building! Some of these people are very fierce about not getting involved with anyone else." He contrasted them with another family that sponsors a yearly party for everyone in the neighborhood. "They pay a DJ and a magician and invite the whole block. Most people come, but not all."

Noting that cul-de-sacs and winding streets that go nowhere form the dominant plan of Marywood, I wonder if some of this desire for distance among neighbors might result from the lack of privacy afforded by this arrangement. In contrast to the street grid, which allows broad access to a variety of streets, the cul-de-sac restricts the notion of neighborhood to four or five families. I mentioned this to Jamnicki, and he agreed. "I think what happens in a cul-de-sac is, if you get even one obnoxious or antisocial person, it disrupts everything because the unit's so small. We see it all the time: someone expresses hostility by putting up high bushes to block their neighbor's view. The neighbor files a complaint, and soon this nice neighborhood is a battleground. Living fences (strategically planted rows of trees) are the big thing now, and there's lots of arguments because of them. It's funny, everyone wants to be around people in their same income bracket, but they also want to have their own world, to walk into their house and just shut the door. I think people feel *entitled* not to have to deal with anything when they're home, because they work such long hours and have a lot of stress. So they're trying to buy themselves an escape. Also, some of the paranoia comes from worrying about crime. People want their places secure, they don't want anyone crossing their yard. They'll call the police if they see it. And you should see the security systems people around here have installed!" Jamnicki ponders the paradox: "Here they spend all this money to make their place look as inviting as possible, and then they say, don't you dare come near my house!"

Certainly the demands of work today are such that many people don't want to confront the unexpected or complex in the limited hours they have at home. Stephanie Pace Marshall, director of the Illinois Institute of Technology in Aurora, lives in what she describes as "a very private development, really like a house in the woods, in one of the newer sections of Wheaton." She says, "I have people all day at work needing things from me, wanting to talk, lots of demands. It's exciting and gratifying, my work, but when I get home I need to get away from everything, just be alone or with my husband. I really want to be anonymous."

As I drive around Marywood, it occurs to me that the sheer grandeur of houses in the new neighborhoods may lead to unrealistic expectations of home as a haven. It seems inherently problematic for people to expect total privacy when buying a house on half an acre, yet when residents are spending $400,000 or more, they feel they deserve it. In addition, the affluence enjoyed by most people in Naperville means that they can supply all of their own wants, instead of having to depend upon their neighbors. Again, this contrasts with the modesty of the Organization Man era. Whyte's Park Foresters were always borrowing tools or lawnmowers or barbecue equipment from one another, or watching television on the set at a neighbor's home. The sheer number of *things*—audio equipment, VCRs, computers, intercom systems—that are taken for granted by people in Naperville would astonish suburbanites of the 1950s. Many of these goods, of course, could not have been purchased without dual salaries that couples earn today.

Here again is evidence of the democratization of upper-class tastes. Thousands of people in Naperville now have the means to attempt to re-create the kind of spacious, private, and luxurious way of life that only the rich could enjoy in Whyte's day. Nevertheless, the minuscule acreage surrounding even the largest houses serves as a reminder that in fact these dwellings are not as exclusive as their marbled bathrooms or soaring entrance halls might suggest. This is perhaps the first time in history that we have seen true affluence on such a wide scale, and while it is truly affluent, it is also very broad-based, which keeps real estate values frighteningly high and so necessitates awkwardly small lots.

Another contrast between the new "estates," as their advertisers call them, and comparably sized houses from a generation ago is that there are no retinues of servants to keep them running. Of the scores of women I interviewed, some ensconced in 7,000 square feet, not one employed a full-time housekeeper. Weekly cleaning ladies are common, of course; agencies bus Polish women in from Chicago to sweep and scrub DuPage County homes. Yet it remains an extraordinary paradox that ever-smaller suburban families are occupying ever-larger suburban houses and doing so without full-time help. The average U.S. household size in 1996 was 2.72 persons. Yet just the three-car garages common in places like Naperville require 700 feet of floor space, which is the size of entire finished interior of that icon of mid-century suburbanism, the Levittown house.

One major reason that people seek grandeur and size has of course to do with resale values. Conventional wisdom in Naperville holds that the larger the house, the easier it will be to sell. It is a truism that local realtors have no wish to refute. Despite the slowdown in the frequency with which people move, which results both from the increased ratio of small business to corporate employment and the daunting complexities of relocating a two-wage household, Naperville remains a relatively transient place. Much of the movement now is the result either of people making major career shifts or couples "trading up," as Barbara Casey did when her advertising business quickly became successful. Barbara says, "We made a good profit on our last house, so we figured we'd invest in something larger. This house is right for us, and it gives us room to grow. But we also knew it was a place that we could sell easily if the time came. That was definitely a consideration."

The always-present concern with resale value, predicated on widespread mobility, is also in part responsible for the popularity of neo-traditional styles, as well as the emphasis on impressive, even showy details at the expense of structural solidity—what builders call "big halls and bad walls." The grand foyer and luxurious kitchen are obvious resale lures, easily shown off when buyers become sellers. Resale considerations also explain the impersonality of many homes, which amounts to a kind of generic grandeur and seems paradoxical given the pervasive view of home as a highly personal retreat or haven. A number of people asked if I had heard that a certain color of paint and carpeting was known as "Naperville Beige," in tribute to the prevailing wisdom that beige interiors are the easiest to sell.

Because of the need to "keep it beige" in the largest sense, individuality of style tends to be manifest either in competitively luxurious surface touches or in the wide range of housing models from which people can select, the Elizabeth and the Savoy both being popular choices that offer a broad range of custom variations. Again, the contrast is striking between these houses and the bland and often identical "little boxes" that first-generation suburbanites bought in Whyte's Park Forest. As always, the contemporary emphasis is on choice, on personal preference, although always within the context of a carefully predetermined, and indeed focus-group tested, range of options. The niche-marketing orientation of our Starbucks culture is evident in the new developments, as is the dominance of corporate control, because prefabrication takes place on a national scale and residential zoning is both rigid and complex. Thus neighborhoods like Marywood and Ashbury offer broad individual selection within strictly defined parameters, similar to what one finds in upscale national chains like Williams Sonoma or Banana Republic, which lie not far away in Wheaton Town Square.

Gary Jamnicki observes that people are so concerned with resale value that many are willing to buy houses that stretch them almost beyond financial endurance. "They look at it as the best way to increase their net worth, so they're willing to risk a lot on the investment." He discretely points out a Marywood house that looks raw and unfinished, but which has been occupied since the previous year. "See that place? The owner had to cancel the order for the shutters midway through. They're paying $350,000, and they can't afford the shutters! Plus they haven't done their landscaping yet, which is going to be a problem, since there's a requirement that you get it done by a specific time. Who knows if they have the money to make the deadline. You'd be surprised at the number of people in these houses who can't even afford to put up curtains." And so Jamnicki gives credence to stories I have heard since my arrival in Naperville of people so impoverished by their investment in housing that they live without furniture for years or camp out in two rooms of a nine-room dwelling. "It's in the two-fifty range that people are most stretched," he says. "That's where you'll see sheets hanging in the window a year after they've moved in."

The widespread hope of riding the wave of escalating real

estate values explains the surprising number of couples in their fifties who move into these big new houses after their children have grown. As Jamnicki observes, "They've been saving for twenty years, and now they're looking for a tax break." This of course adds a measure of diversity to the neighborhoods that was missing in the Organization Man era, when families of the same age tended to cluster together. The number of recent immigrants in neighborhoods like Marywood compounds the variety. Standing on the expansive deck behind the Savoy model, where one looks out on huge neighboring houses that are startlingly close, Jamnicki says, "That house over there belongs to Pakistanis. Across the street are people from Hong Kong. We have all kinds here. With the Asians, you as a builder mostly deal with the men, the head of the house, and maybe with his son or his father. Even when the women work, they stay under wraps. But with the Americans, you deal with the women. They make the decisions, they have the ideas, and they want to be involved even if they are very, very busy."

The Filofax Way of Life

The tenor of life at home in Naperville today can perhaps be most accurately conveyed by a calendar page I glimpsed on a refrigerator door in a south side development. The page for October 30, 1996, read, "5 P.M.—make dough for Halloween cookies. 5:30—decorate with kids. 6:15—bake."

Extraordinary measures are required in order to manage a neo-traditional home life in a physically isolated contemporary suburb, while also meeting the demands of employment in a time of lean organizations and rapid change. The effort of achieving this complex balance has led to a professionalizing of domesticity, or what might be called the filofax approach to family life. Only the precise scheduling and intricate organizational skills which in the past characterized the management of a business can wring a semblance of order from this challenging task. And so a managerial approach has invaded the haven of the home, with complex implications for American life.

Grace Pastiak, the director at Tellabs, has three children under the age of eight. She and her husband, who also works at the company, live in the largest house on a circular road in White Eagle, a country club development off the Plainfield Road. "Our whole group of neighbors moved into our houses at the same time," says Grace. "Fourteen houses with 39 children between them." As an active member of this little community, who plans Fourth of July and Memorial Day celebrations and last year produced the group yearbook; and as a Brownie leader and soccer coach and reader to three-year-olds at Saint Raphael's Sunday school, Grace is a woman of daunting energy and purpose who brings professional-level skills to bear in managing her multiple roles. After a long workday and an evening filled with children's activities and demands, Grace is often to be found in her basement office, revising and printing out the elaborate and precise weekly schedule she keeps for her family on a home computer. Such schedules, she says, are common among families she knows, especially those with working mothers. "I've been in houses where you can hardly see the refrigerator door for the schedules. But having everything planned out is critical, because the logistics are so hectic. You need a system just to get it all done."

When each of Grace's children was born, she stayed home for between six and eight weeks, then put them in a Kinder-Care that was on the way to her office. "I never liked leaving them, but I felt it was a good environment. Plus I was really nervous about the idea of having someone I didn't know in my home. At Kinder-Care, the people are used to dealing with small children. With my first daughter, they knew when she was sick before I did." When that oldest child was ready for school, things became more complicated. "I thought, now how do I do this? How do we pick up one at school and one at Kinder-Care?"

Grace and her husband shared driving duties, managing in large part because her husband's mother spent many weekdays at their house, cooking and shopping and looking after the children whenever they were sick. Grace notes that the children's frequent yet minor illnesses have posed her greatest logistical problems, because they throw off schedules and require last-minute adjustments. "We rely on grandparents for emergencies." Like many women I interviewed, Grace said her life would be unmanageable if family had not lived nearby. Of those who had grown up around Naperville, many had returned to the area when they had children, so that their parents could help with their arrangements. Again, the contrast is striking with the Organization Man era, when almost universal stay-at-home motherhood made being transient less of a challenge.

Also like many women I spoke with, Grace said that family life required more precise scheduling once the children started school. The Naperville district provides school bus service to its many far-flung developments, but that does not solve the problem of what to do in the hours before and after class. Grace says, "Every year, it's something different. This year, we have the older ones in an excellent program at the Y. The bus picks them up after school and drops them off there." She ferries the children back from the Y, while her husband drives the youngest, who is still at Kinder-Care.

Grace finds that children's lessons and activities pose the biggest challenge and are the prime reason for her family's complex schedule. "Different ones of our kids do different things, according to their interests—ballet, jazz, karate, soccer, music lessons, swimming. The Naperville Park District is great and has lots of programs—safety town, science events, things like that. But you have to carpool everything, and that means coordinating schedules with other families. I solved the Brownies by having them meet at our house, but you can't do that with everything. And for the popular activities in a place like Naperville, where there are a lot of kids, you have to schedule when to sign up for things. You make an appointment just to stand in line!"

Again, the contrast with the Organization Man era is profound. Most of the children in Whyte's Park Forest just played in the neighborhood after school; some took piano lessons, and boys might join Little League, but this was pretty much the extent of formal activities. The proliferation of extracurricular opportunities for children (especially those relating to sports) is a reflection of today's niche-oriented Starbucks culture, in which individuals, even if they are six years old, pursue pastimes that reflect specific interests and talents rather than just making a generic choice.

Grace admits that all the activity can take a toll. "I guess it's true, there can be a lot of stress. And I suppose we don't really *need* to do all these things. But the children are so *capable* at this age, just like little sponges, so you want to expose them to all you can—especially when there's so much around, so many choices! Plus there's that guilt thing: will I be a bad mother if my kids don't have swim lessons until they're four years old?" She does what she can to keep things relaxed. "Most evenings, we just grab something for dinner and eat on the way to some activity or practice. But Friday night is family night for us. We stay home and play games, make popcorn, just hang out together. And we try to leave some time free on Saturday. I don't work on Saturdays, no matter what, though sometimes I go back to the office later at night." Social activities are essentially family activities: "When I get together with my best friend, it's with our kids." A number of women noted that adult social relationships usually had to be sacrificed in order to manage everything else. As Jenny Potanos observed, "Family and work, that's about all you have time for. If those are your priorities, there's not much room for anything else."

Grace says that her pace is very different from that maintained by her mother, although her mother also worked outside the home. "She was unusual in that she worked, we always felt that, and I think it made us very independent." Grace and her four siblings were active in scouting, cheerleading, and Little League, but they walked to all their activities, or rode bikes, or took the city bus. The family lived in Berwyn and later Wheaton, both of which were far more centralized and accessible in that era of modest developments and small downtowns. "Everything was convenient, including public transportation. Sometimes I feel it's too bad my kids are growing up with no bus experience. They aren't developing those skills, figuring out how to get around on their own." And with the heavily traveled roads around White Eagle, "there's no place for kids to ride their bikes except right in the neighborhood. So it's for exercise, not for transportation."

The dispersion of developments such as White Eagle and Ashbury adds to the challenges that women like Grace face. Zoning regulations prohibit commercial business in residential neighborhoods, requiring that people drive to supermarkets and convenience stores located in strip malls off busy access roads, even if only to purchase a carton of milk. One seldom-recognized aspect of shopping today is the extent to which the proliferation and variety of goods makes a simple journey to the market time-consuming, for even petty purchases demand decisions in this niche-dominated era, when computer-aided manufacturing makes countless varieties cheap to produce.

Twenty years ago, if one wanted rice, one chose between Uncle Ben's and Carolina; if one needed dental floss, one picked it off the grocery shelf. Now there are fifteen brands of rice, each processed by different methods, and each variety available plain or in a host of flavors. Buying dental floss can be perplexing, with up to thirty-six varieties on display, counting the various sizes, flavors, and shapes. Simply finding what one wants amid the clutter takes extra minutes, which when multiplied for every purchase makes even a minor shopping trip a major enterprise, especially given the size of suburban supermarkets. The complexity engendered by the multiplicity of choices particularly affects women, because they do a large proportion of the family shopping.

Most of the women I interviewed said that they could not have done what they did if not for their partnership with their husband. Husbands in Naperville shop and cook, fetch children, run errands, and attend school conferences, duties which few of them assumed in the Organization Man era. Nevertheless, many women pointed out that the overall *responsibility* for running the household fell on them. "I figure out what needs to be done, and then we split up chores," said Barbara Casey. Grace agreed with this assessment. "*I* work out the schedule. *He* volunteers his time. Part of it's because of carpooling. That's a big part of scheduling, and he's not going to be calling the other mothers. It's the women who do that, the women who figure it out."

Scheduling also determines how residents of Naperville use their leisure time. Indeed, the persistent feelings of being pressed for time that many feel today are exacerbated by a widespread tendency to approach leisure with more rigor and purpose than in the past. The Naperville mother who noted that her neighbors only pursued activities that were of particular interest to *them* attributed this to everyone's being determined to wrest intense satisfaction from whatever free minutes they could manage to find. Because people are so busy, they do not wish to squander their hours on generic pastimes that are only minimally rewarding, and today's Starbucks culture provides them with plenty of options. Again, the contrast is acute with Whyte's Park Foresters, who used their guileless leisure hours for aimless family drives and spontaneous cake parties lasting all afternoon.

The rejection of generic leisure coincides with an increased focus on physical well-being, which means that many spare time activities are also a form of self-improvement. Women I interviewed ran, worked out at the gym, studied yoga, and signed up for stress reduction classes. The self-help movement, tenacious over the last twenty years, has thrived on that 1970s mantra, "I owe it to myself," so that at every turn people are exhorted to take time for themselves. This is fine, except that doing so requires them to schedule in the hours needed for exercise, for writing in a journal, for *working on themselves* in various ways. This has made many individuals astonishingly accomplished and certainly more athletic than suburbanites of the 1950s, but there is nevertheless a paradox inherent in using leisure so purposefully. When one must schedule in even activities that one truly enjoys, these begin to assume the character of tasks, of commitments, so that even attempts at relaxation end up aggravating one's already antagonistic relationship to time.

The fluidity that now characterizes people's jobs and careers and the swift pace of evolving technology make further demands upon leisure. Because few feel confident that their present skills will be sufficient in the future, people are always promising themselves to use spare hours to master Quark or Quicken or become proficient on the latest version of Windows. The task, of course, is endless, for no sooner does one upgrade skills than the next generation of software appears. Many extraordinarily busy women I spoke with confessed to constantly feeling as if they were somehow slacking off. They felt that they *should* be reading the new literature in their field that was piling up on the nightstand or doing the coursework required for their next career. Even when they clearly had no time to do these things, they scolded themselves for falling behind.

In a place like Naperville, the purposeful approach to leisure reaches its height. Indeed, a reference guide compiled for marketers reveals that "career-oriented activities" rank as *the* most popular "lifestyle pursuit" for both women and men in all three of Naperville's zip codes. The contrast is stark with zip codes in, say, Kansas, where the women favor pastimes such as knitting or "grandchildren" (a taste that speaks volumes about the exodus of young people from rural areas), while the men relax with fishing or puttering around the garage. Such activities are hardly likely to be scheduled onto a calendar or filofax, and those who pursue them display the more relaxed and less controlling relationship to time that typified domestic life until recent years.

Vacations also tend to be relatively ambitious, again in contrast to the Organization Man era, when driving to visit relatives was the principal activity during holidays. In Naperville, single women and childless couples tend to focus holiday time upon self-improvement or undertake travel in demanding parts of the world. Pam Lenert enjoys exploring Asia; Karen Keough makes spirituality and health retreats in the desert; Betty Reed, the director of a large mental health clinic, has taken classes that meet in remote parts of the world. Those with children pack the family off for Disney World or places like the Grand Canyon, often accompanied by an extended group that includes siblings, in-laws, nephews, and nieces. In general, these journeys entail fairly complex logistics and so extend the need for constant scheduling to vacation time.

The women rarely complain about their lack of leisure, however, although a number said they regretted not having time to read for pleasure. "That's the one thing I really miss," Grace Pastiak admitted. Those who have children rarely get into Chicago to see a play or hear music, though they do take their children to museums and to movies. When asked about the lack of cultural richness in their lives, most echoed Jenny Potanos: "If you want to have children and also work, that's about all you can handle." This is hardly surprising when one considers that employed mothers in the United States expend over 85 hours of labor every week. But the women are philosophical, saying they look forward to cultural activities and reading in the years ahead, when their children are older.

Given the nature of life in Naperville, the need to plan and schedule also affects women who do not work outside the home. This is partly because their husbands are likely to share less of the burden of household duties, and partly because women for the most part run the after-school programs, which in today's edge cities are many and demanding. But it is also because of the unremitting nature of work at home in an era of self-service and high standards. Research shows that the amount of time spent on housework has actually *increased* over recent decades, in keeping with a century-long trend. The proliferation of household machines and ready-made clothing was originally expected to save domestic labor, yet capital equipment and technical sophistication have instead added to the amount of time spent doing household chores. For one thing, much of what was formerly provided by professional services is now done in the home. For example, when refrigeration put door-to-door ice vendors out of business, it contributed to the rise of the supermarket and a consequent demand for self-service and travel time.

By freeing housewives from drudgery, new technologies have also contributed to an increased work load by permitting a rise in standards of mothering, cooking, cleaning. As Jo Ann Vanek has documented in *Scientific American,* a full-time housewife without help now actually spends more time doing laundry than in the 1920s, despite washing machines and dryers, because her family has many more clothes and expects them to be cleaner. The popularity of gourmet cooking and greater emphasis on individualized interior decor have also raised housekeeping standards. Indeed, the cult of Martha Stewart, with her strenuous programs for domestic perfection, has raised the standard exponentially in recent years. In Naperville, one can identify a "Martha fan" by the wreath of ribbons and dried foliage on her front door, not to mention the hand-drawn stencilling on her walls and the pitcher of lemonade squeezed from real lemons. In addition, the expansion in the size of houses, so characteristic in the fast-growing neighborhoods of Naperville, contributes to the increased amount of time women spend on household chores, because houses this big *have never been lived in by people who do not keep full-time servants.* As Juliet Schor observes in *The Overworked American,* "Just as the capitalist labor market contains structural biases toward ever-longer hours, so too does the housewife's situation."

Finally, the creation of what Vanek calls "a culture of mothering," which mandates that intense attention be paid to children at every stage of their development, leaves today's mothers less leisure than mothers in previous generations, even though they have fewer children. Here the contrast between home life today and that in the Organization Man era is perhaps most glaring. A continuing fascination of Whyte's study is the extent to which children seem to be in the background, entertaining themselves with minimal supervision. Of course, parents helped out with homework and assumed duties as den mothers, but there was nothing like the degree of parental involvement of today, when children's activities, psychological progress, passing interests, friends, and education are monitored every step of the way by anxious adults.

This is in part the result of the trend toward customization in every area of life: With so many options available, decisions can hardly be left to children, and generic decisions ("if he likes sports, he'll of course join Little League") are increasingly difficult, given the bewildering variety of choices. Constant parental involvement is also in part the result of scarcity and bureaucratization; certainly mothers in Park Forest never had to stand in line to register their children for local events nor fill out elaborate forms for children entering kindergarten. It is also a response to the fear of crime, the presence of drugs, and to greater psychological sophistication, all of which will be explored in the following chapter. But the primary result of this increased intensity has been to place further demands upon parental time and energy, with mothers, as the chief domestic organizers, bearing the brunt.

Kelly Morgan, who lives in the Chicago suburb of Evanston and is at home with two small children, observes that the nonworking mothers she meets in playgroups and in her neighborhood often seem as busy and highly scheduled as working mothers. "They tend to be very professional in their approach," she says. "A lot of them had high-powered jobs before they quit to stay home with their kids, and they bring this incredible expertise and ambition to being mothers and running the house." Kelly also points out that, because staying at home is now regarded as a choice, women feel the need to justify it;

they keep very busy in order to prove to their husbands and to the rest of the world that they have a reason for staying home. Again, this is in sharp contrast to Whyte's more easy-going era, when home was a woman's unquestioned domain, and she felt no need to rationalize spending her days there. Whiling away the afternoon at a kaffee klatch with other neighborhood women was in no way considered a reflection upon the industry of mid-century suburban wives nor evidence that any among them should be regarded as a slouch. No doubt the relatively light work schedules enjoyed by the Organization Men themselves made their wives more comfortable simply succumbing to the easy if often stifling rhythms that govern the housebound flight of time.

Lou Cabeen, from Saint Charles, just north of Naperville, and the mother of teenagers, agrees with Kelly Morgan's analysis and adds that she has observed stay-at-home mothers who over-schedule in order to justify their choice, often falling prey to "a kind of female macho." Lou says, "It gets very competitive. You'll hear them, 'Yes, well, I've got *three,* and one is A.D.D. and the other has chronic ear infections, plus my daughter is in competitive gymnastics!' Then someone else pipes up, 'Well, *my* daughter has ballet class every night!' There's also a lot of competition about how well they organize a lot of minor chores, some of which seem pretty pointless. For example, a lot of the women where I live seem to go to Dominicks, Jewels, *and* the Blue Goose (all local supermarkets) in order to get whatever is best at each place. I have to ask myself, *what's this about?* Sometimes, I truly believe that it's an atavistic thing at work in the female psyche: the impulse to be out foraging and gathering in spite of the incredible inconvenience."

Lou thinks the kind of competitiveness she sees also serves as a means of enabling women to cope "with the fact that life in the suburbs is essentially organized around other people using our skills. No buses means *we're* expected to do all this driving; no delivery service means *we* have to pick up the cleaning. When you think about it, the situation is really exploitive, but no one thinks about that, they just assume the way we live is best for the kids." Lou also believes that women who indulge in competitive griping do so because they feel devalued by a culture that is ambiguous in its regard for women who stay at home after their children have begun school. "It's like they imagine that if they're busy enough, they will somehow get points for all their effort. But points from whom? From their neighbors? For their *husbands?* I'm sure the husbands could care less that their wives are driving all over the place, exhausting themselves so they can get the best pork chops while also managing to save 99 cents. Do the men even acknowledge all this effort? I doubt it, really. The husbands probably assume the women enjoy it, because they, the men, would never spend substantial time doing something *they* didn't enjoy." Again, Lou sees in all the driving around "a kind of atavistic expression, a ceremonial taking our children out to meet the world. Sometimes, I imagine the women sitting around in a circle, telling their stories, and beating their staffs like members of some primitive tribe." As an artist, Lou has often been tempted to craft one of these staffs. "It would have fetishes hanging off it, ballet slippers and soccer balls and of course a set of car keys on top. All this activity has got to fill some psychic need. I mean, you can do it all, and I guess you can do it perfectly if you work hard enough, but at what cost, really, and why?"

The Holiday Mom

A recent article in the *New York Times* portrayed many women today as almost unraveling under the strain of trying to create idealized holidays worthy of Martha Stewart, while also meeting the unrelenting demands of the contemporary work-place. And indeed, almost every woman I interviewed empha-sized the efforts she made when it came to the holidays and her determination to re-create either the warm family celebra-tions she knew as a child or the warm family celebrations she felt she missed out on. However, although most agreed that the holidays entailed a degree of stress, most also approached them with enthusiasm, even reverence, and a profound belief in their importance.

Barbara Casey, the entrepreneur who started her own adver-tising agency, remarked, "When it comes to holidays, I'm super-traditional. I want the whole bit, a big tree at Christmas, with the presents piled up. And a *real* Easter. In our family, we alternate going to each other's houses, so when it's my turn I have a lot of people here. That's a lot of work, but for me it's both stressful *and* relaxing. It just takes a lot of scheduling. Since I have my own company, I can let up a bit, and I do. But it's worth it. Big holidays are part of our tradition."

Grace Pastiak is characteristically ambitious when it comes to holidays. "We really do them up. I like *two* trees at Christ-mas and grab bags full of presents. My house is the biggest, so my siblings come here with their families—we have 17 kids altogether! But Dominick's or Jewels do the cooking—Martha Stewart couldn't handle it. Still, I do a lot of creative stuff. I like to make up holidays. I have a Christmas Crafts day in July, bring the neighborhood kids in, and we all make things for Christmas. In February, we make Valentines and hang them on a tree in the circle on our block. The idea is to have some traditions that are ours, that make us who we are as a family."

The sole exception to this enthusiasm I found was Susan Murphy, an entrepreneur who has her own consulting firm, SRM. Susan lives with her husband Mike, the president of College of DuPage, in a new development of large houses between Naperville and Lisle. Now immersed in running a new business in which the family has invested substantial money, Susan tries for a more minimalist approach. "I really burned myself out in the past," she says. "I had the supermom syndrome. For Christmas, I made all my own wreaths and cooked for weeks. It was ridiculous. I felt all this anxiety, this perfectionistic stress. I *had* to pull back, put a stop to it all for a while. For a few years, we didn't even have a tree. Now I do a little decorating, but I'm aware of how easily it can all get out of hand. I see *a lot* of stress now among working women who try to keep the holidays in the old way and dread them as a result. That's not what it's supposed to be about."

Celebration and tradition are the essence of holidays, and many women in Naperville seem willing to expend what might appear an irrational amount of effort on them. But celebration and tradition have always had a particular importance to people on the frontier, reminding them of who they are, where they came from, and why they are putting so much work into carving out a life. On the American frontier, women have always been the keepers of tradition, and holidays are thus strongly identified with women. Indeed, with the decline of farming and hunting, American men have played a continually diminishing role in family celebrations; many today do little more than watch football on TV and carve the turkey. But holidays still give women a chance to display traditional talents, to connect with and indulge ancient female skills.

For many in today's secular world, where celebrations have

become untethered from their religious and agricultural roots, and where nuclear families have become the dominant unit of society, successful holidays have become synonymous with successful families. Indeed, many measure the happiness of their own childhoods in terms of how joyous and close, how celebratory and traditional, their holidays were. Given the pivotal role played in America by women in these celebrations, these remembrances have also inevitably become a way for people to judge their mothers. The women in Naperville know this, and so creating elaborate holidays has become for many an important way of celebrating and affirming their success in managing what tradition expects from them. They do this despite the transformation of their own roles, which make ambitious preparations extremely complex. But, to quote a woman in the *New York Times* article, "Just because I have to work doesn't mean my kids have to be deprived of the kind of traditions my mother made for us." A number of women in that article also admitted that staging sumptuous holidays was a way of proving to their own mothers that their demanding jobs didn't mean that they were selling their families short. And certainly, many such women are bringing highly professional skills to the planning and execution of festivities that far surpass the more modest efforts of earlier eras.

If anything, holidays seem to have grown more elaborate than in the past. Sandy Alcorn of Glen Ellyn says, "I don't remember that holidays used to be such a big deal. They start so early now, and are so *intense.*" Certainly, in developments like White Eagle, the houses are festooned with enough outdoor lights during the Christmas season to rival a department store display. And at lesser holidays, like Halloween and Thanksgiving, front yards are decorated with hand-crafted harvest tableaus, although of course no harvesting is being done in these former cornfields. And so in holiday celebrations one also sees evidence of the democratization of what were formerly upper-class tastes that characterizes life in today's suburban milieu. Indeed, the lavishness of many contemporary holidays hearkens back not to the often pedestrian middle-class festivities of the Organization Man era, but to the prewar, or even Victorian, celebrations of the truly rich.

Sandy Alcorn also points out that women as well as their houses today sport holiday decorations. "It's something you didn't used to see, but now it's everywhere. In the fall women wear sweaters with ghosts or turkeys in orange and brown, and in the winter, with Christmas trees and reindeer. In February you see outfits sprinkled with pink hearts." And indeed, the windows of women's clothing stores around Naperville display an abundance of female seasonal gear, which is worn as if for costume by mothers who bring cookies to school festivities. "A lot of women also dress this way for parties," says Sandy. "It's kind of childish, when you think about it. But the women are probably doing it for their children, as a way of being festive," as a way, in fact, of enacting the part of the perfect holiday mom.

A final reason for the big emphasis on holidays may be that, in the contemporary edge city, where open land and farms are fast disappearing, holidays connect people with the natural world, with a way of marking seasonal changes that go increasingly unnoticed in a landscape dominated by cars, offices, and malls. The sociologist Eviatar Zerubavel, in a fascinating study entitled *Hidden Rhythms*, observes that humans experience time in two entirely different ways: as the cyclical rhythms of nature, governed by recurrent seasons; and the repetitive rhythms of the machine, regulated by schedules, calendars, and clocks. He notes that being able to perceive time as cyclical is essential to our well-being, a crucial manifestation of our connection with nature in which time always moves in cycles.

Of course, since the industrial revolution, the workplace and, to a lesser extent, domestic life have been increasingly governed by mechanical time; only those who do agricultural work still live by the seasons. Yet strong institutions, religious traditions, established communities, and extended families enabled people to keep in touch with organic rhythms by providing rituals that celebrate the recurrence of seasonal events. These rituals, celebrated by families and communities in the same way every year (sameness being essential to ritual), give individuals the chance to reflect upon the year's passing and so discern the patterns in their own lives. Yearly rituals also mark particular days as *different,* lying forever beyond the parameters of mere mechanical time. This sense of mystery, of dispensation, is exemplifed by the question Jews ask each year on Passover: "Why is this night different from every other night?"

Until the last few decades, women's role at home tended to insulate them from the pressures of mechanical time. Cooking (before the microwave), gardening, and, of course, raising children are activities that do not lend themselves to hurry, but rather unfold at a pace more in tune with Ecclesiastes' ancient injunction that everything has its own time and season. As long as women's lives were centered around such timeless pursuits, they could remain relatively in tune with the cyclical rhythms of preindustrial life and so help shield their families from some of the inhuman demands of mechanical time. Indeed, the Victorian idealization of women as "angels of the hearth" owed much to their presiding over the one sanctuary of refuge in a world increasingly dominated by mechanical measures. However, the widespread entry of women into the workforce has extended the dominion of mechanical time into the home, as evidenced by all those refrigerator doors plastered with minutely detailed calendar pages and by Grace Pastiak's devising of family schedules on the computer. The breaking down of time into ever-smaller digital measures, of course, only accelerates the mechanical pace that now dominates life at home as well as in the factory and the office.

One way to alleviate this is to celebrate holidays, which reflect and affirm the recurrent rhythms of seasonal change. Holidays also bind us to timeless traditions, to older ways of understanding our place in the world. That women assume a time-honored role when making holiday preparations only strengthens their connection with the seasons and their cycles, reminding us that the domestic world only recently lay beyond the reach of mechanical time. This is perhaps the real reason that women who are already overloaded will eagerly embrace added duties in order to create holidays that they feel are "super-traditional," and may even be more elaborate than those with which they grew up. It may be illogical by any rational standard, yet it makes a profound kind of sense. The danger is that the tightened scheduling that holiday preparations demand from working mothers can paradoxically defeat this purpose. For when driven by the tyranny of timer and filofax, the holidays begin to assume a mechanical quality and so lose their ancient capacity to restore us.

An Architecture of Gender

The architect and town builder Peter Calthorpe has described today's suburban dwelling as "perhaps the least appropriate form of housing that can be imagined for working mothers." This is hardly surprising when one considers the history of suburban development, which evolved as part of a deliberate strategy for keeping women isolated from the workplace.

America's history exalts the ideal of the single-family house. Home ownership has become a way of measuring success, a means for achieving financial security, even one of the major indicators by which economists judge the country's economic health (those monthly housing starts). The equation of the American Dream with the family dwelling isolated by distance, lawn, and fence derives from Jefferson's ideal of the self-sufficient family farm, which he saw as essential for an individualistic and liberty-loving people. As the nation industrialized during the nineteenth century, the ideal still persisted, although with fewer people earning their living by farming, the family homestead lost its role as a place of labor and increasingly became a haven and a refuge from the world of work.

An early enthusiast of the home-as-haven notion was Catherine Beecher, who published *The American Woman's Home* in 1869. In this hugely influential book, Beecher (the sister of Harriet Beecher Stowe) advocated a strict separation between the genders, with men presiding over the marketplace and the grand affairs of public life, realms that were exciting but also contaminated by greed and the lust for power. Women, as "the better half" were to serve as "ministers of the home," undertaking "domestic labor in the service of men and children" and providing a place of refuge from the harsh realities of industrial life. In Beecher's view, a woman's work was redemptive and provided a necessary balance for her husband's immersion in the often dirty business of earning a living. Only by staying as far removed as possible from this contaminated sphere could a woman hope to secure a reward in heaven, while also serving as an instrument of grace for her family.

Beecher and other reformers of her day believed that the best way to separate the genders was to encourage families to move as far from the rough and tumble of the city as possible. In the early years of this century, as the architectural historian Dolores Hayden has noted, the nation sought to extend this vision by "miniaturizing and mass-producing the Victorian patriarchal suburban businessmen's dwelling for the majority of skilled white male workers." The motivation was often political; as one corporate official noted, "Get the men to invest their savings in homes and own them. Then they won't leave and they won't strike. It ties them down when they have a stake in property." Women's magazines supported the strategy. Christine Frederick, in her 1929 best-seller, *Selling Mrs. Consumer,* promoted home ownership and easy consumer credit as the most effective means for moving families far from the city. She advised producers and marketers to persuade women to equate their husbands' ability to buy things for the house with the feeling of being loved.

After World War II, there was a fierce demand for middle-class housing. America and Europe pursued opposite strategies to meet the demand. Europeans erected large apartment buildings that were convenient to shopping, work, and civic life, while Americans built isolated dream houses in the suburbs. The American approach proved an enormous boon to private developers, who were able to hold down costs by persuading municipalities to supply the infrastructure that supported this kind of housing, as a means of expanding their tax base. It was also a way of keeping women out of the labor market so that jobs could be given to returning veterans.

The suburban strategy reversed efforts made during the war to build housing that served the needs of women who worked. In scores of "Kaiservilles," where women labored in highly productive shipyards, new housing was erected convenient to child-care centers, children's infirmaries, and food services, so that women could fetch dinner and children in a single trip. Houses faced common courtyards, which meant that children could be watched by the community, and the maintenance of outdoor space could be shared. The shipyards where the women worked were within walking distance of housing, and windows in the schools gave children a view of the ships that their mothers were building. Physical space was thus arranged in ways that helped *integrate* family life and work, while still meeting the need of individual families for privacy. In designing cities for women workers, builders drew upon the ideas of early feminists, who were critical of the home-as-refuge notion, advocating instead that women should participate in public life in order to "make the whole world more homelike," thus bringing domestic standards of amenity and warmth to the larger world.

In stark contrast to the Kaiservilles was Hicksville, Long Island, the new town for 75,000 built immediately after the war, when returning veterans were given the first claim on jobs and the family wage reinstituted, both signals to mothers to stay at home. Hicksville's developers gave no thought to issues such as convenient child care, common space, low-maintenance housing, public transport, or energy conservation. Because residents were completely dependent upon cars, and because there were no buses, it was simply assumed that women would serve their families as unpaid chauffeurs. Hicksville was the prototype for the first Levittown and, later, for Whyte's Park Forest; it has of course been the model for American housing ever since.

Dolores Hayden points out that many families today face profound logistical problems in part because they live in a type of housing "originally designed for returning veterans and their families in 1947." The difficulties of this mismatch are apparent in the demanding schedule that Grace Pastiak must juggle, and in the complexities that compelled Jenny Potanos and Barbara Casey to start working from home. Yet despite the entry of massive numbers of women into the workforce, and the fact that households headed by women are the fastest growing kind in the country today, houses in Naperville (as in the rest of the United States) are almost entirely being built to reflect the old Hicksville prototype.

The mismatch between housing and situation is if anything growing greater, for new developments like Ashbury and White Eagle are even more dispersed, isolated, and costly than the more modest subdivisions built before the late 1980s. Tech parks and office complexes are also being built farther out; the new Tellabs facility in Bolingbrook has risen on farmland almost an hour south of Naperville's center. The big discount warehouses, malls, and superstores also thrive at the distant fringes; as they draw customers, fewer products and services can be procured near the heart of town. And so Naperville is increasingly entangled in a maze of commercial strips, those fume-laden corridors of commerce that are among the least convenient and most frustrating places to negotiate on a daily basis.

The problem of endless driving, cited by virtually every woman I interviewed for this book, is made worse by the lack of public transport that has been a feature of suburban life from its beginning. Here we see the truth of Dolores Hayden's notion that suburbs reflect an "architecture of gender," for given the lack of buses and trains, *someone* must drive, and that someone is typically a woman. Lou Cabeen, the Saint Charles mother, lamented that life in her town is essentially organized around the exploitation of women's labor as chauffeurs. And indeed, one reason for the inconvenience that women experience is that urban economists calculate the layout of roads and allocate funds for public transport based *solely* upon the length and direction of trips made by the male "head of household." Because the daunting complexity of female journeying is entirely ignored by transportation planners, it is hardly surprising that women experience difficulties in trying to overcome the physical separation of work and home and child care that economists and planners have built into the national infrastructure.

Women around Naperville are beginning to improvise solutions to these challenges. One enterprising mother bought up a few Dodge vans and started charging $5 per child per trip to and from after-school classes; within a year, she had several full-sized buses and was running a flourishing enterprise. Obviously, families with several children and a variety of school activities are paying $20 or $30 a day for this service. One wonders how long it will take before some begin to question whether paying $200 a year in taxes for a public system might not be a better solution, although the new developments are so widely scattered that workable bus routes would be difficult to devise at any cost.

One disheartening irony of the continuing movement to ever-more dispersed suburbs is that the increasing amount of time consumed in driving, combined with the longer hours that Americans are now working, threatens to undermine the very family values that suburban life was conceived to support. Pressed as people are for precious time, it becomes harder to build the kind of integrated and family-centered lives that abandoning the urban rat race was supposed to make possible. Living and working in far-flung places leaves individuals little leisure to enjoy the houses they have bought at such expense or to build and maintain the strong communities they say they would like. It is particularly poignant that the expense of maintaining a single-family dwelling in a thriving suburb is a primary reason that women who might prefer to stay home for a few years when their children are young feel compelled to remain in the workforce. Yet despite the inconvenience, many families believe they have no choice but to make the sacrifices required to live in places like Naperville because this is where the jobs are, especially the desirable jobs of the information age. Also, the reliance of school systems on local property taxes insures that well-financed public schools will be found only in areas where relatively costly single-family houses are the rule.

The continuing trend toward women setting up offices at home is a way of circumventing this difficulty, bringing public life into a world that was intended to be private. In some sense, it marks the beginning of a return to the Jeffersonian notion of the homestead as the place where the independent family both lives and labors and an end to the industrial system of separation that undermined this original American ideal. For women, who speak overwhelmingly of wanting to integrate and balance their lives, it provides an especially welcome solution, but it is hardly one that everyone can or would want to implement. And so, as the physical separation of work and home continues to grow more severe in places like Naperville, the neo-traditional home, with its intimations of yearning toward a way of life more centered on family and friends, will have to suffice for a while.

Parenthood in an Era of Many Choices

Choice, variety, multiplicity, intensity, the constant need to schedule—nowhere are these contemporary themes so clearly reflected as in today's approach to parenthood. And perhaps nowhere is the contrast between life in Whyte's Park Forest and life in Naperville today so stark as in the way people choose to raise their children.

The notion of choice is key here, for not only must today's parents make choices at every turn, but parenthood itself is very much felt as a choice. Lou Cabeen, the Saint Charles mother, says, "I think our generation approaches parenthood differently in part because we are so aware of having *chosen* to have children. It was a decision we *made,* not just something that happened because we grew up and that's what was expected of us. This is especially true for women. It has to do with birth control and with our knowing that there are other options, options our mothers never had. Knowing we made the decision to bring children into the world adds a huge level of responsibility. We figure we had better do a good job of it. So there's a lot of tension around trying to be a good parent, a good mother. The whole thing becomes this very big deal, and people approach it with a lot of ambition."

CUSTOMIZING CHILDHOOD

In 1950s Park Forest, few women regarded having children quite so momentously. It was the expected thing, part of the generic experience of marriage and adulthood. In William Whyte's study, children's lives were also somewhat generic, for kids were a generalized part of the neighborhood scene, always off somewhere amusing themselves, their slow-moving days unfolding without undue parental focus. Like adults, children did what was expected. The boys played softball or football, while the girls took dance or piano lessons. Everyone went to the new Park Forest public school and took the classes offered at their grade level, which in the early years were the same for everyone. In high school, students might decline a fourth year of math, take world history instead of physics, or add drivers ed to their schedule; beyond that, they did not have much choice. On Sunday, children went to church or Sunday school, then took a drive with the family, or joined in a backyard barbecue. In summer, they attended the local day camp run by the school district, where they crafted skate keys and potholders and played dodge ball. And so except for illnesses, or the occasional disability, the shape of suburban childhood was pretty much the same for all those who grew up in Park Forest.

Children's lives in Naperville are not all the same. Rather, children's interests and schedules have become as customized as those of adults. The choice to have children is only the first on an unending continuum of choices that parents today must make, the negotiation of which requires constant adult involvement. First, day-care options must be explored. A nearby center? A small group at someone's home? A private nanny? Or will one of the parents stay at home for all or part of the preschool years? Next, the right school must be selected. Given today's emphasis on choice, parents may pick from among Naperville's many outstanding public schools, as well as from a variety of private academies, Christian day and parochial schools, all with different admissions policies and requirements. The arrangements whereby children get to and from school require more decisions. Will some combination of the parents drive? Will they carpool? Will they use the schoolbus, if there is one and if it comes to their development? Or might they take advantage of a private driving service like Kid Cargo or Spare Wheels?

The schools offer an array of classes to choose from, beginning in the early grades, electives now being a feature from the start. Children can customize their education from the first years, concentrating their interest on computers, science, or the arts. At well-funded schools like those in Naperville, counselors work with parents to identify children's areas of special promise, for developing these can make them more competitive when it comes time to apply for college.

There is also a wide range of school sports programs to choose among, everything from tennis and golf to swimming and field hockey, from soccer and basketball to lacrosse and squash, with teams for both girls and boys. Regular meets, tournaments, and practices often begin in the third or fourth grade, and by junior high many of the games demand substantial travel, sometimes out of state. With the plethora of activities, schools can no longer provide transportation to all the games, so parents must drive and carpool, all of which takes yet more scheduling.

Sandy Alcorn, whose sons played football at Glen Ellyn's public high school in the mid-1980s, notes that the school sports scene is far more demanding than even when her boys were in school. "Partly, it's because of all the choices. Everything today involves a decision. What are they best at? What do they really like? What will help them get into a good college?" When told a story about a nine-year-old who announced to his mother he was going to "concentrate" just on baseball because that's where he had the most "potential," Sandy laughed. "That's it! That's how things are these days. The kids have got to choose, and choose *early*. It's the Starbucks analogy again, it's all about making decisions, identifying what's best for you. And then whatever the kids decide on, they've got to be the *best* if they hope to stay on the team. That means the parents have to get involved, find special camps for them in the summer and the like. It takes tremendous energy and commitment, but every parent feels they have a responsibility to develop their kids' talent in sports to the fullest extent. Then, of course, there's the cost. The schools are cutting back—and how could they supply uniforms anyway, when they offer so many different sports? So the parents, usually the mothers, have to run around, buying and fitting uniforms for every sport and every season, in addition to supplying the transportation. No wonder it gets totally overwhelming."

Kelly Morgan, the Evanston mother, observes that children's school sports in upscale suburbs "seem to have become semiprofessionalized. You see four-year-olds being coached at hockey and kids of eight traveling 150 miles for weekend games. There's all this emphasis on being the best. And the worst of it is that, by the time you're ten, there's *nothing* for you to do unless you're outstanding! You've already been winnowed out. The team doesn't want you unless you're terrific. So the whole kids sports thing is not about recreation anymore, it's about finding an area where the child can excel and then developing him or her to the highest level." Thus the arena of children's sports epitomizes the recurrent themes of contemporary edge city life: wide opportunity, customized decisions, private resources, selecting the best. This presents a total contrast to the low-intensity environment and easy-going pace of childhood that characterized Whyte's era, for which Sandy Alcorn finds parents today often paradoxically yearn.

Instruction on different kinds of instruments, and in dance and various martial arts, has also become common for middle-class children, as have specialized camps for music or horseback riding. These involve a substantial investment of parental time, as do applications for popular preschool programs and the college prep courses for which an increasing number of children now sign up. Every aspect of children's lives today also involves an unprecedented amount of bookkeeping. One Naperville mother whose family had moved six times in twenty years felt panicked when she found that, because of an upsurge in communicable diseases, her son's college required proof of every immunization and booster shot he had received since the day he was born. Some of her files had been lost in all the moving, and she had to take several days off from work just to track down doctors' records all over the country.

Again, this complexity reveals the extent to which formerly upper-class ways of life have become democratized. Middle-class children in the Organization Man era did not have ski lessons or private tutors. The customizing of children's activities was reserved for the rich, who had staff to manage the mundane tasks that such ambition required. Lacking such, middle-class parents must now do it all themselves, a daunting requirement in any case, but particularly so when mothers work.

Women like Grace Pastiak rely heavily upon carpooling to help them manage their children's complex schedules. But only families such as hers, who live on streets with large numbers of children, or women like Susan De Young, who lives near the heart of Naperville instead of on the fast-growing fringes, are able to avail themselves of this simple help. Lou Cabeen notes that the layout of today's suburban neighborhoods makes carpooling difficult; because blocks are not laid out in grids, long drives are required even for short distances. "You have to go down these long twisting streets that lead nowhere, and then drive all the way back. There are no short-cuts; you are forced to take this elongated route. And it makes no sense to pick up kids from other developments, even if they actually live quite nearby, because you have to drive all the way out to the highway, and then take all the streets necessary to get to their house. It's as if the developers had made it as complicated as possible. So in our area, carpooling is very rare. When I took my daughter to ballet class, I would see the same mothers waiting around every week. But if we tried to alternate, it just took absurdly long." Lou also points out that carpooling allows for little flexibility, a particular problem for working mothers. "It only works if you know your monthly schedule in advance. There's no *maybe* with carpooling, so you have no flexibility. Your kids' schedule for practice and your own working hours have to be set in stone for it to work. So in a way, it just adds to the general anxiety."

High-Maintenance Parenthood

The customizing of children's activities results from the sheer variety available in a place like Naperville, and from the tendency of American life to become ever more dominated by ever more specific niches. But it also results from parents having become far more demanding than in the past. The baby-boom generation is of course famously insistent on having the best, and this manifests itself among other ways in parental activism, the emphasis on school choice, and—at its most extreme—the popularity of home schooling. This unwillingness to be satisfied with less than the best is of course also what led Susie Alberts to travel halfway around the world to find help for her daughter instead of accepting the advice she got from medical experts. On balance, it is an extraordinarily creative characteristic and certainly one that has transformed American life.

But what lies behind this parental insistence upon the best? Why are today's parents so intensely involved in their children's lives? In part, as we have seen, the physical infrastructure of our communities requires it. Suburban distances are great, and town centers are diffuse, so children can't get around on their own. But the widespread skepticism about institutions that has defined the national culture since the 1970s also seems to have played a role. One is struck, upon reading *The Organization Man* today, by the serene faith people exhibited in the institutions that influenced their children's lives. They rarely questioned the wisdom of teachers, school administrators, or the counselors at local summer day camps; their involvement in the schools was minimal. PTA functions served primarily as social gatherings rather than as scenes for the contentious battles that often erupt today.

Kelly Morgan believes that the tendency to overschedule children that she observes in her suburban community derives primarily from the lack of confidence that people feel in the organizations that shape their existence. "People today feel that they need to control every aspect of life. And that's especially true when it comes to their children. Why do we feel we have to do this? I think it has to do with a loss of faith. I mean, faith that circumstances can be adapted to, faith that we can triumph over adversity, faith that help will be there when we need it. And above all faith in our institutions—the belief that the doctor or the teacher really knows best. Flexibility demands a degree of faith, and we know too much today to have the kind of faith we used to have. So we try to control everything ourselves."

The anxiety people feel in regard to their children also results from the competitiveness of an economy that promises only to become more so in the future, and the extraordinary expense that raising a child now entails. Parents today often fear that children who are not coached to be exceptional at *something* will have a hard time getting into a good college and as a consequence won't be able to land a good job. Nanci Fisher, a counselor in the Naperville school system and the mother of two, says, "The incredible expense of higher education has a lot to do with it. Colleges look favorably upon kids who have lots of activities and kids who specialize, so the schools do what they can to encourage it. My daughter was good at soccer, and by the fifth grade there was pressure for her to *really* work hard at it, so she could maybe get a soccer scholarship for college. If a kid is a good athlete, people expect her to do that five days a week and then spend the whole weekend traveling. It's a kind of professional approach. You hear people saying: 'We're going to swim her this winter.'

When you start talking like that, you're *always* going to over-schedule."

Nanci Fisher also notes that suburban schools like those in Naperville are virtually forced to emphasize high achievement because of the fiscal realities they face. "We've got a lot of very smart kids from very smart families. So everyone gets caught up in trying to keep school scores high, because that makes it easier for the schools to get financial support from the community. Also, don't forget that real estate values in Naperville reflect the quality of the schools. If you don't keep the scores up, you're not protecting your investment." As a result, Fisher says, "I see just an incredible emphasis on achievement in the schools. This keeps kids always focused on the future, instead of paying attention to where they are now."

The stress on parents is also great. "I remember taking my daughter to a swim class. The kids all looked gorgeous, but some of the mothers looked exhausted, even crummy. I see that at school with parents; they have *no* time for themselves, everything is for the children. I had one mother tell me, 'All that matters for me is that I'm clean.' Meanwhile, her kids are dressed in the latest. A lot of the stay-at-home mothers devote themselves *completely* to their children, driving them all over the place, never saying no. If they're not busy, they don't think they have a good enough reason for staying home. Sometimes they get way too involved in things at school, become really intrusive, monitoring every little thing that happens to their child. The teachers and counselors just look at each other and say, 'Will somebody *please* find this woman a job?' But the working mothers are exhausted too. They feel they have to keep up. They don't want their kid to lose out on swim team just because they've got a job. So there's no way of winning—there is only choice."

Overscheduling children also results from busy parents trying to make sure that the time they do spend with their children has real value. Susan Murphy, the entrepreneur married
to the president of College of DuPage, observes, "A lot of
parents around here who are incredibly busy feel that *every
minute* they spend with their children has to count. They have
to be *doing* something, something important. They call this
quality time, the time they spend on activities with their kids.
But when you work hard all day and then come home to a four-
year-old, there is no such thing as quality time—no one is
really at their best. The ideal is to have some kind of balance
between structured activities and the kind of woods-and-
basement time that kids also need." Nanci Fisher agrees that
unscheduled time is necessary for children. "In order to be
creative, a kid has to be bored. If you can't play by yourself,
you don't learn how to use your imagination."

Susan De Young's work in divorce law has convinced her
that overscheduling is bad for families. "I see it all the time.
People schedule every minute, so they have no free time. That
means they have no time for their marriage, and without that
the marriage just falls apart." Nanci Fisher concurs: "This total
focus on kids puts incredible stress on marriages. It's not unusual these days for half the kids in a class to have been
through a divorce. And of course after the divorce, the poor
parents are even more worn out and overscheduled than before!"

The pervasive awareness of crime also contributes to the
anxious, heavily scheduled nature of contemporary suburban
childhood. Naperville is a very safe community, but gangs from
Chicago have tried to colonize Aurora in recent years, and the
drive-by shooting of a popular high school sports star several
years ago in that town still reverberates through DuPage
County. Naperville has never really recovered from the brutal

murder of a grade school student one afternoon in her quiet suburban home several years ago. Because she was sick, the child was left alone by her mother, who worked for the school district, and an intruder broke into the house. "That terrified people," says Nanci Fisher. "Parents just don't want their kids alone anymore. They don't want them exploring the neighborhood or running around with friends. They want them in some supervised activity, because they think that's safe, and they want them indoors or where they can see them. Of course, the kids get the message that things aren't safe, so they're more wary, less comfortable being outside or just playing with a friend." Like a number of mothers, Nanci cited the demise of bicycle riding among kids in Naperville as emblematic of the restrictive nature of childhood today. Indeed, the *Wall Street Journal* has reported that the bicycle, formerly both a symbol of and passport to freedom for children, is giving way to structured and supervised activities all over the country.

The danger of drugs is of course also on people's minds. Beth Finelli, the mother of three in a Minneapolis suburb with demographics much like those in Naperville, says she believes one reason parents schedule their children's time so tightly is that they are convinced it's the only way to keep them out of trouble. "It's the old 'idle hands are the devil's workshop' idea," she says. "Leisure is considered dangerous. You hear parents say, 'Maybe if he's busy every second he won't have time to try drugs.'"

Sandy Alcorn finds a parallel between this fear of idle hands and the social work philosophy that was dominant when she entered the field. "The old group work concept of social work was the complete opposite of the therapeutic model you find today. The idea used to be that you had to treat the individual within the social context and direct resources toward creating a positive and busy social milieu. That's why you used to have such an emphasis on things like after-school sports programs for poor kids: the idea was to create a healthy community and give kids things to do, so they would stay out of trouble." Alcorn is fascinated by the extent to which this approach seems now to have shifted to the suburbs, even as resources to keep teenagers busy in poor communities are drying up. "The whole thing has just moved upscale. It's as if we believe more than ever that we have to keep teenagers busy to keep them out of trouble, but we are only willing to act on this with our kids, and with private money."

GUILT, SELF-RELIANCE, AND SAYING NO

The lack of trust and confidence in institutions, and the widespread belief that children in our competitive society may fall behind unless they are given every advantage, have resulted in what Juliet Schor calls "the most labor-intensive mothering process in human history." That this should be occurring at the same time as women's broadscale entrance into the workplace makes daily life doubly complex. Women recognize the costs of this complexity, but are not always clear about its causes or possible solutions. As Lou Cabeen says, "In my neighborhood, everyone complains that things have gotten out of hand, in terms of all we have to do. No one remembers their own parents being so squeezed for time, and a lot of our parents tell us that we're doing too much. But no one seems to have any idea how to change it." Sandy Alcorn agrees. "Everyone around here talks about how things used to be, the freedom kids used to have to enjoy just being kids. That doesn't exist anymore, and most people think it's too bad. But it's not just a matter of people being afraid of crime and not letting kids roam around because of it: that's not the only reason there's so little freedom. No one is sure what it is, but it has to do with scheduling and the high cost of having kids. Everything has just become so *intense.*"

A number of women I spoke with expressed concern that children in Naperville were growing up deprived of opportunities to become self-reliant because of the constant parental involvement in every aspect of their lives. As Susan De Young observes, "Parents don't know how to tell their kids they can't give them every lesson under the sun. They need permission to do this, but who's going to give it to them?" Lou Cabeen adds, "I really think if some of these women could say no to their kids once in a while, the kids might learn to figure out things for themselves." Lou cites the example of her daughter. "I told her I wouldn't drive her to dance class every day. I would only take her twice a week, to the regular class. But she really wanted to go every day. So she bartered babysitting for a ride, and it has really worked out well. She would never have had the initiative to do that if I hadn't turned her down.

"I'm an outsider here," Lou adds, "in part because my goal is to foster self-reliance in my children. My kids do less stuff, only what they *really* want to do, because I won't make major sacrifices for things that aren't that important. But lots of women around here think they can't do that. There's so much tension about trying to be 'a good mother,' so much fear of undermining kids' emotional development. One of the worst aspects is that it divides a lot of women, makes them feel competitive, or guilty, or look down at mothers who don't make the sacrifices they do. Or they just spend all their time agonizing. That makes it impossible for us to get things done in any kind of communal or cooperative way or to make the improvements we need to make."

The late writer Christopher Lasch observed that the insistence on supervised activities for children deprives them of opportunities for informal learning. He notes that, whereas in the past children tagged along with adults and eavesdropped on their conversations in order to learn about the world, "today it is the young who are constantly observed by an army of well-meaning adults." This gives young people less opportunity to improvise a social life of their own. "They have rather become objects of adult solicitude and didacticism," Lasch insisted.

A number of women in Naperville expressed concern that the emphasis on scheduled activities was creating a generation of children whose personal resourcefulness was limited. A few echoed the mother quoted in the *Wall Street Journal* article about the demise of bicycle riding, who noted that her daughters had difficulty making decisions. "They ask me really simple things. What should I wear to school today? What movie should I watch? It concerns me that they rely so totally on my judgment." Grace Pastiak worries that her children aren't developing the kind of skillfulness in getting around that she learned taking buses by herself in Wheaton. "They're growing up without some basic skills," she says.

Philip Langdon, the scholar of the suburbs, notes that children need a wide variety of experiences in order to become self-confident adults. He observes that there is no corresponding term for the kind of intelligence implied by the term "street smarts" that applies to the modern suburbs. Again, part of the reason is structural. Today's developments isolate children; there's simply no way for them to get to know the world beyond their own block. For children to roam at all, they would need to cross major arterial roads. And while very small children may benefit from the safety of the cul-de-sac, it doesn't offer much for them to explore once they reach school age. Langdon also points out that, although the present era is dominated by knowledge, most of this knowledge is collected, digested, and transmitted by businesses or institutions that have their own agenda. This limits the spontaneity of discovery for everyone, but particularly for growing children.

Adolescence

Surveys reveal that teenagers are the least contented of suburban dwellers. Lou Cabeen notes that "suburbs are really great places for young children. In a way, everything here is organized around children's needs, and most people who live here do so for the children. So it seems odd that, once kids are adolescents, there's so little for them to do. Of course, there's plenty of schoolwork, and if they belong to a country club, that's something. But if they're not great in some kind of sport, they're probably not playing anymore, since excellence is the only thing that counts."

Lou notes that most teenagers reject a social life that's totally organized by their parents, yet there are few places where those not yet in college can just hang out or spend time with their friends on an informal basis. "Unless they have a car, they can't even visit their friends without their parents driving, which means getting even more involved with family schedules. And by the time they're teenagers, most kids today have lost the knack of just running around outside. They don't ride bikes, and they can't cross neighbors' lawns. They can't get to stores unless they're driven, and most shopkeepers don't want them hanging around. And more and more, the malls see them as trouble."

In Saint Charles, to Naperville's north, some fast-food restaurants set a minimum. "The kids see this as specifically designed to keep them away," says Lou. Her son worked on his high school newspaper, which sent adults into restaurants to see if the minimum would be enforced; that it was not seemed to confirm the students' suspicions. Lou draws a parallel between this situation and the recent allegations that Denny's restaurants secretly imposed a minimum on blacks. "I think there's a similarity in the way certain people perceive even local white teenagers as undesirable and the way they are disturbed by blacks. Both groups are perceived as an uncontrollable element by those who value control. There's a funny attitude here about teenagers—not your own kids, but other people's, especially teenagers that you don't personally know. It's as if, as soon as children are too old to regulate and control, they're seen as a problem, a threat. People just don't seem to want teenagers around."

As if to bear out Lou's observation, Naperville recently passed an ordinance prohibiting anyone from driving past the same store three times in an hour. The purpose was to discourage teenagers who had taken up cruising the intersections around Riverwalk. The situation echoes other efforts around the country to suppress this timeless teenage ritual, regarded in more easy-going times as an essentially harmless part of adolescent life. In a West Virginia town, for example, teenagers were corralled into a floodlit parking lot, and told that they could cruise there, under the watchful gaze of a battery of police officers, or face arrest.

Philip Langdon sees mobility as the great problem for suburban adolescents. The nature of contemporary developments, with their rigid zoning and deliberate inaccessibility, keeps young people hemmed in, unable to use their own resources or to explore the environment in any spontaneous way. He notes, "At the very moment when adolescents are trying to establish a degree of independence from their parents, they are made dependent upon them for a car or the money to operate it."

Langdon also remarks on the culture's incessant and lofty exhortations to young people to "be the best" and wonders what they make of this unremitting emphasis on competitive excellence. Do they feel ashamed if they are not the best at something? Does it turn them prematurely cynical about their own possibilities or about life? "There are constant lectures, but few opportunities to ground any kind of ambition in paid work. All too often, the message is, if you are not a sports star or the smartest kid in the class, you are nothing." Nanci Fisher, the Naperville school counselor, agrees with this assessment. "It's so competitive here that lots of time kids are burned out by the time they're teenagers. They've worked so hard, had such demanding schedules, that they don't want to do much of anything. They're exhausted. Also, they've become kind of helpless. Their parents have always been so involved that the kids haven't had a chance to learn to do things for themselves. Now they don't want the parents constantly involved in every aspect of their lives. So they just draw back, retreat into themselves."

Richard Sennett, in his insightful study, *The Uses of Disorder,* observes that adolescents tend to feel incomplete without a certain degree of anarchy in their lives. This anarchy is essential to the adolescent task of wandering and exploration, of enlarging their horizons, of enjoying "the integrity to be confused" about who they are and what they want out of life. Without going through such a period, young people cannot learn for themselves how to organize the complex demands of real adulthood. Sennett believes that the "forum for acting on adolescent strengths is denied to adolescents" in contemporary society in general, but especially in a suburban environment. The parental cocoon of protection and habit of constant scheduling deprives teenagers of the autonomy they need in order to learn to manage the confusing and complex tasks of adulthood.

Sandy Alcorn has noticed that many of the young people who went to high school with her sons have returned home to live after college. "You see them everywhere, hanging around in groups, mostly with the same friends they had in high school. I know in part it's because it's expensive to live on your own on the salary of a first job. But I think it's more than that. I think a lot of these kids are having a hard time organizing their own lives." Kathy Johnsen, a student at North Central College in Naperville, spoke of the extreme difficulty her student group encountered trying to organize a one-day trip into Chicago to attend a few poetry readings in the cafes. "It took years to pull a simple trip together," she said. "Everyone acted like Chicago was impossibly far away. People seemed scared, or like it was just too complicated."

Despite the difficulties, the demanding nature of contemporary parenthood offers substantial rewards, according to the women I interviewed. This is perhaps the underlying reason that parents seem little disposed toward attempts at change. Many women spoke of the deep satisfaction they took in being so intimately involved with their children's lives. "I'm friends with my kids in a way my parents were never friends with me," was a typical comment. Others noted, "My kids come to me with all their problems. I never did that with my mother." These women are proud of the sense of trust and camaraderie they share with their children; their close relationships are a source of delight, comfort, and support. And children provide a profound consolation and sense of focus for parents who have been through a divorce.

Such sentiments reflect a phenomenon that demographers have recently begun to note: the disappearance of the generation gap between parents and children, which flourished most famously in the 1960s and 1970s, during precisely the years when many of today's parents were coming of age. The generation gap, primarily a conflict over values, goals, and tastes, is not much in evidence today, for children seem as anxious to succeed academically and socially as their parents are anxious for their success. Demographers attribute this convergence of values to the fact that parents today have an educational level equal to, or even higher than, that which their children will achieve. This gives parents and children more in common than generations in the past, with regard to aspirations, goals, and, perhaps most importantly, social class.

In any case, the degree of guidance, involvement, and closeness that characterizes suburban parenthood today, demanding though it is, may in fact be well adapted to preparing children for the diverse, fast-changing, fluid, and niche-dominated world in which they will live; a world that will require each individual to constantly negotiate a range of ever-shifting choices and craft a life with its own distinctive pattern and rhythm. Perhaps the easy-going, more generic childhood experience typical of the Organization Man era—despite its nostalgic appeal—would provide inadequate preparation for the extreme complexity that people will face in the century ahead. And although young people today may have problems making decisions and tend to prolong their years at home, this may indicate that a longer period of nurturing is required for the new environment.

Parents recognize this and also understand the riskiness of an economic world in which the once broad middle class is shrinking. And so they stretch themselves to give their children every advantage from the very start. In the process, they assume what were formerly upper-class ways of life, though without the retinues of servants that made such an existence manageable in the past. In doing so, they help to shape a world that is ever more competitive, intense, complex, and demanding—for themselves, for their children, for those who succeed, and for those who get left behind.

CHAPTER SIX

Earning, Spending, Saving

A revolution in how Americans earn, spend, and save their money has been wrought by the same confluence of economic, technological, and social changes that has been the subject of this book. The most important change has been the entry of women into every arena of public life. That almost 74 percent of women over the age of 19 now hold paying jobs is the major reason that some households are substantially richer while others are poorer. This growing disparity is having a profound effect upon people's attitudes toward their money.

Throughout DuPage County, one sees the consequences of today's changing patterns in earning, spending, and saving. Rich suburbs grow richer, while older middle-class enclaves lose their tax base. As earnings are redistributed, old notions of class and hierarchy erode. In the "gutsy little midwestern city" that Mary Jo Lenert remembers, Naperville had a place for everyone: older families, workers at the furniture plant, Bell Lab managers, hardware store owners, farm implement dealers. The relative stability forged a degree of cohesion that instilled confidence and consensus. Most people believed that they were comfortably middle class, felt confident that they could afford their homes, and accepted the need to put a little by in regular savings. There may not have been many opportunities for dramatic scalings up the ladder of social and economic mobility, but neither were there many instances of dramatic and sudden plunges downward. Bankruptcies were rare, as were foreclosures.

That sense of assurance and stability has vanished in an era of fluid careers, frequent economic shifts, and the growing gap in earning power. People today confront unpredictable circumstances: one year may be unexpectedly prosperous, while the next might bring serious financial problems. Huge possibilities open for some; for others, horizons look bleak. Robert Reich has posited the splitting of Americans into three distinct groups, which he calls the overclass, the underclass and the anxious class. In Naperville, the overclass intersects uneasily with the anxious class, revealing just how thin the line between them really is. How else can one explain quarter-million-dollar houses for which the owners cannot afford landscaping?

The economic insecurity that many are experiencing has a host of consequences, among them the extraordinary growth in household debt. A good portion of this debt has been assumed by people in order to finance their education. Many of the younger women I interviewed were carrying substantial college loans, which they constantly had to reshuffle—consolidating the payments on credit cards that offered low introductory rates and then shifting them when the higher rates kicked in. The growth of consumer debt has also fueled the democratizing of upper-class ways of life, as people rely upon credit cards to support a level of consumption that in fact lies just beyond their reach. Finally, people are assuming debt in order to keep up with bills during periods of unemployment, often devising ingenious methods of doing so. These strategies and options were unknown in Whyte's much simpler era, when less than 3 percent of Americans had access to any kind of credit card, and second mortgages were unknown.

The need to cushion one's family in the event of job dissolution, and to find extra financing in order either to make a career shift or to live more comfortably during an unexpectedly lean year, has led Americans to pour their money into investments that promise high returns. The stock market has benefited from an enormous influx of wealth as a result. But people in edge cities such as Naperville also regard the purchase of their houses as an investment as much as a means of procuring shelter. This willingness on the part of a broad range of people to speculate with their savings has contributed to the widening gulf between rich and poor, since only the prosperous can spare the dollars required for speculation.

The deregulation of banking has furthered this divide by putting an end to the low-interest loans for modest housing that were formerly subsidized by savings and loan companies, and enabling the financial services industry to create a wide variety of instruments for private investment. Indeed, perhaps the most vivid example of the democratizing of upper-class ways of life has occurred in the realm of personal finance. Discount brokerages now enable great numbers of people to take advantage of opportunities for enrichment that in the past were available only to those who could afford private brokers and personal bankers. As individuals assume the responsibility and risk for managing their money and use savings to fund new ventures or buy new skills for themselves, the line begins to blur between consumption and investment, employee and capitalist.

OUR HOUSE IS OUR WEALTH

The average price of a house in Naperville in 1996 was $239,071. Given a mean household income of $66,943, this represents a considerable outlay, an average required deposit of $30,000 in cash plus closing costs, and a monthly mortgage payment of around $2,000, or more than a third of total yearly earnings before taxes. Yet new housing continues to find an eager market, particularly at the higher end of the spectrum, for suburban housing values are tied to the local economy and to the quality of the schools, and Naperville excells in both regards. The constant circulation of stories about the soaring price of housing also makes people eager to buy before prices go higher and eager to trade up when the time seems right.

Barbara Casey and her husband are typical of those who have so far thrived in the housing market. When Barbara's advertising business began to take off in 1995, the couple put their 25-year-old, three-bedroom house up for sale. The house was adequate for their needs, but the neighborhood, not far from Naperville's center, had few young children, because new families tend to settle in the newest subdivisions; also, they needed a dedicated office. "We made out very well," says Barbara. Indeed, the house, which they had bought for just over $189,000 in 1991, sold for just under $249,000 less than five years later. Wanting as much space as possible for their money, Barbara and her husband moved to Ashbury, one of the big new subdivisions in Sector G, paying $298,000 for a large four bedroom with a 30-year mortgage. The new neighborhood, says Barbara, "will be filled in by next year," by which she means that all the lots will have been sold. The houses will then presumably begin to appreciate in value.

Of course, this is not guaranteed. In 1995, Sector G was flooded during heavy spring rains. The floods, which affected nearly half the housing in the area, were in part the consequence of so much prairie land having been built upon in recent years; the prairie, an essential part of midwestern ecology, had in the past absorbed the heavy mid-continental storms. That Sector G lies in a proven flood zone may make the houses there more difficult to sell in the future, particularly if the rainy springs of recent years continue. Still, this has not stopped real estate from rising rapidly in value throughout the area. As the suburban commentator Philip Langdon has confirmed, "Many people today are buying into houses or communities that they actually know are flawed because of location or the quality of the schools." And indeed, shoddy construction in expensive new subdivisions is becoming a notorious national problem. Recent surveys suggest that as much as *one-third* of all new housing in the United States may have major defects in the original construction. Such defects may not affect the original sale price, but once they become evident, they can make resale difficult.

Although Barbara Casey and her husband bought their new house because "it was just right for us," resale value was also a consideration. Conventional wisdom holds that one should buy the most expensive real estate one can afford in order to realize the greatest profit on resale. Barbara says that she and her husband bought their house with this in mind, convinced that the excellent new school visible through the front windows would protect their investment. Conventional wisdom also counsels people to buy houses that reflect a sense of grandeur and emphasize luxurious details, and Barbara's house is typical of those that are currently selling well in new developments such as Ashbury, Marywood, and White Eagle.

The new house is very large and open, with few walls or doors downstairs, and a premium kitchen that gives onto an expansive "great room" built around a fireplace. The entryway is two stories high and reveals a three-sided balcony on the second floor. Houses like Barbara's reflect ideas developed by the Berkus Group, one of the country's most successful designers of suburban housing. With soaring foyers, sloping ceilings, and sweeping views of interior space, these are choreographed, see-through houses, built to make a dramatic first impression. In the trade, they are known as "twenty-minute houses," meant to be remembered about that long by people who have seen them. They are, however, often difficult to clean and maintain, and offer little in the way of privacy. Balconies off master suites may be visible for blocks, and noise travels without break through the interior. If the appeal of this kind of building diminishes in the near future, such grandeur may not prove a particularly wise investment.

The emphasis on luxurious details as a key to resale often impells buyers to spend excessively on expensive details that they cannot really afford. When Gary Jamnicki and I toured Marywood, he pointed to a stack of unfinished cabinetry stacked up in the kitchen of the new Savoy model he was completing. "This is typical," he said. "Customized kitchens are supposed to be very good for resale. So this couple ordered $10,000 worth of countertops, the very best. That put them way over budget, so they decided they'd make up the cost by trying to install the counters themselves. It didn't work out, of course; it never does. People think they can cut costs by 20 percent by supplying the labor, but instead they mess up and get in deeper. They put themselves and everyone else through a lot of hell."

For those who cannot afford to buy at the top of the market, housing can cause acute financial problems, and create pressure to make career decisions that may not be in the buyer's best interests. Kim Weeks, the woman who works part-time for the Naperville Chamber of Commerce, found that the difficulties she experienced in 1993 were exacerbated by conditions in the local housing market. Kim and her husband were trying to sell their small starter house, which could no longer accommodate their growing family. *"Nobody* wanted the place. Interest rates were very low at the time, so people were buying as big as they could possibly afford." Meanwhile, the new Hunters Grove neighborhood into which they had moved was proving a financial stretch. "We had a range of prices we were interested in, but we came in above," Kim explains. "We were able to manage, but just barely. We were set against the idea of being house-poor, but the mortgage guy managed to persuade us. He said the new house was a cream puff. But after we moved in, our lawn just *died,* and we couldn't afford to put in a new one." The cost of the new house also made it impossible for the family to afford full-time day care, which led to Kim's unsuccessful efforts to work from home. Several years later, she was still not entirely settled. Thinking of the Marywood development I had visited, I asked Kim if all the rooms in her new house had furniture. *"Most* of them have *some* furniture," she said.

Real estate in Naperville continues to grow more expensive, as the value of local land escalates. In 1948, land constituted 11 percent of the total cost of a suburban house; indeed, the low cost of land was a primary reason for the postwar suburban boom. Although it is difficult to find precise figures, land in upscale suburban areas like Naperville often makes up as much as 35 percent of total costs, a higher proportion of total housing costs than land in most major cities.

This is a potentially perilous situation for buyers, particularly given the vulnerability of suburban regions to the boom-and-bust cycles that govern U.S. real estate and the proportion of wealth that most Americans have invested in their homes. Places like Naperville, despite their economic vibrancy and healthy entrepreneurial climate, still depend far more than big cities or older suburbs upon a few large employers to maintain the value of local real estate. This dependence became painfully clear in the early 1990s, when Stamford, Connecticut, for example, suddenly lost several corporate headquarters, and the local housing market collapsed with frightening rapidity. People were stuck with virtually unsellable houses, even as their jobs followed their employers elsewhere. The fragility of suburban real estate was further demonstrated when IBM began its massive downsizing. The company quickly discovered that its suburban headquarters were white elephants, while its buildings in cities like New York retained their value.

The debacle in Stamford (which was mirrored in many parts of the nation) demonstrated another problem inherent in suburban real estate. Most of those who owned older houses in these regions were able to rent them out, which thus freed them to pursue job opportunities elsewhere if they needed to do so. But those who owned newer houses in subdivisions subject to the covenants of Home Owners Associations were prohibited from doing this by legal stricture. The built-in rigidities of HOAs are in fact one of the more troubling aspects of suburban housing as a long-term investment and present particular problems in places like Naperville, where so much of new housing is incorporated under such covenants.

HOAs may be defined as legal building and operating entities that require owners to support them through dues or assessments, while also compelling owners to follow strict guidelines in regard to design, use, and maintenance. The ostensible purpose is to keep property values high by mandating adherence to certain standards. It is HOAs, for example, that specify a house must be landscaped within a specific period after purchase; it was the HOA that required Kim Weeks and her husband to plant new lawn as soon as theirs "died." But critics have pointed out that HOAs may in fact undermine property values in the long run by preventing the developments they govern from going through the natural cycles to which real estate is subject.

Such cycles are evident in older downtowns, where brownstones and Victorian houses have in recent decades been gentrified. In such neighborhoods, the process of deterioration begins with a downturn in the local economy; following that, houses are broken up, basements rented out, and small businesses are run out of parlors or garages for an intermediate period. When the area becomes desirable again, the properties are restored and values soar upward. But in HOA-dominated edge cities such as Naperville, such flexibility is impossible, because the terms of most convenants require that dwellings must remain exactly as they are or be torn down. And so when the economy shifts, as it inevitably does in the United States, housing in newer subdivisions may lose its value, being both unrentable and unsellable for purposes other than those defined in the original terms of incorporation. This seems a particular drawback in an economy that is becoming ever more mobile and fluid, one in which people need great flexibility in order to take advantage of possibilities that barely existed a few years before.

Other rigidities can make an investment in edge city housing problematic in the long run. For example, the wide dispersion of new subdivisions, their distance from services, and the sheer size of the houses now being built make them entirely dependent upon low energy costs. If these prices were to rise in response to a major political crisis or a cut in federal subsidies, many a suburban house would suddenly prove a poor investment, like a car with a fuel injection engine in 1978. New suburban developments also rely upon the continuation of massive federal spending for new highways to serve regions that until recently were farmland. Indeed, the consequences of the decline in infrastructure spending are already evident in the crowded country lanes that serve Sector G.

The value of suburban housing also depends upon the continuation of present tax policies. These have long encouraged Americans to overinvest in shelter and underinvest in productive enterprise by permitting large tax deductions for the first, and levying capital gains assessments on the second. Differing tax policy largely accounts for the United States and Japan being almost mirror opposites with regard to individual investments: the Japanese save 21 percent of their earnings and spend 5 percent on housing, while Americans save 5 percent and spend 15 percent on shelter. For most Americans, wealth is tied up in housing: getting and spending money for shelter takes up the major part of most adults' lives. In the United States, housing is viewed as a key sector of production, crucial to stimulating the economy, creating jobs, sustaining industries, and maximizing consumption. In other nations, the construction of housing is considered a resource consumption.

Present U.S. tax laws also virtually mandate that anyone selling a house must buy a new one within the year. This ties up large amounts of capital, restricts the mobility of workers, and serves as an engine of inflation by feeding a speculative approach to the purchase of real estate. This approach is now under review, particularly among Democrats, who find that more flexible approaches have particular appeal to women. If policies change, the demand for new housing in places such as

Naperville will decline, as those who plan to stay in the area for only a few years are given the option to rent.

Home ownership has long been the bulwark of political moderation in the United States. Those who recognized early in the century that "the working man" who owned his home would be inclined to political docility have been proven right. But the increasing severity of boom-and-bust cycles, the inability of young families (particularly those headed by women) to buy homes in areas with high-quality schools, and the rigid inflexibilities built into much new housing, have begun to make home owning risky, despite the tax advantages it confers. Many home owners have faced economic ruin by being caught on the wrong side of a cycle; others have unwisely speculated on home ownership in order to live in booming edge cities where good jobs (at least for the time being) are to be found. Peg Price, the former mayor of Naperville, has noted a desperation among many people who have overextended themselves in the local housing market. "These people just cross their fingers and hope that housing in this area will go up forever," she says. "They need to look at what happened in California."

OTHER SPENDING

The entrance of women into the workplace, along with the dispersion of offices into suburbs, has greatly increased household spending on cars. In William Whyte's day, two cars in a family were a sign of wealth; among those in the middle class, men took the train to work, while women acted as chauffeurs, ferrying children about and running errands. The prevalence of single-car families in that era can be seen by the one-car garages that are now a major reason for low housing values in older suburban areas like Park Forest. But just as the provision of housing has become more costly and complex than in Whyte's era, so has the provision of transportation.

Since 1990, there have been more automobiles on the road than licensed drivers; the figure is highest in today's edge cities, where driving is necessary for the simplest of tasks. Virtually all houses less than five years old in Naperville feature three-car garages; as we have noted, this is a major reason for their burgeoning size, since three cars require 700 square feet of floor space. Again, we see the democratizing of upper-class ways of life, for whole fleets of cars and extensive garage space have become routine in today's suburbs. But because these now belong to middle-class people, they are acquired with much effort, and maintained without the benefit of help.

The average cost of daily commuting in the United States is $4,712 each year per person, but again the figure is much higher in edge cities, where families are unlikely to use public transportation because both jobs and housing are widely dispersed. In 1996, transportation expenses in the suburbs consumed 24 percent of household income after federal taxes, which means that couples were working a full 90 days each year just to pay for their cars. The price this exacts can be deduced from the increase in the average term of car loans, which has grown from two years in Whyte's era to five or even seven years in our own. Again, the financial burden is significant and is both the result of women working and a reason that many of them must do so, for the design of today's edge cities makes it nearly impossible for a family to have only one car. This adds significantly to the cost of living.

Automobiles are not the only reason that people today are spending a larger percentage of their income than in Whyte's day. In an era characterized by variety, customization, and consumer choice, there is simply more to spend money on, as well as more ways to finance purchases. The proliferation of home electronic devices, evident when one considers that new houses have an average of *eight times* the number of electrical outlets as those built thirty years ago, requires not just the expenditure of money, but also of time, for their purchase and maintenance and for keeping warrantees in order. Buying a telephone and selecting a carrier requires people to educate themselves about what is available and to suit this to their family's needs, since there is no generic "phone company" upon which they can rely. Purchasing and installing a home computer and the appropriate software is another job that requires the substantial investment of both time and money, yet families increasingly feel that they need to keep up with the latest technology lest their children fall behind in school.

Today's high level of consumption also has a significant effect upon the disappearance of time. As Juliet Schor documents, Americans spend more time shopping than any people on earth, three or four times as many hours each year as Western Europeans. There are 16 square feet of mall space for every American, with local ratios highest in edge cities. The emphasis on shopping encourages consumption, and the broad extension of credit permits people to indulge themselves. When interviewing women for this book, I found few families that lived according to budgets. Many echoed Barbara Casey, who said that although she and her husband had saved diligently for their first house, once they became relatively prosperous their frugal and watchful ways went by the board. "We pretty much do what we want when it comes to money," Barbara explained. "We don't really live according to a budget. We put away a percentage of what we earn and invest it in the stock market. Then if we need money, we sell off some stock. We did that recently, when we bought a new boat, which we dock in Michigan, and use on the weekends."

Susan Calomino, a licensed financial planner who works in the Naperville area, says, "Once people around here are making six figures, they're not so concerned about spending. I've seen couples bringing in $350,000 between them who are spending every cent they make. Their basic attitude is, we're making plenty of money, and we work really hard, so we can afford to reward ourselves." Susan observes that the less affluent couples she sees are often the most disposed to saving. "They always have to think about money, and they're used to doing without, so budgeting is more natural to them."

Personal debt in the United States has exploded over recent years. In 1953, a few years before *The Organization Man* was published, an average of less than 0.5 percent of household income was devoted to making interest payments, exclusive of mortgage; this has recently grown to over 10 percent. The increase is often attributed to unchecked consumerism and the famous American inability to delay gratification, which took hold in earnest during the 1970s, the age of inflation, when thrift went from being a virtue to being considered a bad idea. And certainly, the democratizing of an upper-class way of life (in which money has always been conceived of as "a reward") has encouraged many to upscale their notion of just what constitutes their needs and to rely on widely available and temptingly easy credit in order to supply them. But this is hardly the sole explanation. For one thing, it does not take into account the high price exacted by living on a fast-changing frontier and the financial investment that is often required in order to invent responses to conditions that are continually evolving.

People in places like Naperville assume a substantial part of their debt for reasons that have nothing to do with instant gratification. They take out loans to pay for continuing their education, updating their skills, financing career shifts, and starting new businesses. By doing so, Americans—so often scoffed at as self-indulgent overspenders—are in fact *undertaking personally to finance the nation's growing knowledge economy infrastructure.* The means Americans are using to do this are very different from those of, say, the Japanese, with their vaunted high rate of savings. The Japanese put their money in banks, which then use the capital to finance the nation's knowledge base in ways that the banks and the government conclude are best. By contrast, Americans are taking a decentralized and often piecemeal approach, creating the knowledge base for the nation by assuming personal debt rather than by lending their capital to large institutions.

Such financing constitutes a far more individualistic, improvisational, inventive, risky, and ultimately more capitalistic approach; one that seems particularly well suited to a vibrant entrepreneurial climate and a rapidly changing economy. But it is also an approach that exacts a price. "The whole thing is very scary," says Glenda Blakemore, the prison superintendent from Aurora who, at 48, is faced with repaying $33,000 in student loans for the graduate degree in social work she is earning at night. "If I had actually calculated what it would cost, I probably wouldn't have done it. But now, there's no way out, and I'm glad I made the decision I did. I really *want* to build a new career when I retire in two years. And having this degree opens up a whole new range of things I can do, a lot of new ways I can contribute."

The escalating cost of higher education, and the fact that more adults are seeking degrees, is a major, though rarely recognized, reason for the explosion of debt. The costs can be daunting, particularly when assumed at the beginning of a career. Victoria Myler, a chiropractor in her late twenties, began her practice in Naperville in 1993, after graduating from the Palmer Chiropractic Institute in Davenport, Iowa, and then working briefly at a factory in her Michigan hometown. Victoria deliberately chose Naperville for her place of business after doing demographic studies and deciding that the region's affluent, upwardly mobile, well-educated population was ideal for a chiropractic practice. Today she rents an office from an established practitioner in a storefront in a strip mall; this provides her with consulting space and staff support. She has worked to keep her expenses low, at first renting an apartment in Aurora and only recently buying a condominium in a new development off the Plainfield Road with her longtime boyfriend, who works for Federal Express.

Victoria chose chiropractic over medicine in part because the education costs were far lower, and she chose Palmer in part because Iowa offered especially low-cost housing. By taking classes throughout the year, she managed to complete her education in just over four years. Nevertheless, the cost of her schooling put her into debt by over $100,000. She has deferred some loans, and begun paying off others. Recently, she consolidated many of her loans and signed onto a 30-year plan, which will enable her to make larger payments once her business is more established. Susan Calomino, the financial advisor, says that it is no longer unusual for people to take out what amount to 30-year mortgages in order to finance the debt accumulated on their education. Victoria's debts make saving difficult; what she does manage to put aside, she says, "is all for my business, never for anything personal. Everything I do financially is about establishing my career."

Victoria has no real regrets about having assumed such a large debt, because she believes chiropractic is the right field for her, and does not plan to enter another career, but rather to build her practice and perhaps later branch out into teaching and research. But in some ways, her stability is unusual and derives from her position as a state-licensed professional.

Given today's fluid environment, in which people change jobs and careers with increasing frequency, it may be worth asking whether assuming substantial debt in one's early twenties in order to pay for an expensive education before even starting to work is the best approach. Because fluidity requires that people acquire new skills throughout their work lives, it might be wiser to spread costs more broadly over a lifetime, rather than making a large expenditure at the beginning. This goes against popular wisdom, which holds that, in today's competitive environment, only those with degrees from prestigious four-year colleges will have flourishing careers. In fact, this may not be true at all.

Kim Weeks, for example, at the Chamber of Commerce, does not see much of a fit between her preparations for life on the suburban frontier and the real demands of living there. To start with, she doesn't think she got her money's worth from her education. "I went away to school (to Iowa State) because that was the thing to do. You were considered a loser if you stayed at home. And I had a lot of fun, a real typical college experience—football games, dating, all of that. But I'm *still* paying for it and will be for years. And I don't really see much connection between what I studied as a communications major and what I actually do. When I look around, I see people who are doing very well who don't have college degrees, or who went to their community college and just got certain skills. If I had known what I know now, I would have stayed at home and gone to the College of DuPage or somewhere like that, then got out and started working. Maybe I would have gone back to school when I had a clearer idea what I wanted to do. If I had done that, I wouldn't be saddled with debt for the next ten years, and I could be more creative in my approach to work."

Kim does not believe that a degree means as much as it once did, particularly in our entrepreneurial era when people have to adapt to circumstances, and when technology is changing very fast. She points to her sister, who began working at Yellow Cab in Chicago as a dispatcher while attending community college, and is now a senior vice president at the company studying for her MBA. "What my sister did makes sense in terms of today," says Kim. "She's on a clear path. She knows what she's doing, and the investment is worth it." For the time being, Kim cannot discern a straight path for herself. "I have lots of interests. But we're locked in financially, with the loans and the mortgage. That makes it pretty hard to explore."

Americans are also assuming personal debt in order to start new businesses. The credit industry has seen a surge in recent years of people financing new businesses with personal loans, second mortgages, even credit cards. *INC Magazine,* which focuses on entrepreneurs, seems every month to feature a story about some independent spirit who started a now-thriving enterprise using MasterCard. Such borrowing of course contradicts time-honored notions of fiscal prudence, and given the failure rate of new business, it is indeed a risky practice. Yet the popularity of this method of financing makes clear the extent to which Americans are willing to rely upon themselves rather than large institutions in creating the infrastructure of the future. As Susan Murphy, the Naperville entrepreneur who started her own company three years ago, observes, "If you feel you should be doing something, you *have* to do it. So you find a way to finance your dream."

Like many of the women I interviewed, Susan Murphy began her professional life as a teacher. She quit work when her first child was born—"I was completely traditional in my views"—but found staying at home profoundly dissatisfying. "I was extremely unhappy. To this day, I don't know how women do it." Her husband Mike, now president of the College of DuPage, was an ambitious young college administrator. "I found I was very jealous of him," she says, "because he had this interesting professional life, while I was stuck at home. I used to wait at the door for him every evening. And if he'd had an interesting day, he'd be in trouble!" Susan decided to return to school, and took a Ph.D. in clinical psychology, completing her orals when she was nine months pregnant with her second child. She began teaching at a community college in the Baltimore area, where the family then lived, and eventually became the chair of her department.

When her husband accepted a job in St. Louis, Susan decided it was time for a career change. "My kids were older, and I felt a pressure to fulfill myself. I wanted to see what I could do, how far I could go." She took a position as a professional trainer for a large company that served Fortune 500 corporations. "As soon as I started, I became fascinated by the business world. I had always been in not-for-profits, and this was so fast moving, so exciting." The company gave her its biggest and most challenging project, developing training on service quality for Shell Oil. "I just threw myself into it, did nine months of research. I ended up writing three books on the subject—one for senior marketers, one for sales people, one for dealers. I developed a video. I trained 25 professional trainers and 4,000 dealers. I became the company's guru on service."

Susan loved the work, but soon felt frustrated. "I wanted to take things a whole lot deeper. Service requires deep involvement; you really have to *care* for service; motivational tricks and quickie trainings won't get it done. But the company I worked for wanted to mass-market their programs, so a superficial approach was built into the process." Slowly, Susan began to recognize that, "I could do things better. I could develop a template of training for managers that would really *work*. So just like that, I decided to start my own business. It was an incredibly naive decision. I didn't know what I was doing, I just knew what I wanted to do. Starting a business is like getting pregnant. If you really knew what was required before you actually loved the child, you would never go through with it. Well, if I'd known what starting a business would involve, I wouldn't have done it, but now I love it. I've invested everything in the last three years to make it work."

Susan's company, SRM, employs subcontractors to create extensive training materials for businesses, which she then draws upon to create customized service programs. She also hires professional market researchers to survey markets for potential clients. "It all takes money. I have an office in St. Louis. I pay my subcontractors on time. I have to do a lot of traveling to develop my client base. The clients have started to come in, but this is the first year I'll break even. People tell you when you start a business that it will be three to five years before you make money, but you don't believe it, you think you can beat the odds. Well, I'm finding out that's hard to do. My not earning any money these last years has been a real struggle for us. My husband is an academic, and we've had to put two children through college."

While Susan did not use her MasterCard to finance her business, she and her husband took money from their household savings and his retirement fund in order to set up SRM. "My husband has been very supportive, but he's not inherently a risk-taker," says Susan. "Plus he has very traditional views about retirement. He wants to be able to provide for his family's future security; he believes that's part of being a father. His money is at risk now, so he feels he's not really doing his job. We have gambled everything on this business. I have never even considered that it might not work out, because it *must!*

We've given up so much that I have to do whatever it takes to make this a success." Part of the difficulty now, she notes, "is that I'm starting to realize that it doesn't make sense financially to keep the business small. That was my original intention, but it means that I have to do all the client work. You can't clone yourself unless you're willing to grow. So there will be more risks in the future."

Investments like Susan and Mike Murphy's have the potential to add tremendous value to the development of the knowledge economy, both at the local and the national level. But using private means to finance the creation of companies like SRM actually turns the acquisition of personal debt into an instrument of public investment. And so what often gets classified as consumer debt becomes in reality venture capital, and debtors like the Murphys in fact become capitalists, assuming risk in order to create and redistribute resources.

MANAGING MONEY

Just as today's fluid economy demands that people take a creative, varied, and entrepreneurial approach to their earnings, so must they also when managing their money. The trend toward product proliferation and customization in every aspect of life is nowhere more evident than in the way people now conduct their personal finances. Just as one cannot walk into a gourmet coffee bar and order a simple "coffee to go," but must instead make a specific choice, so one can no longer simply open a generic bank account, but must select from among a variety of financial instruments.

The contrast with *The Organization Man* era here is particularly vivid. For Whyte's suburbanites, managing money essentially meant maintaining a checking account, making regular deposits to passbook savings, filling out a brief tax form once a year for a single salary, and paying the mortgage each month to a savings and loan at a fixed rate. Beyond this, there were simple utility bills to be paid, along with a single auto loan and perhaps an account at the local Sears and a life insurance policy. The stock market, bond funds, retirement accounts, margin calls: These were for the rich. Nor were there many opportunities to learn about investing since personal finance journalism was unknown, and middle-class financial advisors did not exist. Even credit cards had yet to be invented. The lineaments of the simple routine described above reveal yet another reason for the more spacious approach to time that characterized Whyte's era, for in a single evening Dad could balance the family accounts.

No more. The democratizing of upper-class ways of life is particularly apparent when one contrasts this simple picture with the complexities of financial management today. "Regular" accounts no longer exist, not making a specific choice has become impossible, and every aspect of managing household money has become complex. Mortgages are held at sliding rates and frequently refinanced on more favorable terms. Several cars require several auto payments. Utilities are customized and often packaged in multiple bills. Credit cards constitute 35 percent of monthly expenditures. The tax code has also become more elaborate, permitting the itemizing of deductions, providing various choices for reporting two incomes, and requiring those with home-based businesses or significant investments to file quarterly vouchers.

Individuals must also make complex financial decisions involving investments, for in this era of low interest rates and deregulation, bank savings accounts are no longer an option for the savvy edge city dweller. Most of the women I interviewed for this book said that either they or their husbands were active investors. Barbara Casey and her husband keep their savings in the stock market, a strategy that demands constant monitoring and the following of financial news; they use computer programs to make their trades. Those who do not invest, like Victoria Myler, still weighed down with student loans, plan to do so in the future but regard it as a somewhat daunting prospect. As Victoria says, "I feel I need to educate myself about it all before I get started. There's so much out there, I wouldn't know where to start."

Betty Reed, who manages the mental health division of a large social service agency, is typical in her experience and her approach. Betty moved to Naperville from Wisconsin in the early 1970s, when her husband, a newspaper reporter, was hired to do public relations for the American Petroleum Institute, headquartered in Oak Brook. The couple still lives in the house they bought when they moved to the area, on Naperville's far south side; it has doubled in value since they bought it. Betty says she and her husband, who have no children, "have been pretty diligent about saving and investing. We have individual stock portfolios and IRA accounts." They use a broker, a financial planner, and an accountant but also do some of their own research on stocks. "We read financial magazines, try to keep up with what's new. It's something we both enjoy."

Having established an admirable degree of financial security, thanks to consistent investments, Betty and her husband, now both in their late forties, look forward to "doing something different with our lives in the years ahead. Maybe we'll start a business together. I'm not sure, but I think there's something interesting out there for us. So I'm keeping myself open, seeing where my interests lead me. So is he." Like many women in Naperville, Betty conceives of retirement as "a time to do new things, try another career. Something fulfilling that would also bring in money." Again, this attitude is in sharp contrast to that of Whyte's Organization Men, who regarded retirement as an absolute break from the world of work. The financial and career partnership that Betty and her husband share is one reason they are able to take this approach. With so much to offer between them, and in an economy that emphasizes entrepreneurship, it's hardly surprising that they would see a range of possibilities for their future.

Susan Calomino, the financial planner, says that most of the couples with whom she works regard investments both as a way to assure some measure of financial security in a fast-changing environment, and a means of financing second careers. Among those who are regular savers, she says, "I see a number who make a practice of putting one of their salaries away for savings. That's a big commitment, but it's an example of how having two salaries can create real financial independence."

Susan herself, who grew up in Texas, first became interested in personal finance when studying for an MBA; she was working for the Santa Fe Railroad, headquartered in Chicago. "I took a class on investments, and it was way over my head," she recalls. "But I was definitely interested. I liked the idea of putting my money to work earning money, so I continued to learn all I could." Susan got her certification as a financial planner while still at her job with Santa Fe. "I felt I would have more control over my destiny if I acquired a specific skill. That seemed a lot more appealing than always having some autocratic chauvinistic department head hanging over me and controlling my fate." She says she loves working independently, out of her small home office. "It's immensely fulfilling. All those years I had a job, I never felt ownership in a project. Now I do. I can see the whole picture."

In her experience, Susan says, women seem particularly motivated to invest because of their desire to explore second careers. "From my vantage point, I see more women than men looking at retirement as a time to try something new. They tend to have a clearer vision of what they want. A woman will say, 'I plan to keep this job until I'm 53, then start the perfect bed and breakfast.' Or, 'I want to quit this job in two years so I can make hats all day and have my own little shop.' I think women are more prone to take this approach because we're used to juggling so much. We tend to overwork, so we always see ourselves as always doing *something*. Even if we like golf, we're not interested in playing it on a full-time basis; we want to make a contribution, be creative, and have some fun. Also, we're used to deferring to other people, to having other people depend on us. That makes us positively voracious for self-fulfillment. The women I see, they're in their forties or early fifties, and they're just ready to explode! They say, 'In two years—in five years—in ten years—it's going to be *my* turn. I'm going to do what I want. I'm going to have my dream.'"

Investing is a means toward the achievement of these dreams. It gives middle-class people the opportunity to shape and customize the future to suit their tastes. It is also, as Susan Calomino notes, "a way for people to take responsibility for themselves, which is especially important for women. It's about being a smart person. People feel that if they're managing their finances, if they are investing, then they're being smart and proactive, really taking charge of their lives." Again, the attitude is very different from that exhibited by the Organization Men, who serenely relied upon the comfortable and secure companies of which they were a part to finance the unambitious and somewhat generic retirement that they fully expected was their due.

Of course, Whyte's Park Foresters had few opportunities to actively manage their money; in 1956 this was difficult for those in the middle class. But changes in this country over the last few decades have created unprecedented chances for people to seize control of their financial fates. In his book, *A Piece of the Action: How the Middle Class Joined the Money Class*, Joseph Nocera skillfully shows how the growing ability of people to make their own financial decisions has amounted to a virtual "money revolution" that has transformed our everyday lives. He points out that the revolution has resulted both from the passing of new laws, and the development of new financial products and services.

The money revolution, particularly as it has occurred among the baby-boom generation and that which followed, has one major characteristic that is often overlooked: it came about largely as a consequence of women's entry into the workplace. For in an era of generally stagnant earnings, it is only women's incomes that have enabled millions of households to take advantage of the innovations that banks and brokerage houses have brought to the market—innovations that would never have developed if there had not been this demand. In particular, the practice of "assortive mating" among well-educated professionals has given large numbers of people the chance not only to become capital investors, but to manage their investments themselves.

The money revolution had its beginnings in the 1960s, when banks first issued credit cards. In the 1970s, the deregulation of banking, combined with sustained inflation, induced middle-class Americans to search for new ways to protect the savings they had always held in passbook accounts that earned 4 percent interest. People looked to CDs, municipal bonds, and treasury bills, which gave them their first experience of selecting from among a variety of investments. Also during the 1970s, discount brokerage houses like Charles Schwab permitted people to open investment accounts with as little as $1,000, while also enabling them to choose their stocks and bonds without the help (or the expense) of a broker. In 1981, changes in the tax code allowed individuals to shelter savings in Individual Retirement Accounts, the first time tax breaks were available to the middle class. Two-career couples in particular took advantage of IRAs, because they could shelter twice as much money per household as families that relied upon one income. According to the credit historian Mimi Leiber, IRAs were the financial device that made clear the extent to which middle-class Americans were going to have to take control of their own financial futures; it was a discovery that made people feel both burdened and empowered.

The 1980s saw the rise of mutual funds, which were originally designed to make investing easier for the novice; they were a way to try on the stock and bond markets for size. But as Don Phillips of Morningstar has noted, "One of the great hidden advantages of the fund industry is that, by packaging investments in consumer wrapping, mutual funds tap into the consumption skills baby boomers have spent their lifetimes refining. Funds make investing very much like shopping." In part because of this, the amount invested in funds has soared, from $90 billion in 1980 to more than $3 trillion in 1996. This exponential increase has both benefited from and fueled soaring stock prices. Indeed, the bull present-day market is the first in history that has owed its existence to the infusion of middle-class money, an infusion made possible largely by two-income families. Thus the baby boomers have done with stocks in the 1990s what they did with housing in the 1980s: driven up prices by driving up demand. By the early 1990s, the culture of investing had become such an abiding part of the American scene that ordinary people automatically thought of world events in terms of their potential to affect the market. Mimi Leiber has observed that, as a consequence, Americans have become "both more sophisticated and more anxious. They know more, and it scares them more."

The cascade of new financial products has enabled those not born to wealth to think about and use their money in ways previously reserved for those who were. This appeal was explicit in Fidelity's promotion for its first tax exempt bond fund, which boasted that "bonds aren't just for the wealthy anymore." The democratization of financial investment has been chiefly a do-it-yourself phenomenon. As the province of the rich, it was dominated by private bankers, lawyers, and accountants, whereas middle-class people tend to make their decisions themselves, reading financial magazines, like Betty Reed and her husband, or seeking information and making trades over the Internet, like Barbara Casey's family. Again, this direct approach helps to break down barriers between work and home, public and private, as the active management of investments now typically takes place in the family den.

The spread of sophisticated money management also contributes to the pervasive disappearance of time, in part because it is financed by what Alvin Toffler has called "prosuming." By this, Toffler means the participation of the consumer in customizing the product or service being bought; we see examples in the widespread use of ATMs, and the popularity of investment software such as e.Schwab. These products save money by requiring people to spend their own time servicing their bank and brokerage accounts; they cut costs in return for customer labor. Prosuming, as Toffler notes, is characteristic of postindustrial economies that emphasize the niche rather than mass production and consumption, and make sophisticated use of digital technology. To the extent that today's economy continues to do both, people will continue to prosume, thus expanding the scope of their consumption while also saving money. The benefits are great, but the cost in terms of precious hours is substantial, as is obvious if one compares the demands of household accounting today with the simplicities of the Organization Man era.

CHAPTER SEVEN

Just-in-Time Learning

The knowledge economy thrives upon the constant increase, expansion, accumulation, and refinement of knowledge. The knowledge economy is thus by nature dynamic; knowledge is never dormant, but always being newly acquired. As repositories of knowledge, individuals must continually expand the scope of what they know, for in a knowledge economy, learning does not stop, cannot stand still. The need for continual learning is especially strong in an environment where people shift jobs and careers several times during adulthood, and regard retirement as a chance to pursue long-delayed ambitions rather than a time to withdraw from the paid economy. And so perhaps nowhere are the themes of variety, choice, and customization so clearly discernible as in the contemporary approach to learning. And certainly nowhere are the implications so great for our common future.

The industrial model of learning was *not* by nature dynamic and expansive, but rather static, segmented, compartmentalized. It was built upon the assumption that once an individual had achieved mastery in a specific discipline, he or she would then be fully prepared to make a contribution to the larger world. And so an isolated period of education in youth—high school, college, perhaps some graduate school—was followed by the assumption of adult responsibilities in the world of work. Preparation was one phase of life, activity another. An individual's formal education might be augmented by a brief period of training sponsored by one's organization before a specific job was undertaken, but this period was sharply defined and usually lasted from a few days to a few weeks. The process was orderly and clear, its purpose being to feed into an organization people who were qualified to undertake predictable work and execute specific tasks. William Whyte characterized the system as a pipeline, an apt and suitably mechanistic image.

This system makes no sense, however, in an era of constantly expanding knowledge, when individuals must be ready to adapt to new conditions as they arise. In such a setting, learning cannot be compartmentalized, restricted to the early years of a person's life, but must be lifelong and continuous. For this to happen, learning must take place *alongside* work, rather than being acquired before work is undertaken. It must thus be integrated into the work of every day.

This integration, this pattern of back-and-forth between the acquiring of knowledge and the doing of knowledge work, can be characterized as just-in-time learning. It is well suited to an era that has moved beyond mass marketing and mass production to an era in which people must create jobs that serve highly specific, and ever-changing, needs. Just-in-time learning suits present-day requirements for the same reasons that the just-in-time system which Grace Pastiak helped put into place at Tellabs proved so effective in managing inventory: it is flexible, adaptable, and potentially far less costly than the centralized, one-size-fits-all industrial model. Just-in-time approximates a niche approach to learning that is both customized and improvisational, and allows scope for individual interests and changing conditions. Just-in-time learning can adapt to circumstances as they arise; thus it spurs the creation of new kinds of work.

The transformation of learning, and its integration into the work of every day, is occurring on three fronts: in colleges and universities, which increasingly serve and depend upon adult students; within organizations, where training and development is playing a more central and wide-reaching role than in the past; and privately, among individuals drawing on a variety of self-help resources—books, tapes, workshops, groups, seminars—that has grown informally but rapidly during the last few decades. Typically, these three fronts of learning are becoming intertwined, as they overlap in purpose, mission, funding, and approach. And typically too, resources from all three are being combined in customized programs that individuals cobble together to suit their specific interests and needs.

In Naperville, we see this process well advanced, for the edge city job market is highly demanding in regard to knowledge, and opportunities for learning are as a consequence varied and rich. Interviewing a wide range of women, I was constantly struck by the number who, as adults, had either returned to school for another degree, were planning to do so in the future, or were taking classes for professional development or personal enrichment. Most of these women also participated in seminars and workshops that were offered by their companies, or by the professional associations to which they belonged. In contrast, it is fascinating to note how classes, courses, and other forms of self-development played in the lives of Whyte's Organization Men, who seemed to assume that the learning and growing phase of their lives was over once they had taken their place in the world of work.

Many of the women I spoke with said that some of their closest personal relationships had developed within the context of learning. As Betty Reed, the mental health director, noted, "My husband and I tend to make a lot of our friends through taking classes. That's how we've formed our social circle. It makes sense—we share real interests in common. They're not just people who happen to live in the neighborhood." Sue Ross, the self-described "social worker for organizations" and a veteran giver and attender of workshops, agrees. "There's something intense about the experience of going through a class or seminar together," she says. "You can get close to people very fast. It seems to bind you together in a special way." Thus the acquiring of knowledge also enables people to customize their social lives to suit their individual tastes in a way that earlier suburban generations, relying on the simple proximity of neighbors, never did. This sorting of people into communities of learning creates new social forms that are particularly suited to the dispersed and decentralized nature of contemporary edge city life. The confluence of needs and solutions characterized by the knowledge economy thus provides an example of the American genius for tactical improvisation at its best.

Women are pioneers in this transformation. Their fluid and unpredictable careers create an urgent need for new kinds of learning, while their tradition of moving in and out of the workplace creates a hiatus that often provides the opportunity for seeking out more education. Many of the women in this book—Susan Murphy, Bonnie McLaren, Nanci Fisher, Jean Ellzey—ended their periods of staying home with their children by returning to school. This has become a common approach, a way for women who have been at home to ease back into the public world while also undertaking the necessary preparation for a career switch.

But women are also pioneers in new ways of learning because of their traditional role as teachers. Particularly among the women I talked to who were over 40, a substantial proportion had begun their working lives as teachers. This is not unusual, as I found when researching *The Female Advantage,* for of the 45 women who were senior executives or business owners that I interviewed, 33 had begun their careers as teachers. Given this background, women are particularly prone to seek out corporate work that enables them to draw on their teaching skills. Thus women are disproportionately represented in the field of training and development, and have put in place many of the strategies for integrating work and learning. Women are also more likely than men both to give and to attend conferences and seminars for which they, as opposed to their companies, have to pay.

Before examining how the just-in-time approach is changing the nature of learning, it is helpful to consider the problems facing Kim Weeks as she labors to repay student loans for a costly education that has not proven especially suited to her needs. Considering her struggle in light of just-in-time principles, it is obvious that Kim has been caught between the highly compartmentalized approach to education that is the heritage of the industrial era, and the more integrated approach that life on today's frontier requires. In essence, Kim's dilemma results from her decision (made when she was eighteen) to allocate a disproportionate amount of her resources to acquiring knowledge before she had a chance to put that knowledge to work. She thus had no chance to judge its relevance to her situation and ambitions, or to the opportunities that would confront her. At the age of thirty, Kim has come to recognize that she might have done better by attending a community college, starting a job, and *then* returning to school with clearer goals—an approach that would have been more appropriate given the fast-changing job environment she has encountered. In some ways, her expensive but somewhat generic four years away at a large state college (the epitome of the mass-market approach to learning) was as unsuited as preparation for the life she has found in Naperville as the education in fancy needlework and tea party etiquette that was given to girls in settler families in Nebraska in 1888. Both reflected traditions that were no longer appropriate for fashioning a life on the frontier.

Once one begins to think of learning as a life-long proposition, one begins to recognize that it may be unprofitable for those without extensive resources to spend a disproportionate amount on full-time schooling during the earliest years of adult life. This is especially true when making a large investment during this period will deprive an individual of the resources that he or she might need during later and potentially more productive periods, or will be stuck in an undynamic job because of the need to repay student loans. Such a strategy may work in some cases, especially because the classic four-year college education fulfills many needs in addition to simply imparting knowledge. But given the need for customization, the one-size-fits-all approach to learning is no longer necessarily the best, and the costs may inhibit the flexibility people will need in the future. This is not to dispute the importance of a college education, which if anything has grown far greater in recent years, as is evidenced by the widening gap between the earnings of those who have a college degree and those who do not. It is rather to observe that the industrial-era approach of isolating learning from work may not be the best strategy for the years ahead, particularly given the growing expense of a university education.

THE EVOLUTION OF COLLEGE

Five important trends are reshaping higher education: the extraordinary increase in the percentage of adult students; the breakdown of barriers between departments and disciplines and the reintegration of formerly separate fields of study; the tailoring of curricula to meet the needs of specific companies and institutions in which graduates will be placed; the development of distance learning, which is delivered by new technologies to off-site locations; and the increasing role of community colleges as a resource both for regional economic development and for life-long learning. All five trends are complementary and are driven by characteristics of the postindustrial economy that have been thematic throughout this book: the need for people to adapt to and support constant technological change; to focus on the niche rather than mass markets; to customize products and services; to work through a variety of partnerships; to remain flexible and responsive to circumstance; to contain costs and operate leanly.

Naperville and the surrounding region offer an unusual number of learning resources, which are both a cause and a consequence of the area's dynamism. North Central College, a private liberal arts school, was founded in 1895; its comfortable old buildings form the heart of Naperville's historical district and give a focus to the downtown. North Central currently enrolls just over 2,400 students, of which more than 45 percent are adults, an unusually high proportion that reflects the local demand for continual learning.

North Central works in partnership with local corporations to customize its curricula in ways that meet their specific requirements. Barbara Knuckles, the school's vice president for development, works to foster these relationships. Barbara's own background lies in business, not the academic world. She directed the Chicago office of the Wirthlin Group, an economic and demographic research firm; she also started and later sold a company that supplies nannies from downstate farms to families across DuPage County. Barbara serves on several corporate boards in the region, in addition to managing her family's farm in southern Illinois. She believes her diverse and unorthodox background prepares her well for her role helping North Central form closer partnerships with the business community.

"Corporations are becoming much more clear about what they need and want in terms of employees," she says. "And that means colleges have to become much more résumé-specific. We just started offering a double major in computer science and Japanese; we're the only school that does that, as far as I know. Motorola (in nearby Shaumberg) wants to hire *all* of the graduates of the program, and at big salaries. We are going to offer a Chinese and computer science major next. Our med school gets 100 percent placement in some of the best teaching hospitals in the country, in part because of our partnerships with local companies. Hewlett Packard and Amoco give us all these analytical machines, and the students use them in their lab work."

Carol Dunn Brown, dean of North Central's School of Continuing Education, says that over the last three years she has seen a much greater recognition in the corporate community of what colleges and universities have to offer. "There's a real hunger for what we can give. It's a great market for schools and for individual faculty." Carol cites a recent call she received from a Dun & Bradstreet executive, who was concerned about the quality of letters that some of his employees had sent out to customers. "He wanted a faculty member to review and critique them. I arranged a meeting with someone for him and went along. He had something pretty limited in mind at first— he really just wanted someone who would correct the grammar. But the faculty member persuaded him he was missing a big opportunity to attract customers because of the poor quality of the letters. She suggested that, instead of just doing a review, she work regularly with the company to improve people's writing and communications skills, using material drawn from the company. She laid out a program that was much more comprehensive than what the executive had in mind, but by the end of the meeting he was thinking much more broadly."

For colleges to be successful in creating partnerships with companies, says Carol, "they've got to concentrate on specific niches and learn to customize their offerings. A school shouldn't try to be all things to all companies but develop specific areas of expertise. For example, we're concentrating on leadership studies and Japanese culture. We're also developing finance courses for nonfinancial managers, which is particularly important today, given the breaking down of barriers that's taking place in companies. Engineers need to understand finance in a way they never did. North Central also offers a minor in conflict resolution—I understand we're the only school that does—and that's perfect for partnerships with companies. We can supply the professionals who use mediation skills in dealing with complex business situations."

The focus on adult learning promotes the interdisciplinary approach that colleges and universities have been experimenting with over the last thirty years. As Carol Dunn Brown observes, "When you're dealing with adults who function in the work world, the traditional barriers between different disciplines don't make a lot of sense. Adult learners really push you to consider the relevance of what you're teaching. Corporate partnerships push that even further, because the focus is on students getting exactly what they need for the real world, instead of satisfying an arbitrary academic requirement. All this gets the faculty out of their ivory towers: they have to think of the relationship between the real world and their material, which means finding new ways to give it context." Carol cites North Central's recent emphasis on problem-based learning as an example of the interdisciplinary approach at its best. "You study a specific problem from different perspectives: for example, the social, financial, and legal aspects. The student enrolls in a cluster of courses that address these perspectives and gets a very broad sense of all that's involved. We also do something like this in our History of Ideas curriculum, which looks at the development of a specific philosophical idea from different angles. This creates a very integrated approach."

Because almost half of North Central students are adults, Carol notes that the faculty has a lot of experience in taking a practical, as opposed to theoretical, approach to subject matter. "The instructors tend to focus on real-world applications, which makes them good at forming corporate alliances, since this is what the companies want. Also, the adults in class often end up recommending their professor to do some training at their company because they're so impressed with a course. They'll talk about what they learned in a class they took here, and all of a sudden their boss wants to offer the class inside the company." North Central also supports a wide variety of internships in organizations throughout the region, which further breaks down barriers between adults and students, education and work.

Carol sees increasing integration between work and learning

as a natural consequence of the knowledge economy. "As knowledge expands, colleges and universities will have to take a much more active role in keeping people current with what they need to know. And that's an ongoing task. A lot of the jobs students will have in the future don't even exist now, so if you restrict education to a brief period of their lives, you have no way to prepare them. People will need to maintain their learning and their skills. And they'll increasingly have to take responsibility for their own careers, which means that they'll have to be responsible for learning what they need." Technology will play a role in this ongoing process, Carol notes, and points out that North Central is part of a consortium of schools in the western suburbs that has set up a distance-learning lab that will deliver classes and lectures both to companies and to students in their homes. "Obviously," she says, "the Internet is going to play a major role in distance learning. That is already happening in more of the isolated and rural areas downstate. The resource is incredible. We are definitely moving toward ATAP learning—learning that occurs anytime, anyplace."

In recent years, community colleges have begun to emerge as a major resource for life-long learning and regional economic development. States such as North Carolina have used them to great competitive advantage, attracting thousands of new jobs to the area by offering training in specific workplace skills in fields such as metallurgy, electronics, and telecommunications. The College of DuPage, as the largest single-campus community college in the world, provides extensive just-in-time learning for people all over the Naperville region. It seems logical that such a school would thrive in this area, because community colleges are well configured to serve the needs of a fluid and well-educated edge city workforce. Indeed, the second largest community college, in Cherry Hill, New Jersey, just east of Philadelphia, serves a population with a similar demographic profile.

COD, as it is known locally, occupies a large complex of buildings spread amid prairie and parking lots on a stretch of road between Naperville and Glen Ellyn. It is as anonymous and impersonal in appearance as North Central is intimate and rooted. As Judy Wagner, the school's reference librarian, points out, "COD is a lot like Naperville as a whole. We're well funded and have access to many resources. That's because of the strong tax base here. And you know how people are today: they want their money's worth when it comes to taxes. That means we have to be *very* responsive to the community. If people don't see directly how we're useful, they're not going to vote us the funds we need to meet our budget."

Of the more than 34,000 students enrolled at COD, 76 percent are over 21, and nearly 40 percent are over 32; just under 26,000 are presently working. Fifty-nine percent of the students are women, which also seems logical, given the fluidity of women's careers. COD has proven especially adept at tailoring its curriculum for adults who are preparing to make major career shifts. Programs like those offered by the Business and Professional Institute have a specific mission to help individuals in the community "metamorphize themselves," as the director Bonnie McLaren describes it, by providing classes, information, and resources, as well as individual counseling to help people identify their particular interests and skills. The Institute gives special attention to women through its Women and Business Ownership program, which brings local women business owners together to share their experience with others who would like to follow in their paths. Several years ago, the Institute established a program to pair mentors with protégés throughout the region. Bonnie McLaren creates the matches.

"I constantly keep people in mind, thinking who would work out with whom. It's a personal and intuitive approach that seems to work especially well with women," she says.

COD also provides a broad array of offerings that give people a chance to explore personal passions and perhaps turn them into the means of earning a livelihood. As I interviewed women in Naperville, I was struck by the number who used enrichment classes as a means to explore potential new careers. Betty Reed, the mental health director, has taken classes at COD on subjects ranging from Native American religion and literature to meteorology and the history of the Middle East. During a recent summer, she and her husband signed up for a five-credit biology course, which held two class meetings in Naperville and then journeyed to Alaska for several weeks of study in the natural environment. "Biology has always been a big interest of mine," Betty explains. "It's something I might want to get involved in professionally in the future. Taking classes helps me figure out what might be out there that I would enjoy." Betty's husband, who is in public relations, is presently completing a program in flower shop management at COD. She says, "He's pretty sure he wants to do something with plants in his next career." Karen Keough, the Lucent manager, is another COD enthusiast. "I take courses mostly for professional development or personal growth, but also as a way of thinking about what I might like to do next." Karen has taken classes at the BPI on starting a small business, has studied French and art, and has explored becoming a travel agent or a social services counselor.

COD's enrichment classes often overlap with concerns that have traditionally been viewed as lying within the province of self-help or even religion. The Gathering, a joint effort by the Psychology and English departments, brings women together to find common spiritual ground. I attended a meeting of The

Gathering, held in an ordinary classroom. Most of the women present were returning to the workplace after a number of years away; several had recently been divorced. All were searching for a new sense of where they might fit into the world and a new understanding of what the world might have to offer. Class exercises focused on helping participants uncover a sense of continuity with their own pasts by articulating what they had learned from their mothers, sisters, and aunts. The instructors urged class members to keep journals and to read their entries aloud. The women did so enthusiastically, even when the material seemed embarrassing in the classroom context—such was their eagerness to connect, to trust, to form close bonds. Occasionally, the instructors would put the readings into a quite radical feminist context, with an emphasis on goddess theology that those present appeared to take in stride. It was extraordinary to witness the openness of these women, most of them suburban housewives, to the ideas they were encountering in the class. It makes it hard to take seriously the claim that "ordinary women" are unsympathetic to feminist ideas; rather, they seem mostly to object to the idea of calling themselves feminists, a reflection of the general discomfort with labels that Americans, with their distrust of ideology, so often feel.

"It's become as much a support system as a class," Judy Wagner explains of The Gathering. "And it's typical of how events here spawn networks that then take on a life of their own. The course has been offered for a couple of years, and a lot of the women who attended still get together regularly. It's become their primary group." Judy's observations highlight the important social role that COD plays in a decentralized region, where services are often minimal and people find it difficult to come together. She notes that many of those who make use of COD live in the unincorporated villages and townships that make up much of DuPage County. "These places have no libraries, no real facilities, so the residents use us instead; in a way, we've become their municipal center. We have a jazz group, an orchestra, an opera and choral society, and an art center, just like a town would have had in the past. For a lot of people, we *are* their town, in the sense of being where they gather and in the sense of providing a central place." That this is so again emphasizes the favor suburbanites show for private spending on what were formerly assumed to be public services and functions.

By offering courses for professional development, personal enrichment, and self-discovery, schools like COD are helping people to find, or to create, jobs that reflect their passions and interests, thus setting the notion of a career within the more personal and profound context of a vocation or calling. As Peter Drucker has observed, the freedom to match one's means of livelihood with one's personal passions is characteristic of the knowledge economy, in which individuals give shape to their organizations, rather than being shaped by their organizations themselves. Being thus able to shape the larger world gives individuals greater scope to define and recognize their own unfolding existence as a journey. And as is obvious from myths and fairy tales, learning is never just a preparation for the journey, but an integral part of how the journey unfolds.

UP THE ORGANIZATION

Just as adult learning in colleges and universities has grown more prevalent and more far reaching, so has the nature of learning at work also changed. As a result of the constant demand for new products and services and the rapid pace of technological change, the need for learning within organizations has become deeper, broader, and more specific. Because the learning curve is so high, particularly in the information-based companies that dominate today's edge cities, and because the need to operate leanly requires that people be able to assume many different kinds of jobs, training can no longer be compartmentalized, isolated from the performance of work, but must be integrated into the tasks of every day. This necessity is returning many organizations to a new version of the old master-apprentice model, in which work and learning take place side by side. Much of the present-day focus on mentors suggests the extent to which this is true, "mentor" simply being a more egalitarian (and less sexually loaded) way to express the notion of "master."

The contrast with William Whyte's era is fascinating in this regard, for highly compartmentalized modes of training were just beginning to find acceptance when he wrote. Whyte strongly lamented this, recognizing it as symptomatic of the increasing bureaucratization of organizations. His comparison between the old and the (then) new kind of training is particularly instructive. The following passage neatly sums up the transition, while also giving unwitting testimony to the extent that the workplace at mid-century was assumed to be the sole preserve of men.

> In [the older type of program], the young man is hired to do a specific job; his orientation is usually brief in duration, and for many years what subsequent after-hours training he will get will be directed at his particular job. If he proves himself executive material, he may be enrolled in a management development course, but this is not likely to happen until he is in his mid-thirties.
>
> The newer type of program is more than an intensification of the old. The company hires the young man as a potential manager and from the start he is given to thinking of himself

as such. He and the other candidates are put together in a central pool, and they are not farmed out to regular jobs until they have been exposed, through a series of dry-run tasks, to the managerial view. The schooling may last as long as two years and occasionally as long as four or five.

The older style of training, which Whyte goes on to describe at some length, emphasized on-the-job learning. The typical "young man" was paired with an older man, immediately given a job to do, and expected to learn about the company in the process. In the newer kind of training, the "young man" takes a different course, undergoing a highly centralized and rigidly compartmentalized program of preparation in order to become an all-purpose professional manager. Whyte compares the spirit among organizational trainees to that of "fraternity brothers," enjoying a golden period of camaraderie and group bonding far removed from the actual business of the corporation. More than anything, Whyte's picture gives evidence of the extraordinary comfort enjoyed by American companies in the immediate postwar era, when they had virtually no competition from any quarter. These companies could afford to expend huge sums on long and almost contentless periods of initiation, the sole goal of which was to produce a loyal and cohesive group of men deeply inculcated with the corporate values. This strategy of course created precisely the kind of self-regarding and inbred conformists who would lead many major American companies to the brink of disaster during the 1970s and early 1980s. Whyte denounced this new approach, which he believed reversed traditions of self-reliance, individualism, and entrepreneurship that had made the nation great, traditions that he feared were disappearing.

He need not have. The rise of global competitors that was spurred in part by the complacency of America's mid-century triumph put a fast end to these luxuriant practices. And with the rebirth of entrepreneurialism, on-the-job training is back in style. As Barbara Casey says, "Everything I know, I learned by working. My earlier jobs were invaluable in terms of giving me the training I needed to start my own business. There's no school, no training program, that could have taught me what I know. It's all been learn-by-doing."

Within larger companies also, Whyte's "traditional" approach of on-the-job learning is now in ascendence, as we can see in Karen Keough's experience at Lucent. Karen would never have made the management grade in Whyte's day. To begin with, of course, she is not a young man. Nor was she a college graduate when she joined the Bell system, a necessity if one hoped to be selected for the professional manager's finishing school. In addition, as Karen is the first to note, she has never conformed to the image of the Bell system manager, has never really been a team player, but has always operated as an outsider in management.

Karen started her career as a telephone operator in California. After four years, she was made an installer, as part of an initiative to put more women into technical jobs. "I wore a tool pouch, did soldering, climbed the wires," she says. "I was one of two women in the job. My boss was convinced I would never be competent with my tools, but I became the lead person on my work team." A big part of her education, Karen says, was learning how to handle the doubts of the men around her, to work amid extreme skepticism without getting discouraged. But she managed to do so and kept getting upgraded to technical jobs that involved different kinds of switches, which broadened her range of experience within the company. Finally, she began working with the software programs used to route calls.

At one point, Karen was supervising a team of 13 male technicians. "That made for a lot of bad feeling," she said. "It was very uncomfortable, a major case of backlash. I needed to get out of there." So she did something almost unheard of in the company. She took a demotion in order to join the training support staff and began to work on creating instruction programs for the various technical personnel. She was the only person in the department who had actually held a technical job, which proved to be a great advantage. She became a course developer and was transferred to the main training division. She designed courses for installers and courses in ISDN technology, traveling extensively and working with customers. "I discovered I loved teaching," she says. "I had really found my calling." She was eventually transferred to Naperville as a product manager for software. "Now I do the documentation and training for the 5E digital switch, which is the company's flagship," she says, adding that she both manages the department and trains all the people.

Grace Pastiak would not have made it through management finishing school in Whyte's era either. Her first jobs out of college were managing a youth conservation park in Utah and creating programs for girls who had joined a boys club in California. She landed an interview for the purchasing department at Tellabs upon returning to her home area near Chicago, because she had done the purchasing for a gourmet cheese and wine shop while in college. "I was the first professional woman hired at Tellabs," she notes. She rose quickly in the company because she held a lot of different jobs. "I like to move around," she says. "I don't like doing things twice. I've worked in engineering, operations, design, control, training, and recruitment. I get my hands dirty. When business is changing fast, you've got to do your learning on the job." In order to keep herself learning, Grace does without an office. "It forces me to keep moving around the place, seeing what is going on."

———

The emphasis today upon on-the-job learning and the mastering of specific skills does not mean that management training has gone by the wayside; indeed, the budget for corporate training and development programs in America in 1995 was $55.3 billion. But this training has undergone an extraordinary evolution, moving away from the emphasis on conformity and team spirit that prevailed in Whyte's era in order to find ways to tap creativity and spirit. The constant need for new ideas, and the recognition that staleness and the acquiescent mentality of yes-men got companies from the Big Three automakers to General Electric and IBM into serious trouble in the 1970s and 1980s, has inspired a generation of management thinkers who have drawn from a rich vein of philosophical, psychological, and scientific thought. It is not uncommon for people in organizations today to have been exposed to insights from fields as diverse as quantum physics, environmental science, psycholinguistics, and systems analysis in the course of attending management seminars.

Art Kleiner, in his wonderful book *The Age of Heretics: Heroes, Outlaws, and the Forerunners of Corporation Change*, has documented the role played by early "t-groups" in creating the climate that led to profound change in organizations of every kind. T-groups served as forerunners of the quality circles and, later, the self-directed teams that have transformed management practice in our era. The ultimate effect, in Kleiner's view, has been to make the world safer for the kind of heretics who improvise change in companies large and small. Interestingly, the t-groups' methods paralleled those of the early women's consciousness-raising and support groups, which at their best encouraged participants to undertake a rigorous self-examination in order to help them to be more clear about how they were conducting their own lives.

In Whyte's era, the vast array of professional development conferences and seminars that we now take for granted as part of business life was nonexistent—one reason that the Organization Men spent relatively little time in travel. But the conference and seminar business has been growing rapidly during the last two decades. Thousands of professional development companies have sprung into existence, and the field has proven particularly attractive for women, with their long tradition of teaching. As a result, people like Betty Reed, the mental health division director, attributes her own development as a professional to both on-the-job learning and the scores of seminars she has attended over the years. "I find it's a way to keep up with new kinds of thinking, as well as a chance to get to know other people in my field," she says. "I've created a whole network of people because of this learning." And indeed, the spread of seminars has led to the creation of virtual learning communities across the United States and is forming the basis for thousands of computer-linked networks.

As seminars continue to broaden the range of their offerings, the line between education, skills development, and self-help is increasingly blurred; the psychological or t-group origins of the current management development work have built this overlap in from the start. Yet it is fascinating to note the extent to which learning programs initiated by organizations, professional development networks, and individuals themselves are not considered part of the nation's educational infrastructure. Just as there is no easy way to account for value in knowledge organizations, so there is no way to quantify the value of the diverse educational infrastructure that is making the knowledge society a flourishing reality. People lament the shrinking budgets that education commands, and certainly this is having an effect upon the quality of how children learn, although a variety of studies suggest money plays a relatively small role in this failure. However, the focus on education budgets only reveals that people are still regarding learning as something that takes place in the years *before* work life begins (a distinctly industrial-era approach), rather than as a lifelong enterprise.

CHAPTER EIGHT

The Search for Spirit

Spiritual life on the postindustrial frontier is difficult to categorize because, like work life, it is increasingly fluid. Americans have for years been remarkably willing to change their religious faith; an estimated 30 percent of adults now do so at least once during their lifetime. Americans are also unusual in regarding the search for spirit as an intensely individual matter, rather than an aspect of identity that descends from and is inescapably linked to one's family of origin. In Naperville's mobile, shifting environment, where the emphasis is on variety and choice, these uniquely American characteristics can be seen in high relief.

Three very different—indeed, even opposing—trends seem

simultaneously to be at work. First, people are returning to various forms of old-time religion, fundamentalist or evangelical traditions that exalt faith as the basis for salvation and demand strict adherence to a defined set of beliefs. At the same time, there is widespread interest in what the scholar Harold Bloom calls "Harmonial religions," essentially New Age creeds based upon (in Bloom's words) "a form of piety and belief in which spiritual composure, physical health, and economic well-being are understood to flow from a person's rapport with the cosmos." Bloom notes that such forms of faith have a long history of being particularly attractive to women; my interviews indicate that this is true. The third trend shaping spiritual life is the growing popularity of nondenominational megachurches, those huge and fast-expanding temples of the spirit that emphasize service, cater to the niche, exploit contemporary marketing techniques, and speak a familiar American language of pragmatism and self-help. Taking these conflicting trends together, and adding a strong dose of traditions ranging from Shinto to Sikh that recent immigrants are bringing into the regional mix, one comes away with a picture of religious diversity and complexity that would have astonished and bewildered suburbanites in an earlier era.

The diverse effects of these different trends are evident in the landscape. The Center for Scientific Spirituality lies down the road from the Danada mall, between the Fox Valley Bible Church and the Korean Christian Assembly. North of Chicago Avenue, a group of Moslems from Pakistan—many of them AT&T employees—recently converted a former Jehovah's Witness Kingdom Hall into a mosque. Upwardly mobile blacks and mixed couples have joined the fast-growing Celebration Fellowship in Bolingbrook south of Naperville. And on Plainfield Road out past Sector G, the Assemblies of God, one of the most rapidly growing denominations in the United States, has opened the Calvary Temple, a kind of high-tech amphitheater that seats 2,500; it seems as vast as an airport (in fact, a small airport lies adjacent) and is as busy on Sunday mornings. Just down the way, the half-built ruin of a huge and elaborate Hindu temple rises surreally from amidst the cornfields; the project was abandoned when its too-ambitious builder ran out of money. In Wheaton, long a stronghold of traditional Scandinavian evangelicalism, as exemplified by Wheaton College, the huge Billy Graham Center is the most visible building in town, proclaiming in huge letters, "For Christ and Kingdom." Yet, as if to keep an observer from drawing any pat conclusion, a theosophist bookstore does a thriving business not far away. Such juxtapositions exemplify the contradictions of today's religious scene, for even as the most fervent brands of Christianity grow in scope and gain more followers, so is there also a movement toward more experimental, less strictly Christian, forms of faith.

The landscape also reveals the extent to which religion, like other aspects of life on the frontier, is moving out beyond the periphery of town and in the process abandoning much of its symbolic civic role. In traditional Westerns, the building of a church at the town's heart was the classic signal that the frontier was being tamed, that private improvisations were giving way to civilized values, that what was once a mere settlement or encampment was on its way to becoming a full-fledged town. Thus, solid-looking churches near the center of towns both big and small have always functioned in America as expressions of civic pride and local achievement as much as signs of religious faith. As the architectural historian Philip Langdon has noted, the placement of churches reveals a lot about what people expect from religion, what place they give it in their lives, and the extent to which religion is tied to civic feeling. A church at a downtown intersection makes a memorable impression. It helps to define the town, its shape, its look, and its style; it thus belongs not only to its members but to the community as a whole. A church with a central location also serves to remind people that the center of life involves values higher than money-making, shopping, and domesticity.

Naperville's downtown is still distinguished by several grand old churches, which give the historic core some of its individual flavor. But with the exception of the Catholic Church of Saints Peter and Paul, where there is standing room only for the weekly High Mass, these venerable buildings are drawing ever-smaller congregations. The new churches are all being built on distant fields, off interstate highways, near big malls, or along feeder roads. The realities of suburban land economics, as well as the desire of churches today to draw congregants from the broader region rather than serving any single town, have taken precedence over religion's symbolic civic value. The new churches remain untied to any municipal unit, glad to be nowhere in particular as long as the land is cheap. This dispersion indicates a radical decentering of faith, the loosening of its ties to notions of place, of geographic community.

The diversity of faiths is, of course, one reason for this decentering; the new churches must draw people from all over if they are to survive because the region offers such variety. The diversity derives in part from increased non-European immigration to the suburbs, but its primary cause lies in what is perhaps the most important religious phenomenon in America's last half-century: the massive and rapid decline of mainstream Protestantism. Since the late 1960s, the Episcopal, Methodist, Presbyterian, Lutheran, and American (as opposed to Southern) Baptist denominations have lost more than a third of their members; for example, 48 percent of young Presbyterians drop out of churchgoing altogether, while the Methodists have lost an average of 1,000 members each week for the last thirty years. Among those who have left these faiths, at least a quarter have joined evangelical or Pentecostal churches, such as the Assemblies of God, which was widely regarded as a fringe sect, primarily rural and southern, only 25 years ago. Others who have left mainstream Protestantism have joined nondenominational congregations, independent churches that for the most part deemphasize any kind of dogma; of these, Willow Creek, the 4,500-seat megachurch in South Barrington to the north of Naperville, is the classic prototype. Still other former mainstream Protestants (as well as Catholics in large numbers) have rejected organized religion altogether, although this certainly does not mean that these people are no longer engaged in a spiritual life. And so in faith, as in everything else, the late twentieth-century emphasis is on diversity, variety, individual taste, customization, fragmenting institutions, and the importance of the niche.

The contrast with Whyte's Park Foresters is striking. The Organization Men were overwhelmingly members of precisely those faiths that have witnessed the most dramatic decline; fully 64 percent were Protestant, and only 8 percent of these were members of other than mainstream denominations. Twenty-five percent of the Park Foresters were Catholic, 8 percent were Jews, and a total of only 1.5 percent were listed either as being "other" or as having no affiliation. In general, then, the Organization Men and their families entrusted the practice of their religion to large and established institutions—an extension of their approach in every area of life. They also viewed spiritual values as synonymous with organized religion; their religion was thus highly compartmentalized and reflected the easy-going conformism that characterized them broadly. Rather than undertaking individual quests, the Park Foresters tended to follow whatever religious tradition they had been brought up in. Whyte especially stressed the social role that religion in Park Forest played, for the similarity of people's religious practices and beliefs helped knit the transient community together and so give it a measure of coherence.

By contrast, the variety of faiths practiced in Naperville today is so great that it is difficult to find accurate statistics. Each year, fewer of the local residents belong to one of the five mainstream Protestant denominations, and nearly 30 percent are officially "unchurched." But how, for example, does one account for the followers of Thich Nhat Hanh's philosophy of peace and meditation who meet regularly in the living room of a $350,000 house in Sector G? Or for the informal "women's spirituality circle" that Juanita Seavey, a local insurance executive, started after leaving Willow Creek in disillusionment? Private practices are widespread, and fragmentation rife, which is one reason good statistics are hard to come by. The difficulty is compounded by the extent to which people today customize their religious practices to reflect the needs and issues of the various stages of their lives. Because of this, spiritual life on today's frontier is much like work life: extremely fluid and liable to adapt over time to suit circumstance and opportunity, rather than being a firmly fixed aspect of an individual's identity.

Another notable aspect of spiritual life today is the lack of attachment that many people feel to the religious traditions in which they were raised. This is partly a consequence of the pervasive value placed on individual choice and partly a result of the frequency of mixed marriage. Couples who marry outside the faith of their parents seem especially eager to establish new traditions that will mark and distinguish their own new family unit. This practice of course strongly undermines the role of the extended family, already weak in our transient and dispersed culture, by giving the generations less of a common bond.

Pam Lenert was raised a Catholic, but now attends the United Church of Christ. She says, "I feel more comfortable in this setting. There's no hellfire and brimstone. It's a very friendly place, and they have a woman as pastor. They bring in wonderful speakers, and I love the time I spend there." Like many of the women I spoke with, Pam went through a long period of not attending any church, but resumed going because of her son. "I want him to have a Christian upbringing," she says. "The Catholic faith gave me a faith, although that faith is no longer Catholic. I want my son to have the same experience."

Grace Pastiak, raised as a Methodist, stopped attending services in the seventh grade; she is now active in Saint Raphael's Catholic Church on Naperville's far south side, where she teaches Sunday School. "My husband grew up Catholic," she says, "and I like the Church's sense of tradition. Plus, for some reason, my mother never had us baptized as Methodists because she thought we might grow up and marry Catholics. She turned out to be right—most of us have!" Susan Calomino's family was Methodist, but Susan became a Southern Baptist in high school; she and her husband, originally a Catholic, are now members of the Naperville Baptist Church, where they are regulars at Bible study classes. Sandy Alcorn grew up in a traditional Evangelical Reformed household, but now attends services irregularly at First Presbyterian. Barbara Casey was raised Episcopalian, but turned against that faith after the minister who performed her wedding questioned whether her family qualified as members because of their sporadic attendance at the church. Barbara and her husband have visited a variety of local churches but haven't yet found the "right fit." She says,

"In a way, I'm drawn to the Catholic Church, which my husband grew up in, but I'm not sure I can buy all the doctrine." Barbara feels little urgency about making a decision just now, because her son is still very young. "When he's a little older, we plan to join a church and make that more a part of our life."

A number of women objected to the equation of a spiritual life with formal religious practice, again in contrast to Whyte's Organization Men. Betty Reed, who describes herself as "a mid-life religious flop," grew up in the United Church of Christ, was active in a Methodist congregation during the early years of her marriage, but has rarely attended services since she moved to Naperville in the early 1970s. Yet Betty feels that her studies in Native American religion have returned her to the sense of deep spirituality she felt as a child, when she lived in close proximity to an Indian reservation in Northern Wisconsin. Reflecting the widespread tendency to customize religious practice in accord with life's stages, Betty observes, "If my husband and I had had kids, we would probably have made more of an effort to find a church. As it is, we'll probably get more involved with religion as we get older."

Karen Keough, the Lucent manager, also views her spiritual search as related to a specific stage of life; she says, "Religion has become much more important to me as I've gotten into my forties. I've built my career, done well, and I can take satisfaction in that. Now it's time to explore other things." Karen's growing spiritual involvement has in fact developed in tandem with her search for a second career, for a new way of life that she will begin at around fifty. "My spiritual interests sort of evolved out of my fascination with alternative medicine, a kind of healing quest I've been on. I've had to deal with a lot of stress, and that got me interested in meditation, herbs, and natural healing methods." Karen has considered getting a degree in this field or making a career some time in the future;

but for now, her studies are private, undertaken informally and on her own. Karen makes regular retreats to Sedona, Arizona, with a group of friends, which she says has given her an awareness of the connection between body, mind, and spirit. She has also attended meditation classes at the Center for Spiritual Science near Danada and recently joined a small Unity congregation in nearby Batavia. "The idea at Unity seems to be that we are all worthy. I grew up a Catholic, where the idea seemed to be that you *weren't* worthy, that God was always looking to punish you for some shortcoming. I don't think it's like that at all. I've come to believe that we are all spiritual beings, who are just at different points on the path."

Jenny Potanos also grew up Catholic; her husband is of Greek Orthodox background. Together, they attended Presbyterian services when they lived in nearby Lombard, but they have not sought any formal religious practice in Wheaton. "It's partly this community," explains Jenny, noting that, given the town's deeply religious roots, "there are a lot of people who are very involved in the church, but don't really lead the life at all." Jenny's children attend a Bible camp in summer—"I think it's Baptist," she says—but she also tries to "give them an awareness of things like Hanukkah, other traditions. I think it's important to give children a lot of freedom to explore, so they can make up their own minds. That way, they won't have a lot of the prejudice that sometimes comes with religion." Instead of formal services, says Jenny, "We try to put our values into practice by helping people—sponsoring a poor family or taking food to people who need it." She points out that, although Wheaton is affluent, several subsidized housing projects are nearby. "It's important for kids to get some perspective about that."

Susan Murphy, who grew up in a traditional Baptist household, also prefers to think of spiritual practice in terms of social action. "That's what interests me, not a lot of dogma. When we go to services, we go to the United Church of Christ in Glen Ellyn, because it doesn't have a strong Christian focus and is more involved with helping people in need. I no longer consider myself a Christian at all—I've rejected that. But I have very strong values and a strong moral compass." Like Jenny Potanos, Susan Murphy believes that the search for spirit is an individual matter, and so has tried to avoid "imposing any religious practice" upon her children when they were growing up. "We exposed them to different things—the Unitarians, some Quaker meetings—but nothing really seemed to connect. I'm not confident that we handled it as well as we could have, but the children have very solid values. And my daughter, who's now in college, has gotten interested in religion and is taking a course. Maybe she wouldn't have, if we had forced it on her."

The social (as opposed to social action) aspect of religion seems less important to these women than it did to Whyte's transients, although a number of those who are members of Kendyl Gibbon's Unitarian Universalist congregation noted that the church was central to their social lives. Another exception is Jasbir Singh, known throughout the area as Rani, a former medical technician and the wife of a surgeon at Saint Edward's hospital in Aurora. Rani lives in an enormous new house that looks out over a golf course on a high-priced cul-de-sac in the White Eagle development.

Rani grew up in India and describes herself as having been "a real rebel" as a girl. Nevertheless, she entered into an arranged marriage and quit medical school at the request of her husband. The couple moved to suburban Forest Park in 1969 and in the mid-1970s to Aurora and later Naperville. Rani describes her early years as a wife and mother as passive and retiring. "I just did what others asked me. I was never aggressive. I lived an isolated and very traditional life. I felt lonely much of the time. I wanted to do volunteer work, but I would always have family responsibilities or people coming from India. I had a hard time making commitments."

Things changed when her three children started school. "They were the first Sikh children in the schools around here. It was difficult, especially for my sons, who wear the turban and don't cut their hair in the traditional Sikh manner. My husband was always very accepted at work and in the community, but it was different at first with the children. Other children didn't know how to react. I saw that I would have to become the spokesperson for my children. This meant I had to get involved at the school, in order to help them feel they had a place there. So I did. I became a den mother, the picture lady—anything that I could do. People thought I was Spanish. There weren't many Indians here then. Now, it's very different."

Rani Singh realized that she would have to create a support system for the family, because none existed. The challenge was to help her children adjust to and thrive in America, while still holding onto and honoring Sikh values. "That meant we had to learn about American traditions. We started having a Christmas tree, decorating the house. The children would hunt for Easter eggs. It helped that we were adopted by a family from my husband's hospital. We spend the big American holidays with the same group every year—the people are Spanish, Filipino, and black. They have become a part of our family life. But I also hired a teacher from India so the children could learn the Punjab language. And we have a prayer room in the house and sit down for prayers every night."

As she learned to negotiate the challenges of multiculturalism, Rani Singh found herself in demand by other Sikhs, who needed both information and support. "I started being invited into Sikh communities in Chicago and Detroit and going to visit Sikh summer camps. People wanted to ask me questions about how I did things. They were anxious about their children. They wanted to understand how to be Sikhs but also Americans and didn't know who to ask." Rani notes that Indian immigrants to the suburbs in the 1970s and early 1980s were mostly affluent and educated. "Our community was mostly doctors or engineers." But as the numbers grew, people with less education began to arrive. "These people could be very shy, especially when it came to the schools. They didn't know how to speak for their children. Often, the mothers were working very hard. I said that I would be their advocate." As word of Rani's activism spread, she received invitations from church groups all over the region. She also began lobbying in Washington about issues of concern to her community.

"I have discovered," she says, "that in America you can learn anything." And indeed, in addition to learning to manage all her family's investments, Rani has taken courses in real estate and in contracting. She served as general contractor for her present house—"ask me about drywalls, about anything!" But the one aspect of life in Naperville that continues to amaze Rani is what she perceives as the talent Americans display for organizing on an informal basis. It is this that has sparked her interest in the social aspect of religion. She says, "American women are the best organizers in the world! It is so easy to work with them. This has been a great lesson for me, and it is something the people in my community need to learn."

Rani has been especially impressed by the religious organizations she has seen while traveling around the region to give her talks. And so, in order to study American women in action, she has become an active member of a Bible studies group that meets regularly in her affluent neighborhood. "It is all women.

They are mostly Catholic, but they have different religious practices. They are very intellectual and very spiritual. They read a lot, and they know how to connect with other people. You can rely on them if they say they'll do something, they are good at distributing work, and they are always punctual. These things are not easy for women from my country to learn, and it is hard for them to organize things as a result." Rani has approached the social aspect of her Bible class with diligence. "I am interested to know about the Bible, but it is also good to participate. I volunteer for things, and I carry through. I ask questions and people help me, instead of criticizing me for not knowing something. The women accept me. They are interested in what I think, though sometimes afraid to ask many questions, as if they might offend me with their curiosity." Being part of the Bible group has strengthened Rani's resolve to help Indian women learn more of the social and cooperative aspects of religion. "This is a very wonderful system, I think."

CUSTOMIZING THE JOURNEY

Perhaps the most widely noted religious phenomenon in today's frontier edge cities is the rise of the huge and usually nondenominational megachurches. These are identified in the public mind by their auditorium-like architecture, their use of light popular music, and their emphasis on enthusiastic and upbeat sermons that often seem indistinguishable in style and delivery from the monologues that open TV talk shows. But what most distinguishes the megachurches, and is probably the true reason for their success, is their ability to customize the services they offer, to reach out in a specific and targeted way to the various segments of the large memberships they serve. The voice-mail list of options provided to the caller at a popular Atlanta megachurch ("press 9 if you've had a death in the family") epitomizes, while also seeming to parody, this niche approach.

The Willow Creek Church, about twenty-five minutes north of Naperville, looks like a large corporate park, and indeed at times the big Saturday and Sunday services, which draw 15,000 people to the 141-acre campus each weekend, have an ambience not unlike that of a motivational management retreat. The language is a distinctively American blend of pragmatism and inspiration, with a strong dose of therapy mixed in, and a notable lack of reference to scripture. The services include spirited preaching on broadly general themes, music live and taped, and testimonials of various kinds delivered by church members. These are videotaped in advance and shown to congregants on giant-screen monitors. One weekend when I attended services, the testimonials came from men in their thirties who were members of one of the many men's groups at Willow Creek. As the huge congregation sat rapt, one burly suburbanite looked directly into the camera and spoke movingly of his struggles to be a good father and husband and of his difficulties in establishing meaningful relationships with other men. "Except for my group," he declared, "there's no safe place for me to be *as a man*. Everywhere else, you're just being urged to buck up, to hold it all in, to avoid ever really connecting. The biggest challenge when you're with other men is to stop talking about the Bulls, the Cubs, the Bears, or the Sox. I mean, you *know* the Cubs aren't going to do anything, so why not focus on what's eternal?"

The line got a big laugh, of course, but the testimony was revealing, for the speaker barely mentioned Willow Creek, much less any traditional tenets of the Christian faith. Instead he confined his testimony to what he had learned about himself by participating in his individual group. This is not surprising, for despite the emphasis on size and growth at megachurches, their real mission is evident in the small groups, of which there are more than a thousand at Willow Creek. These are the true focus of church life: after services, tables line the center atrium and the many corridors, and congregants are urged to choose an affiliation that reflects their situation, needs, and interests. At megachurches, you'll find groups for Young Dads, Prime Time (singles 20–25), Mom's Ministry, Grief Sufferers, Starting Over (divorced), Searchers (not sure), and Late Bloomers. One young man sitting behind a table described himself to me as "belonging to the just-out-of-college, woe-is-me, I-got-no-job-yet group."

This breaking down of people into ever smaller and more precisely defined subgroups mirrors real-estate patterns in the edge city: neighborhoods for empty nesters, for golfers, for the kids-and-cul-de-sac set, starter homes for just-married couples. The incessant theme at Willow Creek may be the need for community, the need, as one preacher put it, "to be with and go deep with other people" and, above all, "to leave our masks behind." But community is defined narrowly here, according to individual niche, which both reflects and reinforces the multiplicity of lifestyle subcultures. As pastor John Ortberg points out, a major goal at Willow Creek is to "get people past being familiar strangers, who stick to neutral topics, and help them really to *connect*." Making such connections is obviously easier when one is part of a small group, and it is assumed that people joining these groups will want to be with others who are like themselves. "It's the comfort factor," explained one woman seated behind a sign-up table. "People can relax more around others who share pretty much the same problems."

Sandy Alcorn, observing several sign-up tables as we walked around after the service, noted, "Why, it's the old Starbucks Syndrome again! It's all about marketing, choice, and demographics. Everybody gets just what they want, something tailored to their expectations. That's why there's such an emphasis on these small groups." Sandy observed that, in more traditional religious communities such as the one in which she grew up, "you had young and old, rich and poor, all worshiping together. So it gave you a sense of all being one because you shared a belief, even if you were all very different." This is precisely what is missing in the megachurches. In their quest to grow ever larger, they avoid almost any mention of dogma or denomination; beliefs are general, fairly undefined, broad. With little in the way of content to hold people together (much less any common history), these institutions must find some other means for creating common ground, and this they achieve by demographic segmentation. To secure a mass market, they practice mass customization, like any other postindustrial enterprise.

What the megachurches offer, then, and a major reason for their success, is a context for choosing the components with which one can customize one's own spiritual journey from among the bewildering array of choices available in today's spiritual bazaar. This task can be particularly daunting for those in today's edge cities, who no longer connect religious identity with family tradition. At Willow Creek, the stages of an individual's life are broken down into defined compartments, and the individual is then able to reassemble them in a way that reflects his or her spiritual concerns. This saves the effort of having to undertake the search alone, as for example Karen Keough has done, developing a spiritual practice that suits her needs from her studies of alternative medicine. In this way, Willow Creek is not unlike the Town Square mall at Danada, which offers a huge variety of goods (everything from Williams Sonoma to Fresh Fields to Sam Goody's to Cozumel restaurant) all targeted for specific niches. In both instances, the array of choices satisfies a broad range of demands, but leaves little room for serendipity or surprise.

Juanita Seavey, a Naperville insurance executive who participated in "The Gathering" at the College of DuPage, was a member of the Willow Creek congregation for three years. She grew increasingly frustrated with the niche approach. "I didn't think they offered all that much for women," she says. "It looks like they do when you see all those different groups, but that really just puts you in a slot. You are viewed either as a mom at a certain stage in raising your kids or as a single person who must be looking for a man in your age group. You're never seen as someone with spiritual gifts of your own. I wanted to put together a woman's program where we could explore some alternative spiritualities, and a lot of the women at the church were interested, but the pastor wouldn't let me do it. He wouldn't give up that control of the program or permit something that didn't fit a defined slot, so I just left. I have this picture of women at churches like Willow Creek going because they think it's good for their families, instead of asking what might be good for *them*. I have this image of women just bubbling up, wanting to understand existence in a way that makes sense of what they're learning about themselves. I think women are spiritually homesick. We know it, but we don't know for *what*."

Sue Ross agrees with Juanita, but she has found sustenance in the DuPage Unitarian church, where Kendyl Gibbon is pastor. "Everything about religion is changing very fast," says Sue. "In a lot of ways, it's like in the companies I work with. They have these new structures, matrixes, teams, whatever. But they can't get away from the old top-down models, with rigid hierarchies, all command and control. That's where the real struggle is these days." Still, Sue can't help feeling hopeful, in large measure because she sees women contributing so much to today's spiritual ferment. "I believe we're on the verge of some really spectacular changes. Again, I see it in my work, the kinds of changes women are bringing about. It's like we're all moving toward some kind of major transformation, a really different world, with different ways of relating to one another. But just now, no one knows what any of this will *look* like, or how we will make ourselves into the kind of people that this new world needs."

The forms of worship evolving in places like Naperville are distinctly American, rooted in native traditions rather than in the ancient disputes that gave historical context to the various faiths of the Old World. The scholar Harold Bloom asserts that the two crucial elements that have marked the American religious tradition from the start are "individuality and the pragmatism of feelings." The Baptist doctrine of "Soul competency," defined as the ability of an individual to determine just how the spirit moves, lies at the root of both these characteristics. One hears an echo of the great Baptist doctrine when women like Jenny Potanos and Susan Murphy speak of their unwillingness to impose any specific set of beliefs on their children, trusting them to find their spirituality for themselves.

Bloom also notes that "an essential creedlessness" is typical of American religions, a truth we see reflected in the megachurch movement. Their lack of emphasis on dogma provides the one strong link between the practice of faith in the Organization Man era and that in Naperville today, for despite the overwhelming proportion of residents who were members of mainstream Protestant faiths, a rejection of denomination also strongly characterized religious life in Park Forest. When the community was first built, the developer donated land for a Catholic church, a synagogue, and an unspecified number of Protestant churches, but a far-seeing pastor persuaded people in the area to subscribe to a single large United Protestant Church rather than dividing up among a number of smaller churches. In order to attract members from the various faiths, the United Protestant Church did not emphasize any specific creed or dogma in its teachings. A variety of common practices were combined to create a one-size-fits-all service, and pastoral counseling vigorously emphasized practical daily advice. The pastor was able to sell nondenominationalism to the community on the grounds of pure practicality: why spend money on a lot of different Protestant churches when one could serve a broad range of religious needs?

The nondenominational and megachurches one finds thriving in Naperville today are clearly descendants of this Park Forest tradition. Whyte noted the UPC's emphasis on the social aspect of religion, and this still remains strong, although the guiding principle at places like Willow Creek today seems more therapeutic, as is evident in the language of the testimonials. Also, in keeping with the small-group niche focus, one finds a far greater separation of women and men than prevailed in Whyte's more homogeneous era. There are groups for "moms" and "dads" of various ages, rather than for parents. Smaller congregations in the area also follow this practice, with women's spirituality classes and men's talk circles. Large-scale women's revivals aimed at the baby-boomer group have proven popular around Naperville, and the Christian men's movement Promise Keepers held one of its largest assemblies in the area.

This kind of gender separation has in part been inspired by the women's movement, which has long urged that women band together in religious congregations, often in order to reclaim some measure of dignity in traditions that have denigrated women. But the effect of the new separatism is paradoxical. To the extent that emotional "breakthroughs" are consistent features both at revivals like Promise Keepers and in

the small groups at Willow Creek, traditional—even conservative and evangelical—Christianity has begun to assume a far
more psychotherapeutic cast. Indeed, many of the basic tenets
of therapy are being spread in heartland communities by nondenominational churches, for in the absence of scripture, ritual, and tradition, therapy has increasingly become the content
of contemporary religious faith. Again, one sees here the
breaking down of barriers, the decompartmentalizing of the
different spheres of life, that characterizes life on today's postindustrial frontier.

Improvising the Future

S ince the 1960s, the broad coalition that constitutes the women's movement has pressed to expand women's participation in every aspect of public life. Starting with simple and concrete demands, such as the drive to eliminate the separate male and female "help wanted" listings from newspapers across the country, women have fought to remove a wide range of impediments to their independence, especially in regard to work and money. During the 1970s, policies that kept women out of professions like medicine and law, and out of prestigious business organizations and well-endowed colleges, were abandoned as a result of widespread pressure. Banks changed their long-held practice of requiring women who sought business loans or mortgages to first receive written permission from their husbands or their fathers. And laws forbidding workplace discrimination entered the legal code.

The change in women's status over the last thirty years has been extraordinary and rapid, especially when one recalls that, just a generation ago, girls were required to take "domestic science" in school, and married women routinely referred to themselves as "Mrs. John Smith." Yet the backlash that has been a feature of political life during the last decade, which first became evident when the Equal Rights Amendment was defeated by a determined minority of activists in 1986, and which has resulted in protracted and bitter public battles over issues such as abortion, has also led many to wonder if the progress women have made since the 1960s might not, in the near future, be reversed.

After all, there have been strong and successful women's movements in the past that, after achieving specific gains, met with widespread resistance and were stopped cold. In the early years of this century, the grassroots coalition that succeeded in securing for women the right to vote went on to press for a variety of social reforms, only to founder during the Red Scare hysteria of the 1920s. Women in the past have also made major gains in the workplace, only to watch them disappear when social conditions changed. During both world wars, women assumed industrial jobs so that production might continue in the absence of men. Yet as soon as these wars were over, women were expelled from the workplace to make room for returning veterans, their talents and energies once again restricted to the domestic arena.

The realization that "Rosie the Riveter," that feisty stock figure of female independence during the 1940s, could so quickly be transformed into a 1950s suburban housewife vacuuming her living room in high heels, has caused many today to wonder, *can all this last?* Particularly given the back-lash against women's public-sphere participation, which so often masquerades as a concern with family values, might not the progress that women have achieved in our own time be reversed? Might not the turn of the millennium even usher in some version of the future depicted in Margaret Atwood's visionary feminist novel, *The Handmaiden's Tale,* in which a resurgent right wing manages to establish an oppressively an-tifemale state, a vaguely Christianized version of the rabidly patriarchal fundamentalist theocracies presently engulfing some Islamic nations?

I believe that such a reversal will not occur for many of the same reasons that the triumph of totalitarianism predicted in, for example, George Orwell's classic futuristic fiction, *1984,* failed so utterly to anticipate or describe our present era. Al-though, during much of this century, people assumed that ad-vances in technology would lead to the centralization of power and control, those advances have in fact had the opposite ef-fect, broadening the distribution of information, diffusing power, and so making it increasingly difficult for any central-ized authority to repress or control individuals. Thus, far from ushering in the reign of Big Brother, information technology has undermined totalitarian governments around the world and is a major reason that so many of them have fallen during the last years of this century.

The shift in the nature of the technology of production and communications suggests another reason that women's prog-ress in the public arena will be extremely difficult to reverse in the years ahead. In the industrial era, the workplace was orga-nized in a way that supported the separation of work and home, and thus of men and women. Reforms could be and were upon occasion made, but any significant movement of women into the public arena could always be reversed, because

243

it undermined the efficiency of a system that thrived on separate spheres. This situation no longer prevails. Barriers have become permeable as the technology of work has moved into the home, decentralizing production; neither private nor public life is still served by a rigid division. Indeed, much of the work done at home now fulfills broad public purposes, as can be seen from home-based businesses and political organizing efforts now run from thousands of dining room tables. To a certain extent, the public/private barrier always reflected an ideal more than a reality, because women participated in public life as members of churches, local organizations, and volunteer groups. They were, however, largely excluded from significant money-making, policy- and opinion-shaping opportunities. It is this exclusion that decentralized technology, an economy based on information, and the grassroots activism of millions of women have now begun to erode.

The Nobel Prize–winning scientist Arno Penzias believes that it is the very nature of digital technology to harmonize apparent opposites rather than accentuating them; in this way, it has the potential to create an environment that serves human needs to an extent impossible in the past. Penzias also demonstrates that digital technology thrives on the principle of integration; quantum leaps in power have been made as the result of systems integration. This directly reverses the prime characteristic of the mechanistic technologies that dominated the industrial era, which grew more powerful as they became more compartmentalized. Thus, the assembly line proved an efficient innovation in the industrial age, while teams are a more useful way of organizing work in the information era. Again, to the extent that today's dominant technology breaks down barriers and reverses the trend to compartmentalization, it favors the involvement of both men and women in public life.

Other key characteristics of the postindustrial economy

make the reversal of women's participation unlikely. Networked technology, because it mandates the sharing of information, gives power to those in an organization's grassroots; as a result, organizations in the knowledge era need to draw from the broadest possible range of talent, skill, and expertise. This penalizes those that limit their field of choice to one half of the human race. Integrated structures are also more inclusive and reflect a biological rather than the mechanical model for which women, because of their historical exclusion, never developed an affinity. For these reasons, too, our digital technology bodes well for the inclusion of women in the public sphere.

In addition, advanced technology has led to the elimination of much of the labor that relied upon pure physical strength and thus gave men an advantage in the workplace. The evolution of heavy-lifting blue-collar jobs into positions requiring computer and decision-making skills can be seen in industries from auto manufacturing to steel production. As a result, women since the late 1970s have been joining men on the shop floor and in the union hall, increasing their participation in nonmanagement jobs in these industries by more than 300 percent in just the last decade.

Women's continued participation in the economic mainstream is also favored by the inherent instability of the postindustrial world. The logic of global capital leads many enterprises to follow opportunity wherever it arises, which means more travel, more relocations, and less job security for employees. This in turn creates tensions that make it harder to keep families together, driving up divorce rates and so raising the incentive for women to work. It is fascinating to note how few conservative commentators have been willing to recognize the connection between unrestrained free markets and the decline of stable families, or to examine the extent to which pervasive market values inevitably undermine values that preserve and strengthen the family. The more closely capitalism has come to be identified with immediate gratification and planned obsolescence, the more relentlessly it has worn away at the moral foundations necessary to center a strong family life. Yet the "creative destruction" that defines the unfettered movement of global capital makes it unlikely that family instability will soon abate.

People also live longer today than in the past and are healthier and far more vigorous after the age of fifty. As a result, the scope of adulthood is being entirely redefined. Work life in the industrial era was compartmentalized in regard to time: those who worked outside the home usually put in about thirty steady years during what was considered their prime, after which they withdrew from the public world. Given today's more active and much longer adulthood, this compartmentalization no longer makes sense, particularly considering the ability people now have to work from home, to work part time, and to move in and out of the workforce. Again, this change favors labor force participation by women, whose domestic focus during their children's youngest years was the rationale for keeping them out of the workforce in the past. When regarded from the perspective of a longer adulthood, withdrawing for a decade does not seem particularly problematic. Indeed, many women today discover their true calling in regard to paid work after the age of forty, which was considered the downward slope of life in the industrial era.

All these aspects of today's society and economy favor the continued participation of women in public and working life, as does, I believe, the institution of a volunteer military in place of the rotating draft for men. There was always something viscerally fair about the notion that men who were drafted to risk their lives in the service of their country should be rewarded in peacetime with the means to earn a good living, and indeed every effort was made to favor veterans for jobs and education after both world wars. But this consensus began to break down after Vietnam. The national ambivalence about that conflict, combined with the economic turmoil that was beginning to develop as manufacturing jobs were either automated or sent overseas, left many veterans to fend for themselves. In the years since, the formation of an all-volunteer force and the growing number of women who participate on the front lines (notably during the Gulf War) have undermined the old notion that "men who have fought for their country" should automatically be given the most desirable jobs.

It is no accident that the contemporary women's movement emerged in the same decade as the antiwar and environmental movements; each attempted to reverse in a different way the basic tenets of Western patriarchal culture. All seemed radical in the 1960s, but all have since become fully assimilated into the fabric of middle-class life. It would be hard in a place like Naperville today to find any educated person defending a toxic waste dump as the inevitable consequence of "progress" or maintaining that a woman's place is in the home—both unremarkable attitudes in the Organization Man era. Again, it is women who are leading this transformation in values. We know from polls in the last three elections that women voters are more concerned about the environment and far less supportive of military spending than are men. Women also exhibit a more communitarian ethic and favor greater spending for social services—herein lies the famous gender gap. And the fact that women in the last decade are, for the first time, voting independently from their husbands has begun to transform our political landscape, along with the issues that shape our debates.

I do a lot of public speaking, mostly to corporate and university groups, and I am often asked if I believe that women are about to "take over" or, alternately, if the glass ceiling will forever hold back women's progress. But I see something very different than either of these extremes: a far greater balance evolving between men and women. As women assume more responsibility in the workplace and the civic arena, men are of necessity assuming more responsibility at home. Thus, women and men today are leading lives that are *more like one another's* than at any time in the past. They share many of the same concerns and, as we have seen, even use the same primary tool, the PC, at work and often at home as well. This reciprocity, this alikeness, creates the potential for people to lead less compartmentalized, and less divided, lives.

This can be seen at every turn in Naperville. Despite the often-observed fact that many women are "trying to do it all," men are far more involved with their families today than in the Organization Man era, especially when it comes to their children. In addition, the movement of people in and out of the workplace in today's unstable work environment means that both men and women are having to integrate phases of time at work with time at home. Many women I interviewed mentioned looking forward to giving their husband "his time"—to stay home, to prepare for a new kind of work, to make a career shift—as a way of reciprocating for having taken time off themselves. Over and over, these women stressed the partnerships they had with the men in their lives: at home with their husbands, but also at work.

It only makes sense that, given the breakdown of longstanding barriers between public and private, work and home, women and men will come to have a more similar approach to life. And it is important, even necessary, that this should happen, for the development of powerful technologies has not simply *coincided* with women's entry onto the public stage, but has in fact been a crucial reason that it has occurred. The potential for humans to destroy themselves has simply become too great for the world to continue along out of balance, with only men making the decisions that shape our public and working lives. It is to redress this imbalance that women have begun assuming more powerful roles, bringing a greater range of human experience to the common pool. Seen this way, women's entry into public life becomes simply the unfolding of the next stage in human evolution, one required by the technological power that our species has come to wield. It is quite simply a way of trying to protect ourselves.

This nation's history has been defined by a succession of frontiers: geographical, technological, social, mythic. We are living in a frontier period today, as the basis of our economy and the means by which we do our work undergo a rapid transformation. Frontier periods are, to borrow a concept from contemporary science, "dissociative eras," that is, times in which individuals are able to influence the larger direction to an extent that may be entirely disproportionate to the actual power that they possess. This is why the notion of everyday revolutionaries has a particular relevance just now, for it is the collective improvisations of individual women seeking to adapt to unprecedented challenges that is giving shape to our common future and forming the basis for the communities of which we will be a part.

Frontier life thrives on improvisation, on adapting methods to circumstances, because circumstances are always evolving; this has been noted by observers since Cortez, who wrote to his patron back in Spain that the new circumstances he encountered required untried methods—as good a definition of improvisation as any. It is hardly coincidental that jazz, America's only home-grown art form, should be based upon improvisation, upon what one critic has called "putting aesthetic democracy in action," through constantly evolving patterns of call and response. For the filmmaker John Ford, who depicted the American frontier with mythic grandeur, improvising an identity has always been *the* characteristic American enterprise; we invent not only our methods, but our very selves as we ceaselessly seek ways to adjust to new conditions.

Men in America have long had the freedom to define the parameters of their lives, to improvise original responses, to "light out for the territories," in the words of Huck Finn. Now that women are no longer confined to the private sphere, they too are assuming this freedom. There are precedents, of course. Sandy Alcorn of Glen Ellyn echoes a number of women whom I interviewed for this book, when she says, "I've felt very alone sometimes, because what I've set out to do is very demanding and ambitious. It's also totally at odds from what my mother's generation pursued. So lately, I've been thinking a lot about my grandmother, who came over from Norway all alone when she was just sixteen. She left her entire family behind and got on a ship that landed in Brooklyn. Once she arrived, she found a job and began to support herself. It amazes me to think of the courage it took for her to come here all alone, and at that age!" Sandy notes that her grandmother left her native land because marriage and inheritance laws made it impossible for a young woman not born to wealth to have any say in determining the course of her life. "She wanted to make her own way, instead of just following tradition. I feel that I got a lot of who I am from her."

Glenda Blakemore sounds the same note when she talks about her southside Chicago upbringing. "I think I got a lot of my attitude from my grandmother, not my mother. My grandmother was what they used to call a 'bloomer girl.' She was very independent. She taught me that you didn't have to be afraid of anything, as long as you were willing to work. Because of her, I've never been afraid to leave a job. I'll be fifty in two years, and I'll be starting a whole new career. But I don't care about age. My grandmother always said age didn't matter. What you really need is a mind of your own."

The identification these women feel with their grandmothers' strength mirrors the experience of Willa Cather, the great novelist of the American pioneer West. In New York as a young woman, trying to make a living by selling stories, Cather felt so alienated from what she had been raised to be that she at first assumed a male identity. Believing that what she was attempting had no precedent in the female realm, she dressed as a man for a time and took a man's name. Yet as her writing propelled her to examine more deeply the Nebraska frontier world in which she came of age, she began to understand that her audacious ambitions were not at all unlike those of the pioneer grandmothers she knew as a girl, women who had carved out a place in the wilderness with their own hands. Recognizing that bravery, creativity, and the desire for achievement were in no sense foreign to her female forebears made Cather comfortable with her identity as a woman for the first time.

As they did on the Nebraska frontier, women today are creating new vernaculars of work and life that seek to reconcile the demands of personal ambition with the need for embeddedness in family and community. This reconciliation is of great significance, for life on the frontier has always brought into relief the American romance with rugged individualism, with the lone frontiersman who pursues his purposes alone, and who, in the classic words of the Texas rancher, seeks to "get while the gettin's good and then move on." But women have long been ambivalent about this approach and about the exaltation of individual fulfillment that it implies. As Max

Weber observed, most women never entirely accepted the premises of industrial capitalism, with its one-sided glorification of achievement and money. The greater environmental awareness with which we are all entering the new millennium also undermines this glorification by forcing a recognition of the costs involved.

By bringing the traditional values of the domestic sphere into the public arena, women are shaping a new synthesis that has the potential to make postindustrial life less fractured than what we have known—more flowing, more concerned with the overall quality of human existence. This presents a chance to "make the whole world homelike," as feminists of the late nineteenth century aspired to do. This is one of the great opportunities of our age. But the present era also offers a variety of dangers, particularly because the transition to the knowledge economy is widening the economic gulf between those who possess valuable skills and those who do not. The increasingly unequal distribution of income that results from this has the potential to undermine our democracy, which has historically drawn strength from a solid middle class. These consequences can be seen in Naperville, as it evolves from the "gutsy little midwestern town" that Mary Jo Lenert remembers into a place where only those who are thriving can live with a sense of safety and assurance, and where they are increasingly isolated from those who do not. Finding ways to close the gap between those who are gaining in this economy and those who are falling behind will be the great challenge of the years ahead. But the industrial revolution at its onset also created huge inequities, which required years of reforms to redress.

Along with the dangers there are a number of impediments to needed change that are particularly characteristic of today's edge cities. Each year, more and more Americans are moving to places like Naperville, booming centers with the feel of the frontier, where individuals can carve out their destinies and test their ideas with relatively few constraints. Such suburban regions have grown rapidly over the last half century because they seem to offer an accessible version of the frontier promise: cheap land, open spaces, individual freedom, economic possibility, and the chance to build an updated version of the Jeffersonian homestead, where the citizen-landowner can dwell in peace and freedom. Yet in many ways, this frontier ambience is an illusion, for both housing and commercial development are controlled by large, and often distant, corporations, and both are rigidly zoned in a way far more suited to a time when strict barriers between work and home still prevailed. The lack of integration between commercial and residential spaces in today's edge cities makes extravagant demands upon people's time, while also forcing them to assume financial obligations that are fraught with risk in an unstable job environment. Also, the traditional boom-and-bust cycle of suburban development makes housing vulnerable to wide swings in value that can be disastrous for those who must move during a downswing. Edge city dwellers are in fact more vulnerable to these cycles than those who live in cities or in the countryside, in part because of the arbitrariness of their location. A trip to Park Forest today offers a sobering lesson: it has become a suburban backwater, which time and fashion have passed by, its somewhat shabby housing stock incapable of the kind of gentrification that can return older city neighborhoods to vibrant life. The ascendance of business travel has no doubt also played a role in Park Forest's declining fortunes; the town is simply too far from O'Hare to play a viable role in postindustrial life.

Finally, the rootless and transient quality of edge city life isolates the nuclear family in a way that may be poorly suited to the demands of the new economy. In his recent book, *Tribes,*

Joel Kotkin observes that the development of the global marketplace presents particular opportunities for groups with strong communal values, long-term loyalties, and a sense of shared tradition. The focus on the group as opposed to the individual, Kotkin argues, has made members of extended clans likely to pool capital and resources and to form fluid networks based upon consensus—highly adaptive strategies in a relentlessly entrepreneurial world. Yet contemporary suburban life, with its emphasis on privacy and the individual family, fosters and reinforces values that can make this difficult: self-reliance and the exaltation of individual preferences and rights.

American life at the end of the millennium is being shaped not so much by highly visible leaders as by the revolutionaries of everyday. The present era is remarkable precisely because it is average women in places like Naperville who are improvising the solutions that will create a common future. This reshaping of life at the grassroots level is, I believe, the great story of our day, although it has been almost entirely missed by the media, which keep their narrow focus on Washington machinations, corporate hot shots, and celebrities of various kinds. But this numbing exaltation of high-profile figures blinds everyone to where the real action is taking place, and to the fact that heroes exist in unlikely places.

Decentralized technology is giving a broad range of people the means to create their own ways of living, transforming their workplaces and their communities to an extent inconceivable in the past. This ability is another manifestation of the knowledge economy's ceaseless drive to draw talent from an ever-widening base: to include broadly, pulling ideas from everywhere. Once people begin to recognize the extent to which this is happening, they will find it easier to maintain a degree of optimism about the future rather than succumbing to the widespread pessimism and doubt that derive from meditating upon today's lackluster political situation. Because I travel widely around the country and spend time talking with thousands of women in places like Naperville, I find it impossible to be discouraged about the nation's ability to address the problems that we face. There is simply too much intelligence, energy, thoughtfulness, and common sense out there in the land, and it is too widely distributed.

It is worth repeating here this book's epigraph from Dee Hock, the founder of Visa, the world's first virtual company. "The real consequence of emerging science and technology," Hock insists, "is not gadgets, whether hydrogen bombs or silicon chips, but radical social change: ever-increasing diversity and complexity in the way people live and work." This diversity and complexity have been evident on every page of this book. These qualities make this a confusing and demanding time to live in; the Organization Man era as chronicled by William Whyte seems almost blissfully simple and secure by contrast. But it was also a time when people's lives and hopes had to conform to the needs of large organizations. Being powerless to improvise one's own life was the price that individuals paid—a price that proved unacceptably high for women.

Notes

Page 10. William Whyte. *The Organization Man.* New York: Simon & Schuster Touchstone, 1956.

Pages 11–13. Statistics on women's increased participation in the workforce come from Howard Hayghe in *Monthly Labor Review,* GPO, January 1995. See also Robert Reich, *Report on the American Workforce.* U.S. Department of Labor, 1994. Reich notes that workforce participation growth has risen the most in recent decades among married women with young children.

Page 12. Figures on the divorce rate come from Robert Schoen, "The Slowing Metabolism of Marriage." *Demography,* November 1993.

Page 13. "Ham-fisted cutting . . ." There is a tradition of praise in the mainstream media of "tough" bosses like American's Robert Crandall, whose overinvestment in the hub system brought his company near ruin, but who appeared heroic to much of the business press as a result of slashing the workforce and holding the line against stewardesses. The most egregious example, of course, is Al "The Chainsaw" Dunlop, of Scott paper, who enriched himself and a few cronies (and the stockholders in the short term) by disemboweling the company and selling it off. See "The Chainsaw." *Business Week,* April 8, 1995.

Page 14. "Our notion of life as progress . . ." As the writer John Kouwenheuven has pointed out, "The basic and unceasing drive within our culture is to lift itself, to be dissatisfied with its limitations, to try—at whatever cost in self-distrust or self-reproach—to discover what indeed is an American." John A. Kouwenhoven. *The Beer Can by the Highway: Essays on What's "American" about America.* New York: Doubleday, 1961, p. 32.

Page 14. For a full and brilliant discussion of the role of the frontier in American life, see Peter Stowell. *John Ford.* Boston: Twayne Publishers. 1986. I have drawn on Stowell's thinking at many places in this book.

Page 14. "As the historian . . ." Sharon O'Brien. *Willa Cather: The Emerging Voice.* New York: Oxford University Press, 1987, p. 432.

Page 15. "This equation of women with civilizing values . . ." Such an attitude would, for example, be unthinkable in Europe, where men have always been identified as *the* primary bearers of civilizing culture. As the great American historian Constance Rourke has noted, one characteristic of our frontier attitude has been the notion that "the vast enterprise of conquering the country would exclude leisure for the arts." In this context, arts were assumed, in keeping with the classical ideal, to spring from a sense of equilibrium, whereas *dis*equilibrium was the major force in frontier settlement. Tom Paine and Ben Franklin also believed that a taste for any but the most practical arts was incompatible with frontier virtues. Such an attitude tends to regard men who cultivate a taste for the arts as effete, again in contrast to European or Eastern cultures. See Constance Rourke. *The Roots of American Culture.* New York: Harcourt Brace Jovanovich, 1942.

Chapter One

Page 17. "Ten fastest-growing cities . . ." Jeff Leitner, "City Growth Still Off the Charts." *Naperville Sun,* October 4, 1995.

Page 18. Nicholas Lemann. "Stressed Out in Suburbia," *The Atlantic Monthly,* November 1989.

Page 19. Adult marriage figures from Patricia Braus, "Sorry Boys, Donna Reed Is Still Dead." *American Demographer,* September 1995, p. 30. On Sector G. Howard Crouse, assistant superintendent, community school board serving Sector G.

Page 20. "Describes this homogeneity . . ." The Levittown quote is from Kenneth T. Jackson. *Crabgrass Frontier: The Suburbanization of the United States.* New York: Oxford University Press, 1985.

Page 23. "The corridor presently . . ." Naperville Chamber of Commerce.

Page 26. Area businesses. Naperville Chamber of Commerce.

Page 26. Regional women in workforce from U.S. Census 1990, Table 149.

Page 28. "American-born blacks . . ." Jeff Leitner, "Naperville's Blacks Among Wealthiest in Chicago Region." *(Aurora) Beacon News,* June 1, 1995.

Page 28. Figures on Naperville workforce from U.S. Department of Census, 1990.

Page 28. "This reflects a national trend . . ." See Robert Manning and Anita Butera, "From City to Suburbia," presented at American Sociological Association, August 19, 1996.

Page 29. "The fact that an individual . . ." The phenomenon of ever-decreasing prices in computer technology is known as "Moore's Law," after Gordon Moore, a founder of Intel Corporation. The reasons for it are outlined in my last book, *The Web of Inclusion: A New Architecture for Building Great Organizations.* New York: Doubleday/Currency, 1995.

Page 30. "Home-based businesses . . ." *Monthly Labor Review.* U.S. Bureau of Labor Statistics, February 1994.

Page 31. "The consumer markets . . ." The commercial practice of niche marketing has had a profound effect on our public life as well. For example, predictive polling based on selective samples, a lifestyle marketing technique, seems to imply that exercising our rights of citizenship is not all that different from buying a product. Indeed, one remembers in the 1992 New Hampshire primary when George Bush used the word "consumer" in place of citizen, seeming to conflate the two or forgetting that there was a difference.

Page 33. "Those bywords of the 1970s . . ." For an insightful discussion of that decade's effect on our culture, see Nicholas Lemann, "How the Seventies Changed America." *American Heritage,* July/August 1991.

Page 34. Mean household income from U.S. Department of Census, Household Economic Statistics.

Page 34. "Falling farther behind . . ." Jon Marshall and Amy Carr, "Rich Getting Rich, Poor Getting Poorer in the Suburbs." *(DuPage) Daily Herald,* October 15, 1996.

Page 34. Growing income gap from Robert Reich, "The Fracturing of the Middle Class." *New York Times,* op. ed., August 31, 1994. See also Reich, *Report on the American Workforce.*

Page 37. "A long tradition of social chroniclers . . ." Robert and Helen Lynd's pioneering study, *Middletown: A Study in American Culture* (Garden City, N.Y.: Doubleday, 1929), told the story of an eponymous middle American town and became the model of many subsequent efforts.

Page 38. "And so it is that the new mother . . ." Such fragmentation reflects what Frances Fitzgerald calls "lifestyle subcultures," which are in fact subtle manifestations of today's sophisticated consumer culture, the entire apparatus of which is aimed at producing and fulfilling the desire for *individual* style and choice. See Frances Fitzgerald. *Cities on the Hill.* New York: Simon and Schuster, 1981.

CHAPTER TWO

Page 42. The Economist cited in "Women Speak," *The Wirthlin Report,* July 1996.

Page 43. On childbearing, see "Sorry, Boys," which draws on Hayghe's analysis for the Bureau of Labor Statistics. Also Diane Crispell, "Dual Earner Diversity." *American Demographer,* July 1995. Reich notes the growing diversity in family life in his *Report on the American Workforce.*

Page 45. Daniel J. Levinson. *The Seasons of a Man's Life.* New York: Knopf, 1978.

Page 48. "So the husbands are having to learn . . ." Grunwald's experience reflects a widespread phenomenon. See Sylvia Nasar, "More Men in Prime of Life Spend Less Time Working." *New York Times,* December 1, 1994; Tony Horowitz, "Jobless Male Managers Proliferate in Suburbs." *Wall Street Journal,* September 20, 1993; Louis Uchitelle,

"Women in Their Fifties Follow Many Paths into the Workplace. *New York Times,* November 28, 1994.

Page 49. "Assortive mating . . ." Citings from "Dual Earner Diversity"; Tamar Lewin, "Men Whose Wives Work Earn Less, Studies Show." *New York Times,* October 12, 1994; Tamar Lewin, "Women Earn Half of Families' Incomes." *New York Times,* May 11, 1995. In "The Fracturing of the Middle Class," Reich maintains that traditional families composed only 18 percent of the households in 1993—a figure perhaps as much attributable to the rapid growth of the elderly among the population as to the more unorthodox family arrangements caused by divorce.

Pages 50–51. On the family wage, see Barbara Ehrenreich. *The Hearts of Men: American Dreams and the Flight from Commitment.* New York: Anchor Press, 1983.

Page 52. "Women's dual roles . . ." Arlie Hochschild and Anne Maching. *The Second Shift.* New York: Avon Books, 1989.

Page 53. "75 percent of all shopping . . ." Dolores Hayden. *Redesigning the American Dream: The Future of Housing, Work and Family Life.* W. W. Norton: New York, 1986.

Page 56. "While researching . . ." Sally Helgesen. *The Female Advantage: Women's Ways of Leadership.* New York: Doubleday/Currency, 1990.

Page 56. "By contrast . . ." Henry Mintzberg. *The Nature of Managerial Work.* New York: Harper & Row, 1973.

Page 57. On women and capitalism, see Max Weber. *The Protestant Ethic and the Spirit of Capitalism.* London: Academic, 1930, reprinted by Routledge, 1992, Chapter Two.

Page 60. "Quantum theory . . ." See Margaret Wheatley. *Leadership and the New Science.* San Francisco: Berrett-Koehler, 1992, p. 17.

Page 66. "In her 1992 best-seller . . ." Susan Faludi. *Backlash: The Undeclared War Against American Women.* New York: Crown, 1991.

Page 67. On men and women's contrasting roles in the workplace and the closing of the gender gap in earnings, see Reich, *Report on the*

American Workforce; also Hayghe. On women's greater satisfaction, see Michael Reiner, "Work Happy." *American Demographer,* July 1995.

Page 69. "The self-correcting nature . . ." The notion of capitalism being characterized by "creative destruction" belongs to Joseph Schumpeter, the Austrian economist whose influential writings have served as a kind of bible among free marketeers who sit at the feet of Milton Friedman. Schumpeter was writing about industrial conditions; it will be interesting to see how his ideas play out in the postindustrial world.

CHAPTER THREE

Page 72. "Yet the miseries . . ." This is fully discussed by Juliet B. Schor in *The Overworked American: The Unexpected Decline of Leisure.* New York: Basic Books, 1992. Schor notes that short work years are characteristic of precapitalist society, because before capitalism, material success was not invested with great significance, and consumer choice was limited by the unavailability of goods and the absence of a middle class. Schor argues that capitalism creates strong incentives for employers to keep hours long, as the result of the need to keep machines operating continuously, and the beneficial effects of long hours on workplace discipline. Again, this may be right for industrial society, but how does it affect postindustrial conditions, when knowledge is the primary value?

Page 72. "The industrial revolution reversed . . ." A vivid demonstration of this process is given in Kirkpatrick Sale's brilliant book, *Rebels Against the Future.* Reading, Mass.: Addison-Wesley, 1995. See also Peter Drucker's classic, *Post-Capitalist Society.* New York: Harper-Collins, 1994.

Page 72. "During the first half . . ." See Hayden for a full discussion of separate spheres in American life. See also Barbara Ehrenrich's insightful *For Her Own Good: 150 Years of the Experts' Advice to Women.* New York: Anchor/Doubleday, 1978.

Page 73. "By distributing access . . ." Drucker describes succinctly why computer technology demands a focus on knowledge. Also, as the Nobel prize-winning physicist Arno Penzias points out, the rigid inflexibility of mechanical systems lent itself to monolithic top-down planning and control, while computer networks excel at moving information sideways. This redistributes decision-making power to those who operate the programs, on the factory floor and also in the office, and so integrates the functions of thinking and doing. Arno Penzias. *Digital Harmony*. New York: HarperCollins, 1995.

Page 76. Home-based business figures in *Monthly Labor Review*.

Page 76. "Decrease in mobility . . ." From "Percent of DuPage Households Living in Same House in 1990 as in 1985," DuPage County Development Department.

Page 87. "While labor force participation . . ." U.S. Bureau of Labor Statistics, Division of Labor Force Statistics Tables.

Page 92. "Almost two decades . . ." See Drucker, *Post-Capitalist Society*.

Page 97. "The brilliant cultural critic . . ." See Kouwenhoven, *The Beer Can by the Highway*. America's role in process innovation is also explored by Art Kleiner in *The Age of Heretics: Heroes, Outlaws, and the Forerunners of Corporate Change*. New York: Doubleday/Currency, 1996, esp. pp. 9–10.

Page 98. "Something they felt 'called' to do . . ." This parallels some of the ideas expressed in Marsha Sinetar's *Ordinary People as Monks and Mystics*. New York: Paulist Press, 1986. Although Sinetar doesn't make it explicit, the common pursuit of the fascinating range of people she profiles seems to be transforming their relationship to time.

Page 102. "Volunteer work, now commonly referred . . ." Jeremy Rifkin. *The End of Work*. New York: Tarcher/Putnam, 1995. Rifkin makes an extremist case, assuming that the downsizing will go on forever; this seems unlikely, given the pendulum that characterizes American life. Nevertheless, his emphasis on the importance of the "third sector" is on target.

Page 105. Virginia Thornburgh quoted in conversation with the author.

Page 108. "At a 1967 hearing . . ." The expectation of a leisure society was documented in "The Office," an exhibition at the Cooper-Hewitt Museum of Design, in winter 1994.

Pages 108–10. These pages summarize the main thrust of the argument in Schor, *The Overworked American*. Schor notes that structural incentives operate against short hours because when working hours are reduced for many workers, the pool of unemployed shrinks. This has the effect of reducing employment rent, and hence undermining labor discipline, because getting fired is not much of a threat.

Page 111. "Juliet Schor notes that . . ." Obviously, the rise in work hours has been exacerbated by the decline in the strength of unions. It is fascinating to speculate on the extent to which this is the result of working people casting their votes for Ronald Reagan in the 1980s, despite his support for right-to-work laws and opposition to the strong enforcement of, for example, federal health and safety rules instituted to protect workers.

Page 111. Kanter quoted in Schor, p. 70.

Chapter Four

Page 118. "As the architectural critic . . ." See Philip Langdon. *A Better Place To Live: Reshaping the American Suburb.* Amherst: University of Massachusetts Press, 1994, p. 152.

Page 121. Household size decrease, U.S. Census Bureau. On garages, see Langdon, p. 150.

Page 131. "The purposeful approach to leisure . . ." A reference guide for marketers. See *Sourcebook of Zipcode Demographics.* CACI Marketing Systems. 9th ed., 1994, p. 82. See also *The Lifestyle Market Analyst,* SRDS, vol. 6, 1994.

Page 132. "Employed mothers in the United States expend . . ." Schor, p. 21.

Page 133. "A full-time housewife . . ." Vanek's study is quoted in Hayden, p. 77.

Page 133. "As Juliet Schor observes . . ." Schor, p. 8.

Page 137. "A recent article . . ." Susan Chira, "Images of the Perfect Mother." *New York Times,* May 8, 1994.

Page 140. "Humans experience time . . ." This is the essence of the author's complex argument. See Eviatar Zerubavel, *Hidden Rhythms: Schedules and Calendars in Social Life.* Chicago: University of Chicago

Press, 1981. Zerubavel calls these two kinds of time "organic or functional periodicity" and "mechanical periodicity."

Page 142. Peter Calthorpe quoted in conversation with the author.

Page 143. On Catherine Beecher, see Hayden, pp. 22–24.

Page 143. "The nation sought to extend . . ." Hayden, p. 33. As Hayden points out, the unacknowledged costs of this kind of housing include wasteful energy consumption, high expenditures in unpaid female labor, and a series of crises of the savings and loan institutions that have traditionally financed it. These costs not only create logistical problems for women, but also build in extra expenses that make it difficult for them to stay home when their children are small.

The separation of work and home as practiced in the United States has also been racially divisive. Because of this, our housing patterns have helped to destroy the basis for any working-class consensus, creating the docile labor movement that has characterized the postwar era, in contrast to Europe's more class-bound politics. Margaret Thatcher, privatizing council houses, used the same dream-house strategy to pry working classes away from their longtime support for the Labour Party and encourage workers to become Tories for the first time in British history.

Page 144. "Americans built isolated dream houses . . ." Cultural anthropologist Michele Rosaldo has found that women's status is lowest in societies where they are most separated from public life. In the United States, the dream house separates women who do not work from public space, thus lowering their status, *often in comparison to that of their own family!* This is recognized (but again in private, not social, terms) by women who feel themselves "looked down upon" because they do not work when they are around women who do see. Hayden, p. 50.

Pages 144–45. For a discussion of Kaiservilles and a comparison between them and Levittown, see Hayden, pp. 6–10. A great analysis is also to be found in Mike Davis. *City of Quartz: Excavating the Future in Los Angeles.* New York: Vintage, 1992.

Page 146. Hayden, pp. 154–55. She notes that urban economists thus overlook women twice: they ignore unpaid work done around the home and the transporting necessary to its accomplishment, and they ignore the fact that more than half of married women are in the paid workforce and so must travel for it.

CHAPTER FIVE

Page 154. "You have to go down these long twisting streets . . ." Langdon explains that much of the inconvenience in suburban life has been caused by the rejection of the grid arrangement of streets and the adoption of a system of arterial and collector roads and minor streets (known technically as a "sparse hierarchy"). The new system results because traffic engineers "judge their work by narrow objectives mainly having to do with how many vehicles they can get a road to carry." Langdon also quotes Walter Kulash, a respected transportation engineer, who notes that suburban transport networks are based on delivery systems for public utilities. However, as Langdon, pp. 27–34, observes, "People do not behave, or want to behave, like water or electricity."

Page 159. On the demise of the bicycle, see Neal Templin, "The Bicycle Loses Ground as a Symbol of Childhood Liberty." *Wall Street Journal,* September 10, 1996.

Pages 161–62. "The insistence on supervised activities . . ." Christopher Lasch. *The Revolt of the Elites and the Betrayal of Democracy.* New York: W. W. Norton, 1995, pp. 123–26.

Page 163. "Surveys reveal . . ." Langdon, pp. 42–48. See also Steve Coll. "Growing Up Suburban." *Washington Post Magazine,* June 10, 1990.

Page 164. "Naperville recently passed . . ." Tom Pelton, "Naperville Cops Take Aim at Teen Cruising." *Chicago Tribune,* September 4, 1994.

Page 164. Langdon quote, p. 45.

Page 165. "Adolescents tend to feel incomplete . . ." See Richard Sennett. *The Uses of Disorder: Personal Identity and City Life.* New York: Norton, 1992. Sennett believes that suburban life deprives young people of the experiences they need in order to handle conflict; without this experience, they withdraw into themselves and adopt a kind of unearned cynicism, as if feeling disillusioned by experiences that in fact they have never had.

Page 167. "Demographers attribute . . ." See Cheryl Russell, "The Baby Boom Turns Fifty." *American Demographer,* December 1995.

CHAPTER SIX

Page 169. "That almost 74 percent . . ." Reich, *Report on the American Workforce.*

Page 169. "Throughout DuPage County . . ." Marshall and Carr, *Daily Herald,* October 15, 1996.

Page 170. "Robert Reich has posited . . ." From "The Fracturing of the Middle Class."

Page 172. "The average price . . ." From *Living in Greater Chicago.* The Chicago Association of Realtors, Spring/Summer 1997.

Page 173. Langdon quote from his discussion of housing quality, pp. 68–72.

Page 175. "In 1948 . . ." The extraordinary growth in the cost of suburban life is chronicled in Hayden, pp. 145–63, and Langdon, pp. 10–16.

Page 176. "When Stamford, Connecticut . . ." Thomas J. Lueck, "Vacated Corporate Headquarters Scatter the Suburban Landscape." *New York Times,* December 7, 1992.

Page 176. Langdon, pp. 86–106, writes insightfully about HOAs, both their real and potential effects on American life. See also, Diana Jean Schemo. "Escape from Suburbia." *New York Times,* May 3, 1994. The definitive examination of private communities is Evan McKenzie's excellent *Privatopia: Homeowner Associations and the Rise of Residential Private Government.* New Haven: Yale University Press, 1994.

Page 178. "The Japanese save . . ." See Jackson, pp. 294–95.

Page 180. "More automobiles on the road . . ." Langdon, pp. 149–50. From "Summary of Travel Trends," Federal Highway Administration, 1990.

Page 180. "The average cost of daily commuting . . ." Langdon, p. 10, figures from AAA.

Page 181. Schor on shopping, pp. 107–38.

Page 182. "Personal debt . . . has exploded . . ." For growth and also percentage of income in relation to interest payments, see *The Federal Reserve Bulletin,* April 1995.

Page 192. "Financing second careers . . ." See also Betsy Morris. "The Future of Retirement: It's Not What You Think." *Fortune,* August 19, 1996. This is the best examination in the popular press of the phenomenon I saw in Naperville of people thinking of retirement as a chance to do more satisfying work.

Pages 195–96. Mimi Leiber quoted in Nocera, pp. 300–1.

Page 195. Don Phillips quoted in Joseph Nocera. *A Piece of the Action: How the Middle Class Joined the Money Class.* New York: Simon & Schuster, 1994, p. 369.

Page 195. "The amount invested . . ." The Investment Company Institute, Washington, D.C.

Page 196. Toffler invents these awkward but incredibly useful neologisms; I think "prosuming" is one of the best. See Alvin Toffler. *The Third Wave.* New York: Bantam, 1981.

CHAPTER SEVEN

Page 205. "Five important trends . . ." See Kirk Johnson, "In the Changed Landscape of Recruiting, Academic and Corporate Worlds Merge." *New York Times,* December 4, 1996. See also Fred Bleakley. "Two Year Colleges Can Help Create Jobs." *Wall Street Journal,* November 26, 1996.

Page 205. Figures on North Central College from Office of the Dean of Continuing Education.

Page 210. Figures on COD from the 1996 *Bulletin.*

Page 214. Quote from Whyte, p. 112.

Page 218. "The budget for corporate training . . ." Data from industry survey conducted by the American Society for Training and Development, 1995.

Page 218. "The role played by early 't-groups' . . ." See Kleiner, pp. 44–59.

CHAPTER EIGHT

Page 221. "An estimated 30 percent . . ." See Stephen J. Dubner, "Choosing a Religion." *New York Times Magazine,* March 31, 1996.

Page 222. On "Harmonial religions," see Harold Bloom. *The American Religion: The Emergence of the Post-Christian Nation.* New York: Touchstone, 1992.

Page 224. For figures on the decline of mainstream denominations and the growth of nondenominational and evangelical Protestantism, see Thomas C. Reeves. *The Empty Church: The Suicide of Liberal Christianity.* New York: The Free Press, 1996, pp. 8–15.

Page 225. Figures on Willow Creek from Mary Beth Sammons, "Full-Service Church." *Chicago Tribune,* April 3, 1994.

Page 225. Figures for religion in Park Forest, Whyte, pp. 365–69.

Pages 233–34. "At a popular Atlanta megachurch . . ." Paul Goldberger, "The Gospel of Church Architecture, Revised." *New York Times,* April 20, 1995.

CONCLUSION

Page 244. See Penzias, pp. 21–29.

Page 246. The changing nature of the military is an important if rarely acknowledged reason for the changing balance of power between men and women. But I also believe that the development of weapons of mass destruction has drastically changed public views about the value of warfare and thus helped to create conditions that have encouraged women's entry into public life. Throughout much of human history, men with strongly martial values were viewed by women as a source of protection—for the tribe, or, later, for the larger nation; they were thus able to command fealty, even subservience. With the advent of atomic capability, however, this began to change. Men, especially those with strongly martial attitudes, are now likely to be perceived by women as a threat to the larger human tribe. Even training in the military services stresses "peacekeeper" virtues these days, and looks askance at the saber-rattling that was tolerated or encouraged in the past. The widespread mistrust of male aggression finds expression in our culture's scorn for "macho," epitomized for all time in the figure of Dr. Strangelove; in the leading-man status of sensitive antiheroes, who have dominated popular culture since the late 1950s; and in the glib notion that testosterone is responsible for everything from criminality to war. The broad awareness of environmental dangers only furthers our culture's mistrust of the all-conquering hero—whether in business or the military.

Page 249. "Frontier life thrives . . ." The interplay between frontier circumstances and improvisation is a major theme in the work of Stanley Crouch. See *Notes of a Hanging Judge.* New York: Oxford University Press, 1990. Also conversations with the author.

Page 250. "Putting aesthetic democracy in action . . ." The phrase is from Stanley Crouch.

Page 250. "For the filmmaker . . ." Stowell.

Page 251. Willa Cather's evolving understanding of women in Nebraska is discussed at length in O'Brien.

Pages 251–52. Weber, pages 62–64.

Index

INDEX